THE GOOD NEW DAYS

Books by Merriman Smith

THE GOOD NEW DAYS
A PRESIDENT'S ODYSSEY
MEET MISTER EISENHOWER
A PRESIDENT IS MANY MEN
THANK YOU, MR. PRESIDENT

Mr. Smith since 1941 has been the White House
Correspondent for United Press International.

Merriman Smith

THE GOOD
NEW DAYS

A not entirely reverent
study of native habits
and customs in modern
Washington

30442

THE **BOBBS-MERRILL** COMPANY, INC.
A SUBSIDIARY OF HOWARD W. SAMS & CO., INC.
Publishers · INDIANAPOLIS · NEW YORK

Dedicated to

JULIET MERRIMAN ROZIER

without whose earlier role this book
would have been most unlikely.

Contents

Contents

A Preliminary
Understanding

Washington once was a town you could count on, but no more. Normally significant social and economic signposts, known among eager eclectics as status symbols, have become about as mixed up as District of Columbia traffic lights.

This shifty situation is owing largely to the advent of the New People, a more satisfactory label for the New Frontier, which is faulty political bannerism because it sounds so much as if John Wayne had something to do with it.

The New People who swarmed into town with President John F. Kennedy brought with them a self-heralded era of change and ferment. But it was only part of an era because the aforementioned signposts were coming down even before Ike and Mamie moved to the farm.

Like many lighthouses now dark, Perle Mesta and Gwen Cafritz have twinkled out. For the lobbyist, a secluded suite at the Carlton has lost some of its magic, and salons of influence and inspiration are now in the genteelly ratty traps of Georgetown. Just when

9

chi-chi Washingtonians thought they had established chablis and soda as a sensible drink, in roared the New People drinking beer from a bottle.

It may be easier to get tee time at Burning Tree, harder to get a tennis court at Chevy Chase. Youth and sweatshirt vigor threatened for a time to be rather important as symbols, but Kennedy came down with back trouble again and the New People spoke decreasingly of touch football and long, hatless walks in the rain.

The In People, who frequently are New People, too, began to be a bit less stoic about their own ailments and it was permissible again to be frail occasionally.

Other signposts and indicators of amounting to something are not only confused, but many of these meters have vanished altogether. In fact, ever since World War II, the mores and habits of Washington have been shifting, and this book is an effort to chart some of the changes.

Once the shiniest possible accolade was found in dinner with Mrs. Alice Roosevelt Longworth, a golf date with Senator Robert A. Taft or scrambled eggs Sunday nights at the White House with the Franklin D. Roosevelts.

Then we ran off the track. The very, very In People played poker on the Yacht *Williamsburg* with Harry Truman and learned that Scotch was for sissies. The next set of standards came in with the Eisenhowers, who pumped considerable life back into Augusta, Georgia, and Newport, Rhode Island. This also was the era of farms and highly bred cattle. Georgetown was left pretty much to old New Deal lawyers nursing their wounds and getting rich; proponents of at least split-the-expenses, if not free love, and the Harvard underground.

Now, however, we have reached a point in history where just about the best sign of being In is to have been shoved fully clothed into a swimming pool at Bobby Kennedy's during a native fiesta for New People. And if one's wife emerges from the pool with throaty laughter as the heavily chlorinated water designs new patterns across her $500 Givenchy original, there, friends, *is* status.

A Preliminary Understanding

The pool, however, is slipping as a sign. Too many have leaped, almost as lovesick Indian maids into blue Minnetonka.

This is the sort of thing historians bobble terribly. To be sure, such history men as McGeorge Bundy and Arthur Schlesinger, Jr., are in the midst of the New People, but because their minds are so often fueled up with buzzing ideas for bettering us, they and fellow historians overlook much of the significance of their times, the Good New Times.

Bundy probably doesn't realize it, but he walks at somewhat of a forward slant and Schlesinger walks with something of a rear leaning. At the precise moment when they pass each other, they make an X. But you'd never find this sort of thing in *their* books.

Now, to improve modern history; a bit peevishly and possibly annoyed at times, but over-all, in jolly fellowship of two Volkswagen owners blinking their lights in fraternal salute as they pull out of the State Department parking lot at night.

And please don't take everything as so darned light and superficial. That man in the buttoned-down, striped shirt drinking beer and crème de menthe over ice in a sticky brick-floored closet known as a garden in Georgetown—he may be in charge of the new death ray. Assuming, of course, that we have one.

M.S.

11

THE GOOD NEW DAYS

Washington is like no other city in the world. It is a living curiosity, made up of the strangest and most incongruous elements. There is a fairy-tale sense of instability about it . . . one vast boardinghouse . . . a city of toadies, always cheering for the party on top.

Frank G. Carpenter in the Cleveland *Leader,* 1883

CHAPTER ONE

Like No Other City

An unnoted philosopher, possibly a night floor scrubber at Agriculture or perhaps a Secretary of State, once said of Washington, "Everybody thinks he can run this place better than anybody."

This is not only true but possible because Washington is the biggest amateur game ever invented. With the entire American population as spectators, side-line coaches and voluble critics, players are assigned largely without training for specific positions. About the time they begin to learn the game, there's an election and seasoned players are thrown out for a new bunch.

This may seem to ignore the Civil Service, which is what many players would like to do, but career people are a class apart and so seldom do they rise to policy-making prominence without political muscle that, when it happens, there's much talk about it.

Washington is a town where thousands of people never unpack entirely. Home is another town for those who arrive expecting to stay four years for sure, and eight at most.

It is a seat of the theoretically mighty; where almost everybody talks incessantly; where status is marked by symbols so odd that they escape such packagers as Vance Packard and Cleveland Amory; where, as Kenneth Crawford once put it, the cocktail glass is one of the more powerful instruments of government.

Probably in no other city of the world do people of taste, means and even a modicum of intelligence demean themselves for free whisky and cold boiled shrimp as do countless Washingtonians several nights a week. This is a folkway and absurd, not for consumption of alcoholic beverages but senseless in the discomfort and effort involved.

It is a glorious town for targets. Congress, of course, is a prime national target for criticism. And the White House, too. But few cities of the world can boast such a supply of ready punching bags.

Lowly employees of the Internal Revenue Service are careful about saying where they work, because even among strangers mere mention of the letters I.R.S. can produce conversational sparks. Take a casual conversation on the bus, for example:

"Look at that in the paper—those fools down at Internal Revenue let some gangster in New York deduct his mistress. How do you like that?"

"I'm sure it must have been an oversight."

"What are you taking up for those bastards for?"

"I work there."

"Oh, you're one of *those* guys. . . ."

Once it was a capital of style and grace, a semi-Southern city where those of standing decently quit work from July to October. During the remaining months, they conducted business of government with relative civility and calm.

This, of course, was before television, air conditioning and jet flights to comfort, for Washington was and continues to be a rather miserable place in summer. In this era of unhurried elegance, one could sit in the Mayflower Hotel lobby and know, without having seen him before, when a Senator passed by, uniformed in a white linen suit and authentically floppy panama hat.

In fact, sessions of the Senate sometimes resembled meetings of hospital interns as lawmakers assembled in their white suits. Senators *looked* like Senators, whereas today a Senator may look like a Congressman or a bank teller or Tony Perkins, and this represents no capital improvement from the spectator's point of view. Marquis Childs will disagree, but Washington was a more stable place when Senators looked like Senators.

It is true, this Golden Age was tarnished somewhat by thousands of Negroes living in some of the nation's worst slums a few blocks from the Capitol itself; some of the more distinguished citizens could, and did, find surcease in whore houses on Connecticut Avenue; on occasion, national leaders were caught pilfering our natural resources. But the town was fun for those with money, tenacity and self-obsession.

So-called Golden Ages or Eras exist largely in minds of nostalgic writers or elderly orators, and if Washington ever enjoyed one it must have consisted loosely of the period beginning shortly after the Spanish-American War and extending until the early thirties when the first New People in many years arrived with Franklin D. Roosevelt. This arbitrary time grouping must, however, skip over World War I, because no war is ever particularly golden except for certain manufacturers.

Washingtonians in the first third of this century, and people of the country to a great extent, wanted, above all, no problems with the federal establishment. There was prestige of sorts to be had in the capital, but even that did not appeal particularly to better families. There was almost an obsessive public concern lest one man attempt to seize or exercise inordinate power.

Admiral George Dewey, still riding high on his Spanish-American war record, told the nation soothingly in 1900, "I am convinced that the office of the President is not such a very difficult one to fill, his duties being mainly to execute the laws of Congress."

Henry Brooks Adams wrote darkly:

"Power is poison. Its effect on Presidents has always been tragic,

17

chiefly as an almost insane excitement at first, and a worse reaction afterwards; but also because no mind is so well balanced as to bear the strain of seizing unlimited force without habit or knowledge of it; and finding it disputed with him by hungry packs of wolves and hounds whose lives depend on snatching the carrion."

Many political leaders, if not most, were regarded by the public as amiable liars and public till-tappers. Most respectable businessmen would not have considered entering government below cabinet or ambassadorial levels. Politician was a dirty word and long before there were such things as civil rights, the taunt, "How would you like your sister married to one?" applied much differently than it does today.

There always have been periods of crisis in Washington, but earlier in this century people of the capital could endure sweaty excitement that gripped the city for days because they knew these things had a way of subsiding. District of Columbia inhabitants, for example, could count on October. The general weather picture has not changed, but other factors have come to bear.

It still is warm during October daytime, but nights bring in faint traces of forest smoke from Maryland and Virginia, and capital residents may sleep again in something approaching comfort.

October once was a blessed time of year with the town quieter and essentially ours, people who live and labor here. No hordes of West Ashton school children gibbering before the White House gates in garish carnival hats with Betty or Buddy stitched on the brims; few if any bewildered out-of-state drivers athwart motor lanes trying to decipher Washington's schizoid traffic signs.

There was a season when even halls of Congress were silent while members talked taxes and tariff to Rotary Clubs back home. And it was a time when society leaders rushed back to the capital from Europe to lay party lines for the season ahead. In short, this once was an uncomplicated and peaceful part of the year for Washington.

Like No Other City

But no more. No such seasons exist. Surcease and relaxation have departed the banks of the Potomac for what may be an interminable period. Or for as long as men and nations speak of wars and weapons that cannot bring victory, but only endless valleys and plains of cindery stillness, twisted and broken places where people once dwelled, and greasy seas where fish float with white bellies upward.

It would be inaccurate, however, to charge the changes in Washington to Russia and atomic scientists. They're only part of the Good New Days. Chiefly responsible for a vastly new capital way of life are the New People. They're like the Golden Age, a rough classification.

The New People, hot-eyed, curious but unconcerned with protocol, and yeasty with shocking ideas, began swarming into town with F.D.R. when he first was elected President. Some came in shirt-sleeves with tweedy, straight-haired wives who leaped at problems of the nation beside their husbands with time out for such sidelines as progressive education and social acceptance of reform-school hoydens.

Others came from campuses, pipe-sucking and a bit bewildered at first, but later strong-voiced, activists, and organizers of long walks beside the smelly old Potomac barge canal.

Given enough time, and this they had with Roosevelt's four terms, even New People will stabilize as their mores and customs cease to stir up amazement. This happened with F.D.R.'s people. As stabilization set in, Southern Senators and senior ambassadors resumed positions of importance, proper young men from the State Department began swimming again in Miss Anne Archbold's ancient pool, and one heard less of Corcoran and Cohen.

Then came World War II when Washington, like other world capitals, was unsettled by the presence of thousands of strangers who came with khaki credentials instead of political license.

Customary values and behavior patterns became hopelessly confused, altered or forgotten. Second lieutenants roomed in base-

19

ments of good families. Diana Hopkins wanly attempted to grow radishes in the South grounds of the White House and Roosevelt spent long hours motoring the upper Hudson Valley searching out respectable housing for refugee royalty.

From 1940 to 1945, capital habits and customs lost their distinctive pattern except for the talking and drinking. The same sort of jumble took place in London, Paris and elsewhere. People who had counted were hard to count.

With Roosevelt's death and then war's end, the high tide of New People resumed as Harry S. Truman and his followers continued alterations to Washington begun by the New Dealers.

Professional Washingtonians and permanent residents who remained in town regardless of political climate began to see and hear of such people as Bull Canfield, the federal marshal in Kansas City; of Major General Harry Vaughan, who, in spite of his closeness to the new President, spurned invitations to the Right Places and went instead to hot-dog suppers of a men's Bible class at a small Presbyterian church in Alexandria.

To the undying appreciation of those who are uncomfortable with less than three forks at dinner, the arrival of President Dwight D. Eisenhower and his followers in 1953 quickly dislodged most of the New People who had come to town under Truman.

Ike and Mamie, although they were definitely Army, brought a great degree of social satisfaction to the permanent colony on the Potomac. For one thing, people in their government tended to be more like the Old People of the pre-Roosevelt era.

Many Eisenhower people were of first generation wealth, but they had been in funds for sufficient time to develop a sheen of financial and social security with taste by Abercrombie and Fitch. Their people were New Newport, but still Newport. They played golf and shot quail and watered in Southern California more than in Florida. They had private planes and new $2,500 shotguns by Purdy. Money did not matter as long as one had it. The frayed-collar idealists went underground or worked with belligerent futility for Adlai Stevenson and Planned Parenthood.

It became fashionable and indicated to read *Nation's Business* instead of the *New Republic*. Walter Lippmann was a respected island, but David Lawrence a better indicator of what the government would do. Wednesday afternoon at the Burning Tree Club became about as reliable a mark of standing in the community as having a Cabinet member to dinner. Mamie was a cute dresser for some of the older, conservative ladies who had stuck it out in their Massachusetts and Connecticut Avenue cliffs after the twenties, but she did entertain people who could be found in Dun and Bradstreet instead of some of the Grant Wood types favored by the Trumans.

There were a few nonconformists within the Eisenhower perimeter, but they were individuals of particular or peculiar talent and their presence derived from political and professional origins. Their influence did not extend into the drawing rooms, although effect of their actions did bob up occasionally in board rooms of corporate America.

While Mrs. Eisenhower may have had a penchant for pink and her husband preferred friends of the golf course, bridge table and hunting fields, they were undisputed society leaders. Any President *is* society; he is status and a cultural guidepost by the mere counting of votes every fourth November.

And each new President, with thousands of followers he brings or attracts to Washington, expectedly produces noticeable changes in the life, and even appearance, of the capital.

Untold man- and woman-hours go into taking down old pictures and putting up new ones. This sometimes leads to removing name plates from certain post offices, even changing names of dams, as happened when the Eisenhowers relieved the Trumans.

When Truman took over for the late F.D.R., people who fancied the lavish display of photographs of those in power were up against it. There's so much wall space in an office of a lawyer or lobbyist. The question was how to fit pictures of the New People in with those of New Dealers.

Some were reluctant to take down pictures of F.D.R. and Henry Wallace right away lest it seem blatantly fickle. The war was still on and patriotism also had to be considered.

But after a few months of getting acquainted, lawyers and lobbyists began shifting New Deal pictures to less prominent locations and putting up fresh portraits of Harry Vaughan, John Snyder and Howard McGrath.

After the 1952 elections, the problem was easier. There was no reason to pick and choose. Down came Truman photographs and up went impressive new pictures of Eisenhower and his crowd.

Easy at the start, the problem of pictures became complicated when it turned out that Eisenhower was a painter. At Christmas, 1953, he and Mamie gave out hundreds of lithographs of his portrait of Lincoln. Picture framers worked far into the night catching up with a flood of new orders, and Eisenhower art work—a bit short, say, of Gainsborough in portrait technique—shone from virtually every respectable wall in Washington, save that of the Americans for Democratic Action.

With exception of one holiday when they distributed photographs of themselves, Ike and Mamie gave a D.D.E. color lithograph each Christmas. One recipient of the entire series complained just after Christmas, 1960, "My den now looks like the courthouse sidewalk during Art Fair week at Stroudsburg, Pa."

The next great picture-pulling came with arrival of President Kennedy, Jacqueline, Caroline, and platoons of their kinfolk in 1961. Nothing since Harry Hopkins and Hugh Johnson did as much to upset and change Washington as New People of the Kennedy Administration.

Towering figures of old Washington simply did not tower any more. A couple known to relatively few Washingtonians entertained the President-elect on the eve of his inauguration. And after taking office, the new President darted around at night to homes of friends for dinner, something almost unheard of in a town where frumpy old dowagers liked to believe they had entertained for virtually everyone of any importance except, of course, a President who was supposed to stay put in the White House.

It was true that John F. Kennedy had been around Washington for fourteen years as a Congressman and Senator before moving into the White House, but his impact on the town was not particularly noticeable. This is no reflection on Kennedy, because all rules of the game change quickly when one is elevated to the Presidency. Prior to the White House, his force and personality were felt largely on Capitol Hill and in certain union circles due to his Senate curiosity about labor racketeering.

But because he and his family were new, attractive and interesting, they became a national fad after the votes were counted. Georgetown real estate prices zoomed upward even though the Kennedys were moving to Pennsylvania Avenue. The town filled with energetic men and women slavering to set the country free after what they regarded as eight years of Eisenhower bondage.

As might have been anticipated, the New People approached Washington virtually as something of their own creation. This is far-fetched, but truly, they wanted little contact with or reference to the past, even Democratic past.

Learning from experience with its necessary transferral of wisdom had been one of man's problems even before Jim Farley. It is a matter of no less vitality today than it was when Archimedes was trying to tell people about the lever.

The New People, circa Truman as well as J.F.K., came to Washington with a certain inbred distrust and often vocal dislike of the past. Roosevelt had not been overly consultative with Truman even when the remarkable gentleman from Missouri was Vice President. Consequently, when F.D.R. died suddenly and Truman was propelled into the driver's seat, people riding with H.S.T. looked almost with suspicion on some of the Roosevelt followers.

The Good New Days

General Vaughan, for example, worried for days about when Mrs. Roosevelt would move out of the White House and what she would take with her.

When the New People of 1961 arrived over the prostrate forms of the Old People, their chief rallying point or nearly common denominator was youth or a reasonable facsimile thereof.

This banner of tennis shoes with small sailing craft rampant produced not only social problems, but some fairly knotty involvements of government.

Young men have an aversion to advice, particularly after titanic accomplishment of the magnitude of national political victory, when so many had said it couldn't be done. They will accept knowledge and teaching of a much older man, but not from one just a bit older.

A thirty-year-old will listen with respect to sage rumblings of a seventy-year-old, but God deliver him from advice of a forty-year-old. This goes beyond acceptance of advice and into basic human emotions.

The New People literally hated Richard M. Nixon, who was not much older than Kennedy; but they merely disliked Eisenhower, who could well have cost them the election if he'd come out swinging for the Republicans a bit earlier in the fall of 1960. Former President Hoover became kindly old Herb to New People and they accepted the stainless reputation of Bernard M. Baruch, whose brilliant economic consistency was matched only by his pronounced preference for virtually all American Presidents since Taft.

Suddenly, it didn't matter what most hitherto and slightly mossy oracles thought. The New People had their own habits, customs and oracles. No longer did crowds shove to the steps of National Presbyterian Church on Sunday mornings for a glimpse of Ike and Mamie. They shifted to Holy Trinity in Georgetown, sometimes standing outside through several Masses before the Kennedys arrived.

Like No Other City

Hair became quite popular. Great masses of it. Crew-cut boulevardiers began to let it grow. Government secretaries spent long hours in beauty parlors where twitchy little men studied photographs of the First Lady and tried to puff up the locks of their customers to a state of luxuriant top-heaviness.

The Kennedy New People, in more ways than hair styles and church preference, wrought vast changes. In their dithering push forward, by hurling themselves at future history and rushing in their brown loafers over sputtering sachems of the past, New People of 1961 mashed into the very skin of the town ways of life first imported in smaller volume by New People of 1933.

Washington continues to be a pleasant place in which to live—no industries to soot the air, wide streets and pleasant parks, good shops and restaurants, advanced public schools. All of which is amazing when one considers that much of the population is relatively transient. There is, of course, a basic population which feeds to a large extent off the floaters. There also are some oddballs with enough money to permit their looking without participating. These are fortunate if sometimes annoying people, for there is no better spectator sport in America than watching Washington.

CHAPTER TWO

The Strangest, Most Incongruous Elements

Washington defies ordinary processes of capsulization because of its diverse human content. Conventional, respectable history certainly does not and cannot tell the whole story. Every schoolboy is told, when his attention can be directed from Cape Canaveral, that the government consists of three basic branches: executive, legislative, and judicial. This is unrealistic and incomplete.

Such classic division ignores some of the more important if unofficial elements of government. The press, for one example. Nowhere in the world are officials as sensitive to what is written and broadcast about them as they are in Washington. And certainly nowhere in the world do columnists and commentators influence destiny as much as they do in Washington, or at least think they do.

And the diplomatic corps. Quite obviously not a part of domestic government but a notable part of government life. Ambassadors entertain about as much as lobbyists, perhaps more. Diplomats seem to receive extra points for the number of canapés they consume in a season. They shrink from conducting diplomacy

The Good New Days

without something to eat or drink on apparent theory that, should diplomatic agreement be impossible, the time spent in negotiation will not have been a total loss.

In fact, during the Good Old Days, Washington aristocracy consisted largely of diplomats and officers of the armed services. Today, however, generals and admirals are too plentiful for their own social good, thanks to unification and creation of a new youth corps known as the Air Force.

As for diplomats, they suffer, too, these days from oversupply. With new countries seeming to spring into being every few days and the New People determinedly recognizing groups of a hundred or more colored people if gathered in orderly assembly on a piece of old French or British territory, the title of ambassador has lost some of its zip.

Frankly, ambassadors have been known on recent occasion to purchase used cars and drive themselves to the drug store, a practice utterly *nouveau* and lamentable to the Old People.

There are other economic, cultural and social divisions of Washington which we will examine in due time, but for the present it might be best to report that the town is more interestingly viewed by performance than from formal tables of organization.

An eminent viewer of the country as a whole, Russell Lynes, has said, "What we are headed for is a sort of social structure in which the highbrows are the elite, the middlebrows are the bourgeoisie and the lowbrows are hoi polloi."

By using elastic tape, Lynes measures his Americans largely by cultural tastes. His highbrows are for the most part withdrawn, snobbish and even effete critics of work done by others. Middlebrows supply the money and join lowbrows in doing the work.

While Washington has all these people, the cultural and social groupings discussed so profitably by Lynes won't work out, because in the Good New Days, what may be highbrow in New York or Philadelphia might be odd as hell in D.C.

The Strangest, Most Incongruous Elements

Kenneth Galbraith might be highbrow to the point of thin air when he's lording it over the economy, but what happens if he's caught listening to Guy Lombardo records? Jack Kennedy was borne into office on the thin, reedy shoulders of highbrows who derived cultural comfort from four-track, full stereophonic recordings of contrapuntal clatter by new masters of dissonance.

But what do they think of Kennedy when they hear that his favorite music is the boopy-doop of Lester Lanin? What then happens to their lip-curled spittle at Ike and Mamie for presenting Lawrence Welk in the East Room? The only recourse for highbrows in this crisis is to regard J.F.K.'s taste for tappy-toe tunes as a dirty Republican lie.

The same sort of thing happened with golf. Because Eisenhower devoted himself so frequently to a losing battle with par, golf and the country club became trademarks of political and governmental deficiency in the eyes of the Democrats. In the heat of the 1960 campaign, Kennedy, himself, began to drop little cracks about how in time of crisis *he* certainly would not be found on the links.

After election, even Secret Service men began to say guardedly how nice it would be to get away from golf after eight years of fairway and green. Then to their sadness, they discovered that Kennedy had been a hot golfer at Harvard. Furthermore, he played constantly at Palm Beach during the weeks before Inauguration. The Democratic faithful shut up immediately with their jokes about Ike and the golf course, and prayed for rain.

Then in the spring of his first year in office, Kennedy's back began to bother him again and golf was out of the question for a time. Party stalwarts were sad about the back, but happy about the golf.

One of the more striking incongruities of Washington is the relationship between national leaders and what might be called the townies. This is even more pronounced with the New People, and this particular division was wide enough some years back.

The Good New Days

There is a reason for the vast chasm with Lyndon Johnson going about his national business on one side and a department-store executive on the other side trying to drum up contributions for the United Givers' Fund.

The capital city consists essentially of those in government or attached to it, and those outside the sphere of governmental activity. It is much like a large combat army with its support or supply forces.

National leaders resident in the capital and so-called civic leaders of the capital have little resemblance, connection or, for that matter, little to do with each other.

A case in point might be a ranking Senator, one of three or four leaders of his party on Capitol Hill. The Senator is much too busy with national and international affairs to want any part of Washington's purely local social or cultural life.

He lives in a world consisting largely of his home, frequently a well-appointed apartment fairly close to town and sometimes a handsome house in the suburbs, and the Capitol with its surrounding compound of office buildings, cocktail lounges, clubs and restaurants. He would be utterly puzzled by a request to address the Washington Rotary Club, but he would not hesitate to walk out on the Capitol lawn to pose for pictures with a group of Girl Scouts from his state.

His wife probably knows a great deal more about life in the city than he does. She may belong to a Wednesday-morning book review or Spanish club with a number of other Senate wives. They also meet each other at the Congressional wives' club, but since there are no drinks served in this handsome building, many of the social affairs there are regarded more or less as necessity.

It is the Senator's wife who must handle most contacts with the nongovernment world, particularly if they have children. She may be a respected amateur artist or musician, and in rare instances she may be a writer of some substance and recognition.

The Strangest, Most Incongruous Elements

But her husband seldom enters this world. Her contacts with culture frequently are outside the home.

When the Senate leader arrives at his home it usually is late— eight or nine o'clock in the evening; he wants dinner; and until bedtime, he reads the newspapers and takes incessant telephone calls. If he plays golf, he may make it to Burning Tree or Chevy Chase on Saturday afternoon or Sunday morning. Sunday afternoons he devotes to television interview shows—if he's not on one, himself—and Sunday newspapers.

A Cabinet officer leads an even more dedicated-to-job existence. If he pulls much weight in the Cabinet, it takes virtually all of his time. Family, cultural interests, life of the city, hobbies, sports —all are heavily subordinated or swept aside before his official duties.

A Secretary of Defense, for example, probably is on duty from about eight in the morning when he rides to work in the back of an air-cooled limousine, scanning the morning papers with a radio-telephone perched beside him, until between eight and ten o'clock at night when he goes home to a large apartment in one of the luxury hotels such as the Sheraton Park.

On the way home, he may have stopped at two or three cocktail parties and never touched a drink, only the hand of his host. His wife learns rapidly to stand clear of as many of these functions as possible, save some of the more important and interesting embassy affairs.

They go out to dinner a good bit together, but largely to stiff, formal affairs. He usually changes clothes at the office and she picks him up there in the limousine.

She may take several guests, usually other women, to a symphony concert where she and her husband are box-holding patrons. But he rarely can make it and when he does, it may be intermission time before he slips into the straight-backed gilt chair held for him.

Wherever he goes, the Cabinet officer must be available constantly and instantly for telephone calls. When the President wants to talk with the Secretary of Defense in the evening, he doesn't say, "Could you see if the Secretary is available for a telephone call?" The President merely picks up his own telephone and says to the White House operator, "Get me the Secretary of Defense, will you?"

The Secretary may be at the Indonesian embassy, in the bath, swimming at Southampton, presiding over a meeting in Bangkok, or at the theater. In any event, within a few minutes after the President makes his request and unless the Cabinet member is exceedingly ill, he picks up a telephone somewhere and says, wondering how the third act turned out, "Yes, Mr. President?"

Sometimes a President, after stating his business, will say, "Did I get you at home?"

And the Cabinet member answers, "No, Mr. President, I'm in Greenland."

Nowadays, a President thinks little of this, knowing that he'll see his man back in Washington next afternoon.

This small aspect of Cabinet service alone would make it difficult to recruit a moderately young bachelor for this sort of work. His courtship of any lady would be relatively circumscribed or she would have to be most tolerant of telephonic interruptions.

(Can't you hear it now: "Mercedes, the reason I've asked you to come with me out to the end of the jetty in this storm—watch that next rock, Mercedes—the reason I've asked you out is to say I love you and I want you to—what flashing light, Mercedes?—oh there, thank heavens I can read code—let's see T–H–E W–H–I–T–E H–O–U–S–E I–S C–A–L–L–I–N–G—oh damn, Mercedes, here, hold our engagement ring while I cut in on my walkie-talkie . . .")

Even with small children, a Cabinet officer might get to the annual Boy Scout father-son banquet; never to a meeting of the troop. He might be able to see his son play prep school football once a year, but he wouldn't be able to stay after the game. He'd have to rush back to the office.

The Strangest, Most Incongruous Elements

He seldom vacations. His wife and children go away and he may join them for a few weekends during the summer, provided, of course, the cottage can be equipped with a straight-line telephone to Washington.

I once knew a relatively minor administration official in Washington who worked for a highly dedicated superior. The top man worked seven days a week; but my friend, being a highly independent soul for official Washington, tried whenever possible to spend part of Saturday and Sunday on his small farm in southern Maryland.

To snatch about twenty-four hours a week away from an incredibly demanding job, my friend was forced to install several extension telephones in all-weather boxes outside various farm buildings, plus an enormous and frightening Klaxon horn which blared in the manner of a fogbound ship every time the phone rang.

Furthermore, these telephone calls went on day and night. My friend fortunately had the temperament for this sort of thing and could awaken at three in the morning, answer the telephone with the bubbly good nature of a used car dealer, carry on an outwardly intelligent conversation, all the while making legible notes, conclude with a towering lie, "Oh, no, sir, I was just sitting here reading and I'm glad you called," and flop back on his pillow, sound asleep as he hit.

If this examination of the incongruities of Washington has become sidetracked by attention to telephones, this is only because it happens in real life. Aside from the toilet, water carafe and occasional tidbits of food, the telephone must rank next as an essential to life of a ranking Washington figure. Sleep is not necessary except at removed intervals. Food if necessary can be nothing more than malted milk tablets or vitamin pills for days on end.

Due to various circumstances—early life, what he regards as pressures of his job, a nagging wife or allergy to certain phases of the moon—occasionally Washington beholds a Cabinet officer who likes to drink. Unfortunately, however, this does not cut his working hours appreciably, nor does it broaden his cultural horizons. He merely has to take telephone calls in some rather interesting places, sometimes shouting at the piano player to tone it down a little.

He may hit a few more cocktail gatherings than some of his colleagues, but not with satisfying freedom, and always at the mercy of a butler or waiter beckoning from the edge of a room and pointing discreetly to a small enclosure where he may answer the telephone.

These government leaders, before coming to Washington, may have been university presidents, corporation executives, labor leaders, and sociologists. Whatever their cultural tastes and status of the past, they are swept beneath the carpet of official duties.

It would be unthinkable for a businessman, the head of a company employing several hundred thousands of men and women in Pittsburgh, to move there and live there for eight years without ever participating in the civic or cultural life of the community. This, however, is quite common in Washington. Sad, but common. A Secretary of Labor might promise and sincerely intend to listen to readings by Archibald MacLeish at Coolidge Auditorium, but what choice does he have if longshoremen pull a wildcat strike tying up the New York harbor two hours before? After this happens to government leaders a few times, they give up planning, or at least setting their hearts on, certain outside activities.

This is a highly erosive process, and while eight years in the Cabinet may leave a man wiser and better known, he's lived in an emotional tunnel for so long that his eyes and ears have diffi ty readjusting to the spectrum of a varied existence on the o side.

The absence of participation in Washington communi life by top federal officials is relieved somewhat by the frequently fervid interest and involvement of lower ranking civil servants.

The Strangest, Most Incongruous Elements

New People will listen on occasion to higher-ranking New People, but they hawk and look fiercely at their watches when trapped into listening to one of the Old People, unless the O.P. happens to be someone like Bernie Baruch or Joseph P. Kennedy, the President's father.

The elder Kennedy, by the way, is quite accepted by many New People, and even admired—not for his millions or for having sired Jack, but for the way in which he studiously avoided crabbing Jack's act. Many New People embarked on what they regard as political and social revolution largely because of domineering rich fathers, and it gives them new hope and a sense of rightness to see J.F.K. whaling into labor, management, Khrushchev, the N.A.M. and the A.M.A. without Dad breathing down his neck.

To approach understanding of Washington, it helps to be a mite prejudiced, because nothing clears one's political vision like bias. This makes it easier to determine right from wrong, because objectivity often equates with weakness in the Good New Days.

This leads us in this particular sermon on incongruities of Washington to what might best be labeled Flexible Sin.

It works this way. A Democrat says on Sunday television that if the Republican President would only stay in Washington instead of traipsing off to Gettysburg, we would not be in a mess with Castro. The Republicans dutifully scream "dirty politics."

Allow a brief interval for changing the cast. Then a Republican says on Sunday television that if the Democratic President would only stay in Washington instead of traipsing off to Cape Cod, we would not be in a mess with Castro. Democrats know their duty, too, and cry "dirty politics."

None of this has to do with malfeasance or neglect, but it does involve Flexible Sin. This is a sin which depends largely on where the witness stands and not particularly on what the sinner does.

Examine the Flexible Sin in helicopters. The Democrats howled waste, budget tipping, and unfairness to our boys in uniform when Ike began using Marine Corps choppers for the Gettysburg run. Now it is the Republicans who speak darkly of expense to taxpayers when J.F.K. goes whirling to Middleburg.

If it's *your* Senator who puts his wife on the public payroll, this is togetherness, the smart utilization of a talented woman. If *their* Senator does the same thing, the rule of Flexible Sin applies and he's a no-good nepotist, not content with looting the Treasury for his own pay but enriching a woman who spends most of her time right in their own home. Eating candy.

Even the most seasoned Washingtonian finds it hard to keep track of sin when one political party controls the Congress and the other party has the White House. In such confusing periods, Flexible Sin becomes Interlocking Sin. This may lead, for example, to a Republican Senator's issuing a statement from his vacation headquarters at Swampscott, Mass., about the unconscionable absence of the Democratic President in Newport.

Even with control of Congress and Executive in the same political hands, vacations always have been sins to those of the other party. Early in the Eisenhower Administration, Walter Reuther, president of the United Automobile Workers and a bristling Democrat, announced that he intended to keep day-by-day tabs on Ike's absences from the White House, even if he only went to the corner for a newspaper which Democrats maintained he did not read anyway.

Reuther, however, did not offer similar statistical services for President Kennedy, but over at the Republican National Committee they happily made little black marks every time Kennedy left the neighborhood. It may be no more than rumor, but understandable if true—the Republicans are said to have given up counting the number of times J.F.K. went to dinner at private homes, because he has been known to sup with Republicans. And the GOP National Committee could score only half an absence against Kennedy on one of his quick trips to New York because he devoted his afternoon to visiting former President Hoover and General Douglas MacArthur.

CHAPTER THREE

Hair by Sealyham, Shoulders by God

The sight of human affairs deserves admiration and pity. They are worthy of respect, too. And he is not insensible who pays them the undemonstrative tribute of a sigh which is not a sob, and of a smile which is not a grin.

Joseph Conrad in *A Personal Record*

Unsobbing: with sighs due only to quasi-enormity, and with an approved if somewhat crooked smile, there should be at this point an undemonstrative stipulation that Washington consists of much more than Presidents, Cabinet members and Senators, although there must be times out in the country when it certainly seems that way.

The capital bubbles and squeaks in polyglot ritual. It abounds, particularly in these breathless days, with breeds and personalities of such high octane performance that their contrails must be observed closely and quickly for proper recognition.

Perhaps this era was spied a-coming by one of the nation's

pioneer psychiatrists shortly after World War I. This New Frontiersman of his day had a spare moment, in fact he had many spare moments in those early hours of psychiatry, in which he spoke to his son. This was significant in itself because the son didn't understand too clearly what his father did for a living. The kid was a little backward about telling playmates that Dad was the only doctor in town with no tongue blades or pills, not even oatmeal tablets for old women with autointoxication.

This may be irrelevant to the narrative, but there is such a demand in Washington today for *true meaning* and reporting *in depth,* even *omnifocus,* that snippets of history are included primarily as defensive measures.

At any rate, this perceptive doctor said to his boy, who has told the story many times since from the reclining leather comfort of his Jaguar, "Son, I want to open my own mental hospital and I want to pick an area where I know some day there'll be a lot of sick people. And son, that place is Washington."

Were it not for certain obscure medical ethics, this man would be memorialized for vision ranking with that of Alexander Graham Bell, the Wright brothers, and the Heeps who figured out installment credit.

This is not to say that Washington has more than another big city's share of square wheels, but there has been in recent years a noticeable influx of those whose behavior, if not hard to understand, certainly is more interesting than that of some of the dreary folk who used to take up space in our town.

Take, for instance, the government official who works fifteen hours a day at the genuinely needed and onerous chore of combating racial discrimination. As government salaries go, he's paid well but the money doesn't cover as much as it might, because he and his wife are strapped by tuition bills for their children at a private, segregated school.

Not all Washingtonians regarded their station so gravely.

Young men with natural shoulders and Wally Cox haircuts

walk briskly to their Hillmans and Volvos at night, speaking earnestly and vibrantly across the nearly empty parking lot about the bully fun of running a government as though it were a spring semester project for Poli Sci 23.

Or, in some of the federal corridors, indelibly stamped products of Radcliffe or Smith in beige loafers, overblouses that tend to blur distracting endowments and Sealyham hair effects which they like to believe are mildly suggestive of Jacqueline. These frequently join forces with the young fellows in Volvos, returning to either his or her castle for marriage, thence back to Georgetown to dismay the disciples of Margaret Sanger. They blessedly thus create openings in government for other Radcliffe and Smith girls. Also, eventually ending up as customers for Rambler station wagons.

The random picture is not entirely frivolous.

Lisping men from new African countries, trying desperately to sound sure of themselves in their new world of still shaky acceptance as they try to build stature and even tradition almost overnight; as they try to state aims and goals without its sounding like wheedling parochialism.

Or the deeply concerned scholars, gray heads and crusted briar pipes together at the Cosmos Club taproom around a communal pyre of knowledge and smoke. The fifty-year-old men who can be seen sometimes in good little restaurants at night, wearing maroon blazers with college crests and trying to read the *Economist* or *Le Monde* by wavering candlelight. The over-age blazer fellows are would-be participants, but actually sad spectators. Eventually and with sufficiently nurtured connections, they may help, but never decide.

These people have their gods and demigods with seldom little doubt about their devils. Not always toweringly intelligent, they're often cunning. They soak up incidental intelligence thirstily and once absorbed, it is forever theirs and only theirs. Two men may read the same anecdote by George Dixon, but if

41

they lunch separately, the story is an individual matter of inside knowledge with amazing disregard for circulation of the Washington *Post* in which Mr. Dixon's essays appear.

Probably as much read as the Yellow Pages are society sections of Washington newspapers, which have a language of their own; a language for which there is no Berlitz save experience; a language which the New People know and thereby base their decisions to feel fortunate or left out of things.

An N.P. knows with experience that if a project, a process or even a meeting is described as *supersecret* or *hush-hush,* in the *patois* of Washington, it means the writer knew something was going on, but not entirely.

If a woman is *attractive, vivacious* or *charming,* chances are that she's a wee bit plain, fiftyish but important. To mention her *attractive silvery locks* means that she has one foot in the grave. To say that she has *prematurely gray hair* can be quite catty.

Should a woman be said in print to be *ravishing* or *beautifully tanned,* her dress showed everything. She was half-naked if the gown was *stunningly cut.* Should she have an *athletic figure,* this is a sure Washington sign that she's disgustingly young but built like a Percheron.

If a man is described as *courtly* or having *charming Old World ways* and a *still-erect figure,* watch for an obituary soon. He's on his last legs and with what breath left to him, he's a frightful old bore, he talks endlessly about Senator Borah and how they quit making good cars when they quit making the Reo. Because of Washington's greatest common determinator, seniority, which we will deal with shortly, the man with *charming Old World ways* must be tolerated even though young ladies shudder at the memory of his scraggly hands on their thighs the last time they sat beside him at dinner.

When a social affair is described as *lavish, sumptuous, glittering,* or *breathtaking,* put it down that the food was tasty and plentiful, and the liquor lasted. If the account contains such clues as *un-*

Hair by Sealyham, Shoulders by God

fortunately rainy, mob scene, loud clatter, or *wedged in,* the canapés were soggy and the whisky was blended, plus the fact that the guests for the most part were second-rate except one former Supreme Court Justice who went there by mistake.

Where there is reference to guests being a *select few* or *only old friends,* the host and hostess were either out of the current swim entirely, suffering a dollar gap, or merely sore at the society writer.

The experienced Washingtonian, N.P. or O.P., also pays attention to descriptive detail. If the affair was *gay,* it was the sort of thing to which you could take the rector. There was only punch, weak punch. Bananas sliced and floating on top. Imitation cut-glass cups. When the gathering was *tres gai,* things are looking up —a few got looped, others went on to finish the job at a quaint gin mill. The hosts were a bit above par.

Occasionally the morning and evening social stock lists display other indices which might be overlooked by any but true students. *Bubbling gaiety* is a dead giveaway. The writer may have been a shade socked-in. It was fun, though; particularly the handsome military attaché whom the hostess discovered going to the bathroom right beside her boxwood hedge. You can't put this sort of event in the paper, but Barbara did the cutest thing. She ran and got the can of Scat which she uses to protect the hedge from her dog and sprayed it all over Tony.

Should an affair be referred to as *daringly different,* this may require inquiry. Either the decorations were shockingly bad or the historian dropped in on so many affairs the same day that he or she isn't too clear on detail. Or possibly, the hostess lived up to her not-so-public reputation.

Survival, acceptance, or at least understanding in the Good New Days involves not only social terminology, but knowledge of strangely differing persons, places and conditions which must be worshiped—or denounced automatically, without question and at all times.

The Good New Days

Some of the adorations are nationwide in scope, some peculiar to Washington and the era of New People.

The Irish, for instance. These are the pets of American politics. One may damn the daylights out of the British, the Portuguese or the Brazilians, but to imply that the Irish or those of Irish extraction are even fractionally short of being mankind's best—past, present and future—is to invite lumps, large ones. This was true in Washington long before the Kennedys. Their arrival only intensified the cultism.

One may say in the course of friendly conversation that a political leader of Irish lineage is a dirty bastard, but better not call him a dirty *Irish* bastard lest the John Birch Society meet in special session and rains descend upon the city for forty days and forty nights.

Saint Patrick's Day is much more of a fete in Washington than in Dublin. Zionists come to work in bright green ties and little white clay pipes in their jacket lapels. It would, however, never occur to an O'Grady to wear a Star of David in *his* lapel on some selected Jewish holiday, just as a matter of squaring up.

The Proper Washingtonian also must bear awed reverence for Indians. Not American Indians, but Indian Indians. They must be regarded and hailed as invariable examples of gentle, honorable, peaceful and wise people, despite Goa. This law of wonderful Indian Indians probably dates back to Mahatma Gandhi, but derives its continuing virility from Washington's generally guilty conscience about the years of American neglect of Asia.

Except for the Bureau of Indian Affairs in the Interior Department and certain geographically involved Congressmen, Washington today shows no particular interest in American Indians on the possible theory that if they don't have oil and send their daughters to Vassar in air-conditioned Thunderbirds, they're a bunch of mangy mendicants.

If an onyx-eyed Indian Indian comes to town seeking five million dollars for a birth-control clinic in Lower Rastrapati, he and his cause are worthy without question. He's entertained at benefit movies and cocktail parties, although he doesn't drink, himself. But just let an impecunious American Indian creep into town asking for water for his reservation or that his twelve-year-old son with one bad eye be exempt from the draft. He's denounced as a dreadful by-product of the welfare state and drummed back to his boondocks without even a *Congressional Record* to read on the return trip.

It once was *de rigueur* to preconize the poor and humbly begun in national politics and equally *pro forma* to belabor the rich and regard their desire for public office as a forerunner of large-scale larceny. This era apparently is behind us forever. The log-cabin types no longer seem to grow in our forests of presidential timber.

The popular acceptance of such multimillionaires as President Kennedy and New York's Governor Rockefeller has, however, produced some curious changes in public attitude which is reflected to great extent in Washington.

Many Americans now seem to want rich men in high public office, but they want these fellows to act like poor men. This may be called, for purposes of particular study, the riches-to-rags political posture or school of conduct.

Leading up to the 1960 campaigns, Kennedy and Rockefeller competed in raggedness. It was not until after the conventions that we often saw them decently clothed. Prior to that time, they posed for endless pictures in raveling blue jeans and frayed deck sneakers. Rockefeller took to eating in delicatessens. Some political scientists believe Rockefeller disposed of Averell Harriman rather effectively in New York City by being jovially more messy in the pizzerias.

Those few votes by which Kennedy defeated Dick Nixon may have come from the hamburger joints and malt shoppes he frequented during his bid for office. Nixon simply was not much of a drive-in man, yet Kennedy successfully dribbled chocolate shakes from coast to coast. Enough voters to put him in the White House must have reacted like indulgent grandparents:

"There goes a kid who could eat at the best places with his money, but bless his down-to-earth soul, for all his millions, he picked *our* place, the Tastee Toastee."

On the other hand, Nixon, with comparatively few dimes to his name, could have gone the entire route eating exclusively at acrid little diners with chalked menus, windowsill hamburger establishments, and squirting mustard on his suit for extra effect. He would not have added a vote to his cause because many voters would expect a man in modest circumstances to eat that way.

Possibly this will convince Poli Sci scholars that rags-to-riches no longer is effective or necessary as a prerequisite for service to the nation. Rags-to-rags might be evocative of votes in years to come, but it's hardly worth a sell-off now.

Success-through-contrast has other aspects. The rich candidate, in addition to old clothes, should savor old things. (This is in no way meant to insinuate anything about the wives of our more successful politicians. Insinuations about women in politics will be contained in a separate and easily identified chapter.)

Although it may seem dissociable to the losers, today's winners are great for old automobiles—until they win, at which time they switch to government limousines.

The greatest vote getter of them all, F.D.R., rattled around in a horrible old trap at Hyde Park and Warm Springs, and had his picture made thus ensconced, at intervals which increased in frequency as Election Day neared.

Rockefeller (we continue referring to him in a Washington book because of his continuing interest in getting there) was well aware of the automobile factor in politics when he moved into the shabby neighborhood of the governor's mansion at Albany.

It is true that Rockefeller took his own $12,000 Chrysler-Gia with him to Albany, but he promptly gave it to the state. Then he was widely photographed batting over rock and rill in an ancient Chevrolet roadster with hair tousled convincingly above a simple sweat shirt. This again gave the voter an opportunity to drumble contentedly in the knowledge that "he could afford anything, but he really prefers a car like *ours*."

Those in the audience who would dispute our riches-to-rags theory by bringing up Stevenson and Eisenhower are dismissed right now as pot-valiant malcontents. Any truly sound political theory must have certain flexibilities.

Adlai was licked by the 24-hour, 24-karat gleam of a war hero. Taking the long view, these fellows are frightfully hard to beat. Ike not only was clad in the shining armor of a winning leader against the foe; he was a calmly confident protector, a highly successful author—and he had the damnedest smile ever uncorked on an opponent.

Stevenson countered as well as he could. Accepting that he couldn't outsmile or outstretch Ike, Adlai turned up with a hole in his shoe, and while the A.D.A. may ask to extend their remarks in the record, that *was* the high point of the Illinois governor's 1952 campaign.

Adlai was a millionaire (and Ike wasn't far from it then, either), but the hole-in-shoe picture said to the voter, "We all have our problems." The response was so electric that Stevenson smartly followed up the lead. He appeared in shirts with slightly peeling collars. He let his Libertyville, Illinois, farmhouse run down to where the dismally gray clapboards resembled his peeling shirts. However, he stopped short. He would not remove his coat. This would have stated the raveling collars with more conviction. Somehow Adlai clung to the incomplete idea that people should choose between candidates on a basis of their beliefs and past performances. Which is no way to win elections.

The shoe was not a total loss, however. He had it half-soled and went on to the United Nations where he now may dress as spiffily as he wants with new shoes every day, without a voter to worry about.

The Good New Days

Even a skimming review of studied inversities of the Good New Days should take into consideration some of the demigods. Their standing in the national community is intrinsic and as worthy of understanding as the acceptables, the *de rigueur*ous and the *pro forma*nts.

In the current climate, one should, without waiting to hear the facts, take a guarded view of any crusader. A crusader is quite different from an idealist or one of Kennedy's professors. A crusader is a nut. He may come to Washington with a cause so clearly just that we stand back from the glare of its simplicity. This in itself warrants quick rejection of the crusader, because if it's simple, it can't be good.

Anything easily understandable should be suspect. If any clod can understand it, why did we waste all those years at the university?

Women's organizations. The cowardly way might be to say quickly, "Not yours, madam." It is true, however, New People seem less impressed by clubwomen than Washington of other years. Mrs. Roosevelt may have started this trend, because she was forever tangling with such outfits as the Daughters of the American Revolution.

The D.A.R. has been against much of what administrations have proposed and much of what government has done since the end of World War II. Even Mamie Eisenhower began to have her doubts about the good times to be had with the D.A.R. This could be a rather serious indictment, because Mamie, when she put her mind to it, could be about the most affable hostess ever to entertain in Quarters 1600.

Women singly and in small groups are ever so well regarded by the New People. But when the ladies begin to shape up in lots of several thousand, drape themselves in officious ribbons and medals which denote little more than tenancy on the local level, and then for certain periods each year tie up Washington cabs and hotel space with their national conventions—if the truth were known, not even the Old People liked it, and national gatherings have grown since those days to terrifying proportions.

It is unfair to blame the D.A.R. for all disfavor which women's organizations may incur with the New People. Some societies make even a greater impact. Frankly, some of them live it up in a manner suggestive of The American Legion before their conventioneers mellowed.

It is an alarming male experience to be trapped in a hotel elevator during a national convention of a more active girls' club and, in bosom-to-back cordiality, be evaluated openly, accurately and depressingly. The late John Foster Dulles once burst from a Washington hotel elevator with a look of hunted terror after a free-wheeling lady delegate piped up, "I think he's cute." The late Secretary of State may have been many things, but not cute.

A state of demigodliness also applies in the Good New Days to certain largely male organizations; not for their conventions, which seem to run much smaller than the female assemblies, but for their innate dullness. Doctors and bankers have fun at their conventions, but there are so many of them that they usually gather away from Washington. What we get are the dull ones— all kinds of engineers, educators, electrical contractors, computer makers. These birds come to Washington wanting something done. Their groups are so small that they're in a Senator's office before he knows it.

Election years naturally cause some shifting in attitudes. The Senator may hide from a delegation this year, but race into the capitol grounds to greet them the next. Congressmen, having to run every two years, cannot afford a slack season, as the Senators can. House members should remain constantly polite, even to ladies with badges and large ribbons.

CHAPTER FOUR

A Living Curiosity

> There are blessed intervals when I forget by one means or another
> that I am President of the United States.
>
> Woodrow Wilson

The curiosities of Washington go far beyond incongruities recently touched upon, but before getting into such things as lobbyists and fairly normal housewives who become political hoboes, it may be advisable to take up a more intriguing question: Why do sensible people, well-fixed, outwardly successful and with time for enjoyment of the advertised pleasures of life, suddenly chuck everything for a place in the unkind, burning political sun?

Power? Few of them ever have it. Prominence? Yes, but of a perishable sort. Money? It is better to have it before coming to Washington, particularly in a position of importance. If there's anything a Congressman, and apparently a voter, hates, it is a well-paid federal employee. Dedication to public service? Thank God, some. Glamor? Particularly for ambitious state capital wives who envision themselves in Washington as forever hobnobbing with royalty, movie stars and David Brinkley.

American mothers, since that ship was off-loaded on Plymouth Rock, have cherished the idea of a son eventually making it to the side of the Chief Justice on Inauguration Day. Today some mothers take Mrs. Roosevelt and Clare Booth Luce seriously and think of little Marjorie as presidential material a few years hence.

This is properly part of the American dream, but so is Elizabeth Taylor, and most of us don't do anything about getting rid of her latest man except think while walking home from the neighborhood movie.

Many Americans do more than dream of the Presidency. Having only superficial knowledge of what realizing the dream entails, they break themselves, their families and frequently their fortunes seeking the American pinnacle.

For thirty-five men who've climbed the road to the White House successfully, there are in history thousands of hopefuls who went to their graves completely but miserably confident that except for mysterious thievery and occult circumstances, they, too, could have made it.

Thus the lure of the Presidency is more than a dream; it is a virus for which there is no known drug except victory. And frequently the victors, although never disparaging the office, rebel and lurch against its confines once it is theirs.

Shortly after ten o'clock one July morning a distinguished-looking man eased out of the White House front door. Clad in a linen suit, white shirt and dark tie and carrying a small bundle of papers under one arm, he paused on the portico and looked about furtively.

Then he started down a long walk leading to the northeast gate on Pennsylvania Avenue. His pace quickened and he sailed through the gate as passers-by stared at him.

He reached the sidewalk and cast a worried look over his

shoulder before heading toward the Treasury building and nearby shopping district. At that moment, the White House doors flew open. Two husky men raced across the portico and down the steps, their coattails flapping as they ran with urgent, ponderous muscularity.

Sizing up his predicament, the man on the sidewalk began to run. Clutching his bundle of papers, he darted around sightseers, murmured soft apologies and sped across the street to the Treasury sidewalk. There the two burly pursuers pulled up beside him, puffing and looking stern, but saying nothing. Their quarry gave up the race and slowed with dropped-shoulder dejection.

"I came very near getting away that time," said President Woodrow Wilson to the two Secret Service agents. His fun spoiled, Wilson then walked to his bank and on to a haberdashery before treading glumly back to the White House.

On another and later occasion, the setting was the north shore of Massachusetts, just outside of Swampscott. The house was a large frame structure on a fairly isolated point beside the beach.

It was early morning. The sun scattered diamonds on the sea and the beach was empty. Even the hardiest New Englanders had better sense than to try swimming on the north shore before noon.

Two men were in the kitchen having coffee and heard a side door slam. They leaped from the table and looked out a window. A man, dressed in a summer wash suit with high stiff-collared shirt, was racing away from the house. Although he ran hard, his progress was slow because of the heavy sand. His primly pointed dress shoes sent up little geysers of sand with each labored step.

One of the men in the kitchen cautioned his companion. "Let him get a start, then we'll run down the hard part of the beach and catch him before he gets to the New Ocean House," he said.

They put down their coffee cups and set out, running easily along the harder sand at the water's edge. They closed the gap handily in less than two hundred yards. Their quarry tried putting on a burst of speed, but the sand was too much for him and he stopped. He coldly surveyed the two agents and turned back toward the house. Sadly retracing his steps across the sand, President Calvin Coolidge turned to one of the Secret Service men and said tartly, "I almost did it."

Once, on the golf course of the majestic old Ponce de Leon Hotel at St. Augustine, Florida, President Warren G. Harding tried to play without Secret Service men following him.

The federal protectors persisted, however, and the next day when Harding played, he insisted that they caddy for his foursome. For the next several holes, he deliberately hit as many shots as possible into the rough so that they spent most of the afternoon clumping over palmetto roots and damning the mosquitoes.

F.D.R. had a small Ford phaeton equipped with special controls so his infantile paralysis would not prevent his driving. He took particular delight in trying to race away from his staff at Hyde Park and in Warm Springs, on occasion driving at breakneck speed up lonely, dead-end country roads and sitting in silence until discovered.

After this happened a few times, his staff and Secret Service men learned virtually all of the possible secret routes and let him have his fun, within limits. After twenty minutes or so, the Secret Service agents would decide to go get him, and then stumble across his hidden car with loud cries of mock surprise. On at least one occasion, the agents were downright nasty and didn't discover him at all, leaving him to emerge somewhat crestfallen from his well-known hiding place. He was as miffed as a child who stayed out after bedtime and returned to find that no one had missed him.

With enlargement of the Secret Service, refinement of short-wave radio and realization of the futility of it all, Truman pondered but never really tried escape, although he did mutter about the White House being a prison. Eisenhower was too well trained as a military man to think of fleeing. He was not the type to start running down a beach (he didn't like beaches anyway), and for most of his adult life, he'd been accustomed to having functionaries around him twenty-four hours a day.

As this was written, President Kennedy had not been on the scene long enough to determine whether he would attempt a break-out, but the emotional climate was there. Kennedy has one strange presidential trait, however. He would not object if an amateur photographer, a complete stranger, took his picture while balancing a kumquat on his nose, but just let a professional photographer get within five hundred yards and the President begins to feel like a hunted animal. He seems to ignore completely the fact that the friendly, harmless amateur, armed with one of the finest lenses available, may trot right to *Life* Magazine with his stuff if it's any good.

These examples of presidential behavior raise a highly difficult question: Why do they seek the job in the first place?

Men who bull and claw their way into 1600 Pennsylvania Avenue have a common quality. During an election campaign, they are so sugary that diabetics would be advised to stand at least five feet away. Repeatedly, they say during campaigns, "When we get down to Washington, you better not come to town without letting Martha and me know—come see us, that's what the place is for."

But the hour after he takes the oath of office, the new President moans to Martha, "Why won't they leave us alone?"

During a President's first term, there is talk by his associates about burdens of the office, how we're slowly killing our elected leader and how the poor man needs all the rest, relaxation and freedom from the White House he possibly can get. Having believed this for many years, this writer is now willing to argue the point with ammunition picked from the battlefield.

In electing a President, we tend to fashion him along superhuman lines in our minds. We forget, unless we're attacking him politically, that he's still human and quite open to suggestion. And here's where his friends enter and add to his misery.

All Presidents seem to have at least one essentially dumb friend, a pleasant fellow with money who can afford to hang around in volunteer service as personal errand boy, punching bag, laugher-at, confidant and companion. If they're smart, these dumb fellows never argue. They are emotional chameleons. If the President feels fine, the friend does push-ups. If the President feels low, the friend comes down with acute yips. If the President says, "It looks like rain," the friend says, "We're in for a helluva storm."

These men really make the Presidency worse than it is. A President says he has a bad pain in his foot and there's invariably a chum at close range who foams about pressures of the job. You tell a President, or for that matter, a school principal, that he's being ground to bits by his job and if you tell him often enough, some of it is bound to sink in.

There also are around every President, in addition to the dumb one who usually comes out of it richer than when he went in, a small cadre of friends who devote most of their time to seeing that the cadre is not enlarged. It's like owning a Cadillac. If they were as cheap as Fords, who would want one? It's the same at the White House. Being in the inner circle isn't worth it if there are too many members.

Thus the cadre members spend a great deal of time discouraging recruitment. They do this by drumming at the President with the suggestion that virtually all outside their immediate circle are dedicated to his ultimate or eventual destruction. Cabinet members frequently have to step around these protective bodies to carry on vital business of government.

In three different administrations, I heard three different friends of three different Presidents say almost identically, "I do wish the Secretary of Interior would leave him alone." And this from men without the slightest official status or responsibility.

A Living Curiosity

Another frequent word from the inside of any administration, "They'll kill the President if they don't stop asking him to make speeches." This is nonsense. A President is a politician and politicians love to talk. A top-flight politician starts talking even before he gets out of bed in the morning and he keeps it up, even while eating and drinking, for about eighteen hours. The strongest part of any President's body are his vocal cords. One reason a President may appear a bit glum when he walks into church is he knows that he'll have to be quiet for nearly an hour. Some Presidents relieve the strain by singing hymns loudly.

A President also has company for virtually every meal he consumes in the White House, and this includes breakfast. Friends say this is another example of the killing nature of the job. A better guess might be that he doesn't want to eat alone, and his wife by this time has turned into a rather unresponsive audience primarily because she's been listening to her beloved day and night for years.

Possibly because of F.D.R.'s death and Eisenhower's illnesses, it became popular to dwell on the killing nature of the Presidency. Without attempting to encompass all of history, facts would seem to dispute the theory that the White House is a well-upholstered death cell.

For one thing, those who maintain that burdens of the Presidency become more pressing and increasingly complex with each passing year seem to forget that with these passing years Presidents seem to survive more successfully. Heaven forbid circumstances require later editing, but as this was written there were three living ex-Presidents—Hoover, Truman, and Eisenhower—and this for the first time in history.

It also is highly debatable whether Franklin Roosevelt's death was hastened by the Presidency. Considering his background of polio and arteriosclerosis, the carefully supervised life he led in the White House may well have prolonged, and not shortened, his life.

The Good New Days

A President who cannot detach himself from his job, or on occasion let some of the air out of his own importance, may be in for trouble. They still tell a story around the White House of Coolidge dropping off to sleep in his office one afternoon. He awoke to see a Cabinet officer squinting at him through a crack in the door.

"Is the country still here?" Cal inquired.

William Hard, writing in *Atlantic Monthly* in 1936, hooted at what he called the "crushingness" of the Presidency. He pointed out that Teddy Roosevelt emerged from the White House saying he had "a bully time," and departed soon thereafter on expeditions to Africa and South America; William Howard Taft went from the Presidency to a long career as law teacher and jurist.

Hard thought in 1936 that other Presidents might have a bully time in the White House, too, if they would "dispense with a little of the mixture of sentimentalism and megalomania which afflicts a good many of them." Hard argued that many of the Chief Executive's burdens stemmed from his aggressive busybodiness and arrogant determination to be all things to as many men and women as possible.

A bit overdrawn perhaps, but close to the truth.

Busybodiness and arrogance are fueled largely by those closest to a President. Theoretically, he is well informed on major matters. Therefore, friends and closer staff members compete with each other to be the first with choice morsels of gossip which they justify as internal intelligence.

There's also a completely nonpartisan organism which seems to infect most occupants of the White House. Call it simply the "right" bug. Because we elect a man President, we expect him to be eternally "right." He begins to believe it, himself, and so do the people around him.

Considering the multitude of problems and decisions that flow across a President's desk daily, how could he possibly be right all of the time? Conduct of the Presidency is anything but a precise science since it deals largely with conduct of humans. To pretend that a former Senator from Massachusetts, Missouri, California or Arizona acquired foot-sure omnipotence and flawless judgment through the magic of national election is time-wasting sham. But we practice it. And we add strain on the Presidency with such an attitude, particularly if the object of our affections happens to believe it himself.

Quite aside from the "right" bug, a President can work up a quick sweat about his privacy, and here again friends are ready to help, as long as he keeps them in the golden corral.

There is virtually no limit on the extent to which a presidential candidate will invade his own privacy. His wife is paraded at airport rallies, railroad station gatherings, and across stages of countless auditoria as a carnival attraction. There are those who maintain to this day that Stevenson would have done much better against Eisenhower if he'd had a wife along to exchange little homekeeper hints and jelly recipes with the lady voters. This probably is not a good example, however, because the first Mrs. Stevenson (at this writing, there is no second Mrs. Stevenson, but Adlai still is quite attractive to many women) was an arty type who supported an avant-garde poetry movement in Chicago and this might not have played well at all with ladies who purr appreciatively over a good jam recipe.

If the Presidency takes some years off the life of a man, it is done during a campaign. By some American mystique, a man is better equipped for the job by having shaken hands with us. While we're planning colonies in space, this is a most unscientific method of appraising presidential potential. A man may go a lifetime with little or no attendance at church, but we forgive the past if he starts showing up at any church with regularity while he's running for office. And he must love animals. Two or three lovable mutts in his family will produce more votes than an M.I.T. degree. This is about as sensible as the handshake, but just try to think of a successful presidential candidate who ran sans dog.

Russia shoots her dogs into space and sends us the leftovers (witness the space dog Khrushchev sent J.F.K.) whereas we tie dogs to our candidates.

A presidential aspirant without children also is dead on the launching pad. Not only must he have children, but like them and all other children as well. He must like them filthy, quarrelsome, kicking, screaming and biting ("spirited little fellow, isn't he, but what's a boy without spirit?"). His own kids must be models of deportment, each daughter an exceptional little homemaker who stitches her own bibs on the tiny sewing machine made for her by her brother, known to his many friends as Scout Bob.

A photogenic grandson is political money, banked and paying interest. David Eisenhower was far better known than his own father, a fine upstanding Army officer who sank quickly from view in the comely appeal of his children.

Anyone with children knows that in the normal course of family life, Goodness Itself, reincarnated in the form of son or daughter, is bound to raise a little hell at times, with the result that Mother and Father bark, rage, throw punches and send the offender away in temporary banishment.

During a political campaign, however, a would-be President who spanked one of his children would be regarded as an arch-fiend. He could do no more harm to his cause by kicking his wife in the mouth.

And eat? This comes just behind handshaking, liking children, and going to church. We want our Presidents to eat, every hour if necessary, to prove there's nothing on this world to beat American home cooking. Which, of course, is one of the great sadnesses of our time. *Some* Americans are good cooks just as *some* French are dandy in the kitchen. But the minute a man declares for President, he declares himself on the side of all native cookery. The food may be so bad the host won't touch it, but the candidate had better go for seconds if he wants votes in that neighborhood.

A President may be utterly allergic to shellfish and break out in zebra stripes when confronted by lobster, but he'd better not say anything about it in New England. Just eat and get to bed early, after sending for the doctor. A President who lets it leak out that he dislikes fried chicken would be President without the votes of countless Southerners.

A potential President also is in trouble when he likes a particular food. If he is so witless as to say in public that he can't get enough coconut cake, he'll find it every time he sits down to a meal for the next twenty years. Long after he's out of office, old ladies will be throwing together soggy confections and shipping them to him because somehow they get the idea that it is *their* special cake he likes above all others.

When the votes are counted and the loser climbs the heights of insincerity with his cheery, sporting farewell, the winner sleeps for a few hours and arises to don the girdle of exceptionality.

One of the first symptoms of victory is to kick reporters and photographers into the street. For months, they've lived with the candidate, called him by his first name and listened to his every thought, repeatedly. These deathless friends go first—OUT. A spokesman roars after them, "Can't a man have any privacy?" Forty-eight hours before, the last thing he wanted was privacy, but things can change rather rapidly when the big board shows more than 266 electoral votes.

Then the winner roars to his staff, "The next person who shoves a piece of coconut cake at me gets it right back in the kisser—and get that goddamned dog out of here."

His wife tries to have a moment with him, but a man she never saw before says, "Could you come back in an hour, perhaps? The President is tied up right now."

Then when she does get to see him she merely wants plane fare home to enjoy a rest on her own, far from the sound of his voice. Besides, four picture magazines want to do new layouts on the kids and interior of the house.

"I will not have our children raised in a goldfish bowl," is a favorite saying of new Presidents. After the election.

Thus we have what has become a fairly classic situation. A man expends so much energy and suffers so many indignities in seeking the Presidency that he arrives at the White House bushed and irritable. His trailing band of sycophants are so distressed by his attitude that they set up a wail about crushing burdens of the job, invasion of his privacy, cruelty of the public. And this before his first paycheck.

To meet this dreadful situation and stand up under burdens which seem to take on more weight with each sympathetic tear, the President then has to begin running away from the White House, from his staff, from the Secret Service and the public. In the job he had before winning the Presidency, he worked longer hours with less staff, rarely more than one day off a week and frequently not that much; he had to do his own shopping at times and pay his own bills, and if he got as much as a month away from the office in the summer, he spent it politicking.

But now, because people tell him constantly that he's working himself to death, his burdens are unbearable, the cruel public will never be satisfied until they can own and examine every shred of him; that he ought to get away as much as possible—because people tell him these things constantly, some of it absorbs. He may even brood about it, at least until time to run for a second term. And after his second term, he spends the rest of his life reliving the Good Old Days.

In departing the White House at the end of his second term, a leaving which is now constitutionally required because Franklin Roosevelt won four times, the outgoing President participates in one of the sadder dramas of our political theater.

Restive Europeans once beheaded their rulers to get rid of them. In a sense, we're less considerate. We simply throw our old ones away. At noon on Inauguration Day, the Presidency becomes a bus at the last stop for the incumbent. It may be high noon to the new crowd, but it's black midnight to him.

Even if succeeded by a member of his own party—which is rather rare, because we have a tendency to switch from side to side in boredom with one administration after eight years—the outgoing President is not treated with the courtesy shown Joe DiMaggio on Old Timers' Day. The White House may give him a car to get to the airport, but little more.

One minute, he can command the services of thousands; the next minute, he may command only a cab driver.

Knowing these things, Alf Landon, Tom Dewey, Adlai Stevenson, Jimmy Byrnes and many others still wish and believe. And, waiting in the wings, still more.*

* A situation also discussed by the author in 1948 in *A President Is Many Men* (Harper).

An Olio

Many years ago, during tent shows and chautauquas the proceedings halted periodically to give the principals a rest, permit the sale of candy, or provide lesser members of the company a chance to display their talents, which were not up to inclusion in feature presentations. This break in the show was called the olio.

Sometimes the purpose of the olio was to lend credibility to or explain the rest of the show. It is within this rough frame of reference that the following is presented. There are times in this book when the hypothesis may seem hypoed. But here we have an unvarnished account of life among the N.P. in Georgetown, with parenthetic remarks by this author in *italics*.

From the Washington *Post* of August 25, 1961:

BACHELORS' BALL LACKS ONE JFK
By Dorothy McCardle

Three lonely bachelors gave a round-robin party Wednesday in Georgetown. They were only sorry that a fourth lonely

An Olio

bachelor, President Kennedy, couldn't come, too. [*The* Post *front page the same day told how the President was deeply concerned about the Russian threat to Berlin.*] But a fifth lonely bachelor, Attorney General Robert F. Kennedy, did come.

The three hosts, whose wives are all away, were Stephen Smith, Special Assistant to the Director of Special Operations [*SADSO?*] in State Department and brother-in-law of President Kennedy; Donald Wilson, Deputy Director of the U.S. Information Agency, and Rowland Evans, New York Herald Tribune correspondent.

Smith, whose wife, Jean Kennedy Smith, is the sister of the President, [*still with us?*] had a "lonely bachelor dinner" together with Wilson and Evans on Tuesday night. They decided to toss a dinner dance the next night. [*That's fighting back, fellows.*] They wrote out crazy telegrams about wives being off in Yugoslavia (Jean Kennedy Smith and Eunice Kennedy Shriver are there). They had the Robert Kennedys' social secretary put in calls to Parties Unlimited and to Ira Sabin to send round his orchestra.

[*Try to imagine the scene Tuesday night. They're in Steve's kitchen eating cold beans out of a can and one of the fellows cries, "Say, I know what let's do—let's write some crazy telegrams about our wives being in Yugoslavia, hire a caterer and an orchestra, and have some fun."*]

The party began with dinner at the home of Evans on O St. [*But not until after a voice on the White House end of a telephone said nothing doing, not with Berlin in such a mess.*] Some 20 young people [*see what we were talking about, Perle?*], including Sargent Shriver, Under Secretary of the Navy, and Mrs. Paul Burgess Fay, Jr., and Senator Claiborne Pell of Rhode Island and Mrs. Pell turned up. [*Were they invited or weren't they?*] Funny speeches about the overnight telegraphed invitations were made by three hosts.

66

The Good New Days

[*Sarge, Paul and Claiborne didn't get their telegrams because they refused to pay the collect charges, but what the hell, they turned up, didn't they?*]

Then everybody adjourned across the street to the Smith house for dancing, coffee, and a nightcap. In the back garden, a dance platform had been set up under the stars and a few threatening clouds. Had the wives been home, they could not have turned out any prettier setting. Butterfly lights had been strung through the trees like Christmas lights. And Japanese lanterns were hanging from the many trees.

[*"I feel sorta funny, standing here stringing butterfly lights through the trees like Christmas lights, with my wife in Yugoslavia," Steve said. "I'm doing the Japanese lanterns and my wife's only on Cape Cod," Don shot back. Rollie didn't have much to say because he was rather busy at the time nailing the dance platform together.*]

Everyone took a fast turn to the strains of Sabin's four-piece dance band.

[*Then they all went over to Allen Dulles' house and rang his doorbell and ran like crazy to their own houses which all are very close. Upstairs, Dulles, in flannelette pajamas with natural shoulders, snapped off his C.I.A. code machine, listened to the doorbell and then to the patter of young people scattering to their homes. With an understanding smile, he murmured, "Ah, youth!"*]

CHAPTER FIVE

Juniority, Georgetown and Chevy Chase

Juniority, sometimes referred to as seniority, is one of the more reliable keys to Washington status, sometimes referred to as rank. Under the accepted arrangement of life-giving properties within the District of Columbia and its environs, first there is blood, then air, and then rank. Determination of status and/or rank involves an impure science of relativity, the theorem for which not even the celebrated Einstein could have mastered. The way our system works, only one man in town has all he needs—the President. From then on, progression is downward.

Status and seniority frequently equate. When there is a difference, it relates to durability. A lobbyist may have status but no seniority except among other lobbyists. Seniority for many in and around government is difficult to determine. One cannot be completely secure as an old-timer because there's invariably an older-timer who never lets a younger-timer forget it through such devices as "I'll admit Coolidge was interesting, but you should have been here a bit earlier when we . . ."

69

The Good New Days

Washington is a great town for deans. The diplomatic corps has its dean, as do the House, Senate, private clubs, the American Automobile Association, and bookmakers. Officers of the armed forces rank each other by date in grade. So do government elevator operators.

Dean of the diplomatic corps is an ambassador with longest continuous service in Washington. This is custom in most world capitals. Other ambassadors rank behind the dean according to day and date, and in some tight cases, even time of day when they presented their letters of credence to the President. Diplomatic seniority gives the possessors better seats at banquets, the right to go through receiving lines first, and access to numerous cocktail parties.

Other deanships also are determined by starting time of continuous service. But there are deans along the fringe of government who are under almost constant attack or challenge. To refer to anyone as dean of the Washington press corps, for example, is inviting trouble, because to determine this accurately would involve a mass meeting of several thousand men and women who are not particularly fond of each other to begin with. The meeting would be utterly without progress, because there could never be agreement on definition of the press. Therefore, the field in Washington journalism is cut up into various deanships—White House, State Department, Congressional, Radio, Television, baseball, football, and even such things as dean of Washington food editors.

To say that a man in Washington is a dean is to cloak him with a certain amount of reverence, knowledge and standing in his particular part of the community. He may be a genius, but if it is said of him that "he's rather junior," he is destined for additional duty below the salt. His opinions and bright sayings may be copied, stolen or borrowed with little or no credit unless it is for someone senior. To complicate matters further, a forty-year-old woman may be senior to a sixty-year-old man, which makes neither

70

of them feel entirely right about the situation except on paydays. Then she feels more right than he does.

In no other sector of Washington and possibly the world does juniority depress, and seniority uplift, as in Congress. Length of service is the one and only commandment. A man who survives election after election moves upward into positions of amazing authority and distinction. Elderly pragmatists become powerful committee chairmen due to superior prostates and rugged livers more than for their knowledge or legislative ability.

Older members of the House and Senate undoubtedly will reject this theory, just as they automatically reject, then study, proposals of their political opponents. The truth is, however, that a man regardless of ability must be blessed with a good prostate and liver to last it out long enough to accede to a top chairmanship. With wisdom of a Disraeli and legislative acumen of a Tom Watson, the same man would never make it without highly durable inner equipment, for the chase is unbelievably long. To the elderly goes the chairmanship; to the rheumy-eyed and palsied, credit for vision and vigor.

Juniority reaches its most humbling state in a freshman House member. In the Washington scheme of things, he's about the lowest form of political and official life, with the prestige of a second lieutenant at the Pentagon. This in fact may be a poor analogy, because there are said to be colonels at the Pentagon who've never seen a second lieutenant.

Junior Senators also have a difficult time. Suppose, for example, New Jersey elects a forty-year-old man to the Senate and, two or four years later, elects another Senator, this time a man of sixty. Assume that they continue to win elections. Twenty years pass. The eighty-year-old man still is the junior Senator from New Jersey. If his colleague's innards stand up under tests of time, politics and Washington food, our old youngster from New Jersey will be saluted on his hundredth birthday as junior Senator while his eighty-year-old senior bobs and spittles in brotherly approval.

The Good New Days

New People see the iniquities of the seniority system, but they know better than to tangle with them. There's always a chance an N.P. will be senior some day. Therefore, New People in their quest for status have concentrated more on areas where their position is determined largely by political achievement and customs of the achievers.

In this situation, status requires certain coloration—housing, clothing, automobiles. Properly housed, clothed and motored, virtually any mildly pecunious product of a good Eastern college can blend into the better people of modern Washington and become one of them with little else on his dossier.

For fuller appreciation of this social osmosis, we return to Georgetown, a residential area referred to earlier in what might be regarded as salacity by some rickety pewholders. Unblinded by the flame of belonging, however, a new viewer would see Georgetown as a strange hodepodge of slum and elegance. Ratty or regal, it is a modern Capital must—a neighborhood detached from which New People tend to be nervous, uncomfortable or disdainful.

Georgetown is for narrow bodies and broad minds. Because the residents are so deucedly proper and acceptably blooded, there's no finer setting for an ugly wife who's a bit on the horsey side and resembles a tweedy woman watching her husband shoot skeet in a *Town and Country* ad. Georgetown also is fine for ugly wives because even pretty ones affect a fashionable ugliness, flitting about shabby stalls and overpriced groceries with no makeup except beige lipstick and a slight scent of Crisco, with full-bodied manes of carefully uncombed hair caught up in pipe cleaners. And shoes from under a spreading chestnut tree.

Streets are narrow, houses are narrow and, necessarily, occupants thereof. In other American neighborhoods, householders proudly display living rooms thirty feet in width. The same pride is shown in Georgetown for a salon eight or ten feet wide. Fifty feet long would be chic, but the width must be restricted lest the home smack of something later than early nineteenth century. Some entire houses are less than twenty feet wide which makes for interesting dinner parties and bed arrangements. With such dimensions in style, hallways must be little more than slits. This makes it almost impossible for fat people to blend into the community with any measure of comfort.

Better known and higher ranking New People circa 1962 live in Georgetown with the controlled sense of *liberté, égalité* and good breeding to say as little as possible about noisy neighbors if theirs is the good noise of Bartók, Jelly Roll Morton, or a potted young diplomat above the rank of third secretary.

President Kennedy is without question the currently oustanding alumnus of Georgetown. During the period between his first election and inauguration, he used his powdery old red brick house on N Street as a base for intermittent operations between visits to New York and Palm Beach. Neighbors looked from their ancient windows with disapproval at the commotion in front of Kennedy's house, but this changed to approbation and even mild exhibitionism when the same neighbors began turning up in background shots for the Douglas Edwards show.

One or two Republicans in the President's block were sore losers and sent maids to shoo sightseers from their stoops, but real estate dealers were bravely nonpartisan and shot house prices skyward. As N Street became increasingly hallowed and well-publicized, the Kennedys made room for newcomers by moving to a house on Pennsylvania Avenue.

After deciding that government quarters would do for a few years, J.F.K. off-loaded the sanctuary on N Street at a good profit, and his tiny hallways then creaked to the proud tread of New People whose position was thus assured.

There must be moments when a cold draft slips beneath the sash windows of Georgetown, even beneath windows of houses rented as youth hostels and salons of influence or comfort by distillers and aircraft manufacturers. These errant breezes carry a disturbing message—Bobby Kennedy doesn't live there.

This can be most unsettling for New People if thrown, for instance, into a conversation among people from Milwaukee who find it hard to understand why Thermopane shrines of the building industry are not preferable to period pieces of Georgetown. But among themselves, Georgetowners know that the case of the Attorney General is unusual and defensible. Bobby and Ethel have, at this writing, seven children. God knows, Doctor Spock himself couldn't raise seven kids in one of those Georgetown houses even with the advice and consent of Doctor Gesell.

Because of high population density practiced by the President's brother, Robert and Ethel are forgiven for living in the Virginia suburbs, as long as they visit the neighborhood periodically for friendly little reunions in the Seventh Precinct.

The reasons for Georgetown's desirability as a neighborhood for New People are not entirely capricious. Living there is rejection of the ordinary. Georgetown antedates most of the capital. Many of the houses may lean somewhat, but they were built in the late eighteenth century. Also, the center of the community is protected against commercial inroads. Zealous civic organizations see to it that commerce remains on the outer edges of Georgetown, and in character. Consequently, the bars and stores are little wider than the houses.

There are other status areas of housing in Washington, but not matching the undisputed symbolism of historic Georgetown. Foxhall Road, which begins on the blurred northwest border of Georgetown, is fine for middle-aged, well-heeled fashionables; for those who entertain by the gross, and thereby at times entertain rather grossly. Dinner for a dozen or cocktails for thirty would be tops for most of the N.P. Georgetowners. On Foxhall Road, the parking lots are larger than the best homes of Georgetown.

Spring Valley, another part of the northwest section of Washington, was excellent under the Republicans. Nixon lived there (he also sold his house at a good profit when Whittier, California, beckoned after 1960). Architecturally, Spring Valley is centuries later than Georgetown, but not many of the residents. Their political ikons may bear the sayings of a Garfield rather than a Roosevelt. There are admirals and Senators in Spring Valley who fought vigorously against construction of a hospital near, not in, their section because a medical facility would attract undesirables—the sick and wounded who never have helped any neighborhood.

Today Spring Valley might be acceptable to New People as the home site for a rather square Cabinet officer who was brought to town because Jack thought he might be good for government. But no real activist of the N.P. would live there for at least two reasons—his wife would feel odd about running across a hundred-foot lawn to borrow a bottle of Vermouth; and also, he would be far removed from Action Central, which is the area of government buildings and embassies—and Georgetown.

Chevy Chase, at the far end of Connecticut Avenue on the northwest side of the District but east of Georgetown, Foxhall Road and Spring Valley, once was good in the accepted sense of officialdom, but no more. Not for the best, at any rate. Chevy Chase is an outright suburb, just on the Maryland border, and New People avoid suburbs when possible. Lawns must be mowed, Scouts must be trooped, parents and teachers must be associated. This is all respectable and necessary, but dreadfully time-consuming.

Consequently, on most N.P. maps Chevy Chase would be marked only as the location of the Chevy Chase Country Club. The C.C.C.C. is the oldest such establishment hereabouts, and has an adequate golf course but better tennis courts, which are more attractive to many N.P. than golf facilities (again, that old business about Ike). But quite seriously, there are N.P. who give C.C.C.C. a wide berth because of such O.P. era hangovers as discouraging the inviting of Jewish dinner guests. This is an un-attractive fact, but still fact without an unlikely and sudden change of club directoral heart before this is published.

Eisenhower was about to accept an invitation to play Chevy Chase early in his White House stay when his press secretary, Jim Hagerty, received not one, but at least two copies of a letter sent by club officials to a C.C.C.C. member suggesting that he not bring Jewish luncheon guests to the sacred precincts again. So informed, Ike continued to concentrate on Burning Tree.

Chevy Chase Club, however, does continue to be a high status symbol for many Washingtonians on the conservative side, even if involved with a current administration. And so does Burning Tree, which has only one severe standard of membership—that the member be male, demented on the subject of golf, relatively important and possessed of about $1,500 with which to pay the entrance fee. The membership is much more informal than that of Chevy Chase, imbued by a gusty locker-room comradeship which hit its peak when members were introduced to the President of the United States—in the shower.

All private clubs are discriminatory. They differ in this quality only as to how much. Washington has some predominantly Jewish country clubs where Lutheran ministers, to stab at an outlandish example, would not be regarded as prime membership material.

Acceptance of private clubs is another of the more curious incongruities of Washington and the New People. There are gentile N.P.'s who delight in the tennis courts of C.C.C.C. But they don't like some of the customs. We have no desire to make Chevy Chase a lonely target for solo invidiousness. A somewhat similarly incongruous situation exists downtown with the Metropolitan Club, which many N.P. regard with awe and acceptance often reserved for temples.

The Metropolitan Club is a midday status symbol, a luncheon haven for thought-makers, White Division. Some of our town's most ardent liberals were disturbed early in the current wave of New People to have it brought out rudely that Metropolitan had not, up to that point, admitted Negro members. Bobby Kennedy wrote a rather mean letter to the club about this; then Secretary of Labor Arthur J. Goldberg quit cold, and other N.P. began to find the delightful luncheon menu something less than complete.

(If the author appears to be burning his bridges to clubland, it is only because he is neither O.P. nor N.P., and his memberships are limited economically to such things as the All-State Policyholders' Club and Blue Cross. For somewhat different reasons, President Kennedy at the time of his election had not a club membership to his distinguished name, much to dismay of the clubs. He plays golf in Palm Beach at a predominantly Jewish country club on his father's membership. Burning Tree has made him an honorary member and he played there several times. He also played at least once at Chevy Chase as a guest and very early in his White House tenure.)

Having touched briefly on status aspects of juniority, seniority and housing, domestic and recreational, we move on to other colorations of belonging or amounting, whichever, as the tax forms say, is larger.

Cut away from the strange protocol of diplomacy, Congress and the armed services, probably one of the more critical status symbols of modern Washington is largely overlooked by non-Washingtonians—parking space.

An assigned parking place on public property, a narrow little white-lined slot that remains inviolately empty on days when the occupant doesn't come to work—there is a mark unmatched even by having been shoved into Bobby Kennedy's pool.

Not even Mrs. Mesta in her heyday had her own parking place downtown unless she paid for it or was permitted to have her limousine ease into the space of another. But the important thing is that she had no space to call her very own. This may not seem much, just at random, to a wealthy author like Merla Zellerbach

77

of San Francisco, whose chauffeur could buy a parking lot if necessary; to Jack Paar, who can park in the basement of NBC; or to an actress like June Lockhart, who has Lassie to rely on for transportation. But an assigned space is shoutingly important in Washington. This is where the little man cuts the big man down. Or at least, has his moments of superiority.

Dreadful feuds develop within government departments over assignment of spaces, and then the loose system of seniority operates. A new administration naturally doles out prime spaces to its own crowd, but not even the new New People can dislodge veteran civil servants who've been occupying the same parking spaces for years. These more or less permanent federalists hang on to what is theirs simply by not telling the New People where *all* the spaces are. Furthermore, parking spaces are so highly treasured that outgoing federal workers have been known to delay their departures from Washington merely to cling to their parking places, until discovered quite late in a new administration.

In fact, office space and stenographers have been held over in the same manner. When the Eisenhower battalions arrived, an official of the Truman Administration lasted for six months in a small, well-hidden office of the old State Department building with his equally Democratic secretary.

They managed well, drew their pay twice a month and supplies as needed, until one day an Eisenhower official blundered into the office while seeking the men's room. The Ike man thought he knew just about everybody on the White House staff and inquired almost humbly, "What do you do?"

"Winding up the affairs of this office," was the straightforward, almost indignant reply. It took another three weeks to root him out. He then went on about three months' accumulated leave while his secretary found a spot in General Services, until the Democrats came in behind Kennedy and fired her for having been an unnecessary fixture of the Republican administration. Having no tattooed serial number to prove her Democratic origin, she took her dismissal bravely and went to work at Commerce for better pay.

Discussions of status can veer sharply as we've done, which makes it necessary to procrastinate on definitive development and return to essential signposts.

(The literary technique of mentioning a situation, then saying it will be developed more fully in a later chapter, is time-saving but must be watched lest the author forget himself and make such promises in his final chapter.)

Concomitant with assigned parking space as a status signal is the automobile, another point at which little men may at least take on colorings of big or important men. Due to a certain amount of commendable utility, the little car, preferably European, is In, in Washington, possibly more so than in other American cities. Partly, this stems from what the *Economist* of London spotted developing in America as long ago as 1958—the coming of "a certain inverted snobbery."

The *Economist* observed on May 31, 1958:

> There are few American families today, at least in the upper income groups with money to spend, who cannot manage with what they have in the way of durable goods; moreover a certain inverted snobbery seems to have developed—keeping down with the Joneses—so that it is now smart to go on driving a 1955 car or washing with an outdated machine.

Current capital cultism follows this theory in a general direction, but not the specific. Sophisticated New People don't wash in any kind of machine, new, outdated or moderately old. Their work is done by laundresses who do not starch shirts as those detestable laundries do. But the cars, yes.

An able practitioner of Washington status would not be caught dead, dismembered or drunk in a 1955 Pontiac, but he'd go to his great reward happily in an M.G. of any vintage. A 1930 Pontiac might be smart, but nothing good came out of 1955. Nothing, do you hear, nothing. Possibly a book or two by men now running State, but little else.

Keeping down with the Joneses is part of the previously mentioned campaign behavior of our millionaire office-seekers. New People may be dense in many ways, but they can spot trends. Hence, a man may drive to C.I.A. in a slightly scabby Renault, knowing or hoping that his appearance smacks of wise and well-behaved humility, but still a clearly understood potential of being able to do better. The man who is forced to drive a dented Volkswagen in Washington may be bothered by realizing that he looks rich but isn't. In such cases, Pontiacs are advised from time to time.

We are avoiding purposely any discussion at this point of limousines and chauffeurs as Washington status indicators because there is untruth in much livery. There may be guidance, but not basic meaning, because limousines are more easily rented than Volvos. One must know the specific limousine to reach what Kennedy calls a judgment. If one possesses his own limousine and hires his own chauffeur, he's deadly rich, usually not in government, and is to be generally disregarded by New People as a crass example of what Washington would have been if the Old People had been allowed to continue.

For one more guide to updated status in the Good New Days, we turn to schools. Probably no class in relatively recent history has fought more for improved public schools than the New People. And from observation rather than tightly statistical study, no group patronizes private schools for their children more than New People.

The established private schools such as Sidwell Friends, St. Albans, Maret, Madeira and others have expanded their plants, raised tuition and still face the longest waiting lists of their histories. New People, it must be said, favor private education primarily because they believe it to be vastly better than public schooling, because the better colleges have the same idea—and because the kids are picked up and delivered.

Parent-teacher associations are on a clubby level of social and intellectual equality with group meetings only once or twice a year, and then with no dreadful reading of the last minutes and incomprehensible treasurer's reports. The parent-principal relationship is on a first-name basis, and who would ever dream of calling a public school principal by her first name, much less running into her on the Cape during the summer?

CHAPTER SIX

How to Tell a Truly Important Person (TIP)

It is one thing to know what Washington status is, another to spot it. Being able to walk into a restaurant and point out Senator Wayne Morse or Jack Logan (once referred to as the town's most eligible bachelor, although he's a white-haired old man) is difficult for the beginner, because so many people in Washington try to look like Senators or eligible bachelors.

The patina, the shapes and sounds of importance, are decidedly vital amongst the New People. Underplaying, as we've mentioned, has its moments of current popularity, but much more is involved.

We have a problem of proper labeling in the District of Columbia which is mildly similar to the difficulties of C. Northcote Parkinson in nailing down just what constitutes the governing class of his native Britain.

The eminent author of "Parkinson's Law" says that the British *Establishment*, the governing class and its tributaries which we are probing from the Washington end, may consist of "the most influential members of the most influential families."

The Good New Days

Writing in the Sunday *New York Times,* historian Parkinson adds: "In the wider sense, it can mean all who speak with an upper-class accent—'they' as opposed to 'us.' But has the expression any meaning? Do the privileged few constitute so defined a class? Is there, in short, a citadel to be attacked?"

There most certainly is, Mr. Parkinson, a citadel to be attacked in Washington. Perhaps attack is not the proper word. Balloon-pricking is better, if hyphenated.

The problem of exploring the Washington Establishment is that so many people try to act and appear as shareholders when they're really not.

Upper-class accent is important in Washington as it is to Parkinson in London. To pattern one's accent on President Kennedy is not advised, however, because the result would be to sound like an Oxford don playing the part of a New England lobsterman in an amateur theatrical.

Aside from Kennedy, the identifying accent of the Washington TIP is theoretically Ivy League. It involves great opening of the mouth in the manner of a gulping goldfish, with volume adjusted a shade above that of your luncheon companion. The broad A is suggested rather than hit hard, the R is relatively soft, and the G is dropped at times. The annoying thing is, however, that none of these are done consistently. The broad A might be used in "can't," but not in "pass." This appears to be largely a device to throw off imitators. Only the real insiders know when to sharpen the "can't" and broaden the "pass."

To a Missourian or Texan, best description of the N.P. accent would be simply this—sissy. This has nothing to do with masculinity or virility. They talk so much more gently, with more refinement than we've been accustomed to for some years in the political arena. This sometimes makes the men sound prissy, if not sissy.

The dials, however, must be shifted for tuning to the voice of the N.P. women. No high trilling ultra-girl voices for them. A lady TIP is deep and throaty, and sometimes in the dark she might run a good octave below a male TIP, unless she's dating beneath her class, in which case it is advised to await better light or location for our survey. A genuine Wellesley, Radcliffe or Bennington TIP had pounded into her somewhere along life's chalked path that a woman's voice should be full-bodied and direct. In another era, it might have been described as a cultivated gin husk.

Choice of vocabulary also can be the straight-off tip on a TIP or N.P. Men and women of the Washington Establishment have glitteringly broad vocabularies. Their use of profanity is utterly delightful and should be taught in some of our greater academies where cursing is rather rudderless quantity instead of quality. Nothing spices a conversation better than well-placed profanity, but only dullards curse profusely.

Listen to a lady N.P. telling of a recent parents' meeting at her child's progressive, private school:

"The wife of the Swiss chargé—you all know Ratsy, I'm shuah—I love her mahdly, but I cannot abide her squinchy little ideas about getting the children to clawss on time. So, ahfter our simply precious clambake, I went to Ratsy and said one word: bawls."

This sort of thing keeps a conversation toned up and is much to be preferred to idly dropped damns and hells.

We might add another note on the audio aspects of the TIP. Their voices may be otherwise gentle, until they laugh. They roar, they spray, they blast when the situation calls for indications of humor. Their laughter tends to the gutsy, diaphragmatic HO-HO rather than the laryngeal HA-HA. Bared teeth also are expected as a matter of free emphasis, involving a certain amount of careful dental care frequently available only to the better families.

It is helpful to be familiar with plumage of the TIP of the N.P.; drab-in-the-day, don't-give-a-hoot-at-night for men; essentially the same for women unless the girls are on display at luncheon, tea or cocktails.

The Good New Days

A flat-chested N.P. woman is a rarity but their pattern is to try appearing that way. During the day, that is. At night, they're quite proud. And outwardly, a true N.P. tries to be untouched by the nocturnal emergence, accepting it as he would any other appurtenance of well-bred family life.

The N.P. man during working or daytime hours, if they coincide, goes in for dark single-breasted suits, cut with undertaker conservatism. Medium grays and browns are acceptable if sufficiently medium. Scratchy herringbone tweeds are fine for winter, seersucker for summer. Casual jackets almost never, except on an occasional economist who still rebels against his New England parents. In short, the N.P. man could go right from the White House or the State Department to a funeral without changing his suit.

Their shirts uniformly have button-down or tab collars. With a shirt, the N.P. trick is to look choked. Narrow, straight, dark ties. Shirts with fine stripes on a white background are much preferred over plain white or blue oxford. The President can wear a plain white shirt because he's President, and Pierre Salinger may come to work forgivably in a yellow shirt because this is the sort of thing one might expect from a Californian. In fact, a Californian could come to work in a breechclout and not surprise the Eastern N.P. whose travel has not broadened him to accepting Westerners entirely as "us."

Away from government compounds and/or at night, the *TIP* male plumage flashes to the point of gold cummerbunds, tasseled slippers, double-breasted black dinner jackets with white buttons and worn with white duck trousers, and bow ties at will. Mrs. Mesta in her book so simply titled *Perle* derived all manner of fluttering mileage by telling how Jack Kennedy as a young Congressman showed up for one of her cookouts in a dinner jacket and—will you ever—brown loafers.

This could have happened to any of us, and Perle probably has thanked her social stars many times that it happened to her, because this undoubtedly was one of her solid contacts with J.F.K. Madame Mesta once was a redoubtable status symbol of Washington, particularly during the Truman days. To dine with Perle was mildly akin to knighthood, but to the N.P. of today she's a virtual stranger except to the Lyndon Johnsons, to whom she sold her house.

Female TIP plumage at night shows something of the pack-following exhibited by TIP males in their daytime clothing. The well-endowed ladies have never been too keen about Jacqueline's preference for high-necked overblouses, but they respect the quality of leadership and follow it accordingly at more formal affairs. It is at the smaller, intimate after-dark gatherings that their charms become evident.

Except for a diplomatic ball, the TIP women currently favor loose, casual and above all, plentiful hair styles. Hair, in fact, seems almost more important than bosom. The First Lady's Mr. Kenneth or Alexandre of Paris may try to swoop styles up and down from year to year, but the N.P. women seem to have gone to such trouble cultivating their amazingly luxuriant mops that they may end up influencing Mr. Kenneth.

Except on formal evenings, a TIP lady frankly looks better in the wind. Loose-fitting and pronounced manes seem more in setting at the peak of a windy hill, standing long-armed and long-legged at the mast of a racing sloop or running across Wisconsin Avenue in Georgetown.

Sadly for the occasional spectator, the outward trappings discussed here occur in more than the N.P. or TIP circles. This makes TIP-watching unsure because of government clerks and stenographers who affect similar grooming. To be certain, it's necessary to listen closely to their voices. No matter how plentifully touseled and overbloused, any girl overheard exclaiming over Fabian's newest album is very un-TIP or N.P. and if her date talks of the wax job on his Chevrolet, move on.

We must not be carried away at this point by idle expectation that virtually all N.P. deserved of the designation also qualify for TIP. They may think they qualify. Only at times do they coincide.

Of obvious mathematical necessity, comparatively few N.P. can have TIP license tags. These are numbers under 1,000 and not preceded by serial letters. The District of Columbia once limited its tags for TIP to 500, but with the 1961 change in administrations, it was hard to tell how much low-tag pressure there would be, so the limit was advanced.

In unkind practicality, the people who want to resemble the TIP have spoiled the license-tag business for just about everybody. Restaurateurs, doctors, lawyers, liquor-store owners and others have wedged themselves into the low-number lists, most of them left over from the Eisenhower Administration. Thus it will take a year or two for the N.P. to weed out these hangovers and get low numbers for their restaurateurs, doctors, lawyers and liquor-store owners, because even the N.P. have occasional need for their services.

With sufficient background, one may detect a TIP by license tag and car considered together. A limousine carrying dark blue plates with white numerals and a number 100 and 125 is a Cabinet member's official car, or that of someone with Cabinet rank. A limousine with DPL on the license plates is hauling an ambassador, his wife, or one of their guests who could not make his way independently. Less than a limousine and with diplomatic tags, pay no attention. These are the vehicles of embassy employees, many of whom are quite nasty about parking astride entrances to supermarkets. When their motoring individualism is pointed out by police or irate shoppers, the drivers merely mutter "Deeplomateek" and go on with their shopping.

Not all limousines are those of Cabinet and diplomatic corps. Some belong to lobbyists; lawyers, when there is a difference; doctors, when they're sure no patients will see them.

A black Cadillac or Lincoln limousine with a telephone in the

How to Tell a Truly Important Person (TIP)

back window and a silver-gray imitation fur laprobe invariably is a Cabinet member. If after checking the license number this proves to be untrue, you know it is a lawyer trying to look like a Cabinet member. If the limousine is gray or blue, probably a diplomat or people from out of town.

Incidentally, I have several friends in show business who rented liveried Rolls Royces in New York and brought them to Washington for Kennedy's first inauguration, thinking it was a class affair and that they would blend in with the N.P., TIP grade. But poor things, they looked like so many British ambassadors.

A black four-door Mercury with two men in the front seat, driver uniformed and other man in civvies, plus three children in the rear seat: Caroline Kennedy on her way to tambourine school with two friends.

Same car, same load minus the man in civvies: children of an assistant secretary (who're called members of the "Little Cabinet") on their way to a birthday party at the home of friends who're outranked by their father. He'd use the family car if they were going to a party at the home of someone who outranked Papa.

One sure sign of belonging or at least knowing how to belong is the grocer. A TIP really doesn't care as long as it is good and expensive. But many N.P. are prudent. They want TIP groceries without paying the same freight. So, the smart ones patronize the virtually hidden little traps which cater to embassies. This can be wildly valuable on Sunday when liquor sales over conventional counters are forbidden. A grocery store with a liquor license can, however, sell whisky to an embassy on Sunday with some degree of safety. Thus the clever N.P. trades at the same place, his wife having made considerable distance with the old crone who runs the store by buying her outrageously high-priced broccoli without complaint. Then, when crisis comes to call on the Sabbath and the cellar is bare, off to the grocery stall for diplomats where the owner graciously credits the Sunday disbursal to the Rumanian

Embassy and charges the actual customer no more than fifty cents or a dollar extra.

The N.P. cannot stand the impartiality of most supermarkets. They must know the grocer; he must be their very own. Being thus owned jointly by many N.P. holds promise to the proprietor of a small interest in Fort Knox.

The TIP has global food and beverage tastes and the N.P. try to. They bake their own bread at home (pretending not to have bought those half-baked loaves at Ancient Charlie's with the Sunday hooch) and slice it on a small board at the table, spilling bits of crust in the *vin rosé* (for which they paid Ancient Charlie $1.19, "ridiculously low," and for which Charlie paid forty cents).

What separates the N.P. from the TIP in the matter of food is shopping. The TIP sends a houseman in a panel truck or station wagon to Magruder's or Larimer's where they occasionally have off-season sales on Beluga caviar or quart containers of Austrian *pâté de foie gras* at $27 the flagon, again "ridiculously low" when you think what we paid for it last Christmas at Maison Money in New York.

The N.P. woman, if her husband's rank possibly permits it, does her own shopping at the neighborhood independent where the prices are higher than in supermarkets, but where Tony saves those special butterfly chops just for us. Tony, it might be pointed out, has a delicate time keeping his "just for us" patrons rotating with sufficient rapidity to preserve the aura of exclusivity.

This may happen in many parts of America. Indeed, it undoubtedly does, but it has added interest in Washington because these same N.P. patrons of the slightly higher-priced mercantile outlets are the noble federal officials slaving day and night at far less than they could make back home in father's bank; slaving to protect us from further increases in the cost of living.

Is this what C. Northcote Parkinson had in mind when he referred to "they" as opposed to "us"?

Ours, however, is not to quarrel but to observe with detachment and avoidance of personalities wherever possible.

How to Tell a Truly Important Person (TIP)

Which brings us to drinking habits of the TIP and N.P., discussed at this point purely in the "how to tell" sense rather than a definitive exploration of Washington cocktail parties which will entail a separate and frightening chapter.

Taken as a class, the N.P. seem to be more moderate than the O.P. The new ones drink a lot of beer and wine. In fact, some of them drink one or the other much of the time when they're not burdened with the often onerous chore of saving us from either Wall Street or the Russians.

A genuine TIP drinks as cautiously as a boxing champion between rounds. He got to be a TIP by having every brain cell bleeping and blooping every waking hour. He drinks primarily as an excuse to talk. Our visitors will never see a verified TIP getting loaded at a public bar or even in the semiprivacy of a party. (What he does in the back of that limousine under his silver-gray imitation fur laprobe between traffic lights is something else again. The car may jingle with old pints, but we never see him smashed. And I doubt he ever is.)

The N.P. may become exuberant and sing the Whiffenpoof song to a point of hoarseness, but he really doesn't get tanked. A friend of mine observed a party at the Robert Kennedys' where the traditional shoving-into-pool-fully-clothed rite was observed more than usual.

"I felt perfectly horrible," he told me, "when I saw before my own eyes these people bouncing in and out of that pool entirely sober."

The N.P. on such occasions can be very much like Indians in India where they congregate by hundreds of thousands to welcome a leader and behave for all the world like a mob of drunks in their eye-rolling, lip-dripping fervor. This involves a form of intoxication or exuberance derived purely from human contact, and a certain amount of trying to outshout each other.

Invariably, books have a circular tendency and here we are again at Bobby Kennedy's swimming pool in Virginia, dangling our shoes and dinner trousers in the shimmering cool water and chatting with a N.P. about Kafka or the Boston Red Sox (it is exceedingly gauche to back the Yankees in N.P.-land).

There on the diving board stands a handsome young man in a soaked dinner jacket, night vapor rising from him in eerie, wispy trickles that bespeak the healthy American heat and vigor churning beneath his prudent wash-and-dry pleated dinner shirt. It is Ted Kennedy, and a cultured, throaty N.P. lady says with a warmly appreciative chuckle to a puzzled man from Mali, "That's five times for Teddy."

Even if Perle Mesta had formed a coalition government with Gwen Cafritz when each was dealing a hot social hand around town and rented the entire Potomac River for a party to end all parties, they could not have approached the status of having been splashed by Ted as he made Dive Five.

CHAPTER SEVEN

The Wonderful Washington Point System

There was a fanciful story some years ago of an enterprising lady journalist who tracked down John Quincy Adams while the old fellow was floating in the Potomac having delightful little constitutional thoughts.

Since J.Q. had been choleric about granting interviews on land, the lady spied his clothes on a grassy bank and squatted thereon, while Adams treaded muddy water and sputtered answers to her questions.

This well could have been the start of the so-called Washington point system. Although history omits the precise dialogue, it is reasonable to assume the lady made for the nearest tavern in Georgetown and, over a mead bought by some lecherous Senator, said slyly, "J.Q. looks so cute with his clothes off." And across the table, a lobbyist for the candle trust whistled softly and said, "Two points for her."

In the early days of railroad sleeping accommodations, President Grant strolled unannounced into a washroom, pulled off his shirt

93

and shaved beside a disconsolate drum drummer (sales were poor because the drum market was pretty well shot after the Civil War). Making conversation, the salesman blamed the recession on that idiot in the White House.

Being well-equipped with whiskers, Grant wanted no more than a touch-up, particularly on a bumpy road bed, but he did take the time to identify himself and tell the drum drummer he didn't know his snarehead from a tomtom.

At the next stop, Ellicott City, Maryland, so the story goes, the drummer leaped from the train to tell the platform loafers, "I just got chewed out by President Grant."

Being near Washington, loafers of Ellicott City were influenced by jargon which they picked up on rare trips to the capital. And one of them is supposed to have said to the salesman, "Bully and a point for you, Clarence."

See how it works? Flexible as hell, but a durable system still in daily use.

Essentially, the point system is a conversational method of determining Washington status. Points are not necessarily cumulative. Perhaps the system is better described as a method of measurement or immediate appraisal. Something like a reviewer giving a movie two, three or four stars. More than establishing rank or status, the point system is a way of expressing one's attitude toward a specific behaviorism or performance. Also, it may cover one's automobile, home, family or personal activities.

We mentioned earlier the advantages of being shoved into Bobby Kennedy's swimming pool. Virtually every columnist capable of putting pen to foolscap also has commented on this status-establishing drippery.

There was a time when immersion at the Attorney General's was good for at least four points. It should be mentioned, by the way, that a seasoned Washingtonian seldom confers more than four points except when exclaiming over amplitude of bosom or cuddlesome qualities of a rear end.

The Wonderful Washington Point System

One of Washington's more revered journalists, weary of riding in buses over thousands of political campaign miles, worked out a system of self-entertainment. Passing through a town with thousands cheering the candidate, this fellow would sit at the bus window, mumbling to himself, "I'll give that one 75 . . . golly, there's a 90 . . . the one in yellow, poor thing, a 50."

But back to total immersion as a system of social measurement. Publicity and the gregarious nature of Bobby and Ethel ruined the swimming-pool dunk as a point-getter. The Kennedys reached the point of having to watch for utter strangers racing uninvited over their suburban Virginia meadows to the pool and social salvation.

Because the water-streaked evening gown became such a symbol, some N.P. women actually selected their party clothes—just in case. One woman, bound for an R.F.K. fiesta in the McLean woods, confided that she had copied one of her Balmain originals in a cheaper material so she could join the fun with little fear of ruining a truly fine dress.

In the summer of 1962, ugly stories began to circulate. A dry cleaner in Spring Valley offered his most trusted clients, including some Republicans, a completely confidential dress-streaking service for the uninvited.

A dusty traveler from Middleburg arrived at the Georgetown Inn with a horrible tale—during the previous weekend, at least two guests were pushed into the pool at Glen Ora.

Down crashed the point-standing of the Bobby baptismees.

Then came more shattering tidings. The President swam daily in the White House pool as a matter of therapy for his occasionally nagging back. Since his swim sessions were entirely stag, he frequently paddled about without the encumbrance of trunks in Y.M.C.A. democracy.

Improving on the manner of John Quincy Adams, J.F.K. was known to have invited an occasional journalist to chat with him as he paddled therapeutically through the 90-degree water. Male journalists, of course. Since J.F.K. bade them enter, there was no need for such foolish derring-do as sitting on his clothes. Besides, the clothes were hung neatly in a locker nearby.

Also, there was word in certain circles that *some* men, high of station in or out of government, had been invited to swim *with* the President.

Clearly four points were justified for a visit with the leader of the New Frontier in or around the White House pool. And with equal clarity, a necessary downgrading of Bobby's pool.

It is difficult to forecast new point-makers, because they have a way of developing rapidly and from an impromptu start. Also, it should be borne in mind that the point system is not always oriented to the White House. Points often are scored among the New People with little or no thought of the Kennedys, unlikely as such a dangerous mental condition may seem.

Having one's home on the Georgetown Garden Tour is a good two points, although it does mean sending the children away for a few days to forestall their opening a closet and unleashing a cascade of overshoes, tennis rackets and ping-pong balls at the feet of visitors.

Having the Schlesingers at a small dinner dance is good, provided there is an upstairs sitting room where brains of government may adjourn periodically to take telephone calls and talk about Adenauer or Vietnam. Since the Schlesingers do get around, however, this would not rate more than a point. If the Bundys were there, too, you might force it to two points, but not a whit more.

Walking with a Supreme Court Justice once made points, but today very little. As they get older, the Justices seem to walk more. Mr. Justice Douglas, for example, walks all over the world; keeping up with him would be too time-consuming to exact advantage at home from the points thereby derived.

Being photographed by Mercedes, the wife of Mr. Justice Douglas, is another matter, perhaps a two-point matter, depending on how many pictures she makes and how well they turn out. Mrs.

Douglas not only walks, but she is an excellent photographer. If she comes to your party with several cameras, photographs your guests dancing the Hully Gully and sends you a batch of deliciously private prints, this would have to be scored indisputably as a two.

A hike with Mr. Justice Douglas along the old Potomac Canal for ten or fifteen miles was once a source of points, but not today. He sometimes is accompanied by as many as a dozen or more walkers. If a heavy rainstorm forced the group to call for limousines and a happy, humid ride back home, a half-point.

Another source of points is being able to do something unexpected and entertaining. This was not often noticeable during the Truman and Eisenhower eras, but New Frontiersmen brought to town a custom of self-entertainment—charades, games, group singing, unusual dancing, imitations.

It has long been held in Washington that a man's professional progress or standing can depend to a great extent on the social charm and ability of his wife. The N.P. wives, about whom we gossip at greater length elsewhere, are an active and entertaining bunch.

As could be expected in most communities, there tends to develop what might be described as social incest. Same guests, same hosts, same houses, on a round-robin basis. Partly because Washington has few attractive night clubs, these folks entertain at home more than going out. After dinner comes a cry for Gladys to do her imitation of Jackie addressing the Girl Scouts. The hostess knows from good experience that Gladys, particularly after her second Stinger, is a walloping good warm-up for the otherwise stodgy postprandial period.

Being rather frequent in her performances and seldom changing her material, Gladys no longer receives points. Just chuckles.

But should an Assistant Secretary of State who never before opened his mouth at such affairs suddenly bounce into a passably good Russian squat dance, he most certainly should have a point.

The Good New Days

Congressman William Green of Philadelphia gets an occasional point from first-time listeners when he sings ancient parodies about the leadership on the Hill.

Currently, the key to the point system seems to be action. The N.P. are intensely active in a physical way. This stems from youth. The only defense against it without seeming unduly O.P. is to be professorial, hellishly long-haired or semi-invalid. Being unable to dance because of phlebitis, or being violently opposed to it as an outdated culture form, might be acceptable. But simply sitting vacantly and watching others Twist has been known to result in minus points.

Take water-skiing. A genuine N.P. activist upon first exposure to the sport would say, "Here, I want to try that." If he immediately shucked down to his skivvies and subjected himself to semi-drowning in the wake of an outboard, his two points would be unquestioned.

Horseback riding? No. This is a form sport. After considerable training in private, the N.P. might get a point or two for a broken collarbone, but nothing for the sport itself.

Card-playing, even with higher New Frontiersmen, has little point value. Most of them are so busy with fate that they're not much for pure escapism. After all, one can discuss Medicare and birth control for India while water-skiing or dancing, admittedly with difficulty but still within some framework of communication. Chances for communication while playing bridge are negligible and, in any case, ill-advised.

There might be a point to be claimed for playing poker with Peter Lawford, who loves the game, but gaining a point in this manner is scarcely worth it. Lawford, being an accomplished actor, easily can cast himself as Ravanel, a Mississippi river boat gambler, and win a ghastly number of pots while other players sit there, dumbly themselves. Only the most point-hungry N.P. would resort to this sort of scoring.

Lawford brings to mind a bit of N.P. whimsy which, under proper conditions, might be worth a point on a dull day. Many of them go barefooted. And not always at the beach or pool. They pad around barefooted because it betokens freedom and a lack of pretense. Also, their feet may hurt but this should be regarded as carping. Lawford plays golf barefooted, which may have led some of the N.P. to their taste for shoelessness.

There are no points for being barefooted, however, if one walks with any indication of tender sensitivity. A clean, firm barefooted stride over hot asphalt or coarse gravel should be worth a half point because it indicates frequent presence at the shore or one's country place.

We may only imagine what might have happened had one of the Crusaders shown up shoeless for a golf date with Eisenhower. George Allen went about as far as individualism could go by playing in sneakers. And only five-star indulgence made this possible.

Lest the Washington point system seem confined to the N.P., it should be noted that the O.P. have their ratings, too. Regardless of administration, membership at Burning Tree is a source of points for men.

Probably more points accrue to a lobbyist than most other Washington males for playing at Burning Tree, one of the tonier fresh-air camps for adults.

Tennis at Chevy Chase is a point; membership, two; but only among more conservative Washingtonians. Lunch at the Metropolitan Club was an entry on many point cards until that public airing of Metropolitan's negative attitude toward Negroes. Chevy Chase does not seem to have faced this particular problem of color. Not even Roy Wilkins of the N.A.A.C.P. would raise a fuss over Chevy Chase; not out of fear or awe, but because it would be a foolish waste of time and invective.

When leading New Frontiersmen curtly quit the Metropolitan, the place went down on the N.P. point scale, but up on the O.P. chart. The O.P. position was not anti-Negro. It seemed instead to be happiness over departure of any N.P. from any scene.

To dine with Mrs. Robert Low Bacon or the brilliantly cognizant widow of the late Colonel Robert McCormick—very strong

O.P. points. Dinner with Fulton Lewis, Jr., with Dean Clarence Mannion among the guests, can be extremely interesting and unquestionably good as a grabber among conservatives.

I know one man who got points all over town for being seated at a dinner next to Robert Welch of the John Birch Welches. The man had several luncheon invitations, even from N.P., to tell his dramatic I-was-there story. Whether this man should have been allowed permanent points turned out to be debatable. Mr. Welch, it seems, had very little to say except that he was impressed by the energetic handsomeness of two men at the same dinner—George Romney and Secretary Ribicoff—before he returned to vote-hunting in Connecticut.

There are scores which few outside of Washington would think of as important. A smacking three points can be given easily for a parking place set aside at the District of Columbia stadium for the District commissioners, members of the Cabinet, and baseball- or football-club majority stockholders. Three points may seem inordinately high, but not when one considers how this is quickly translatable status in front of an audience of thousands. It might rate four points on a dreadfully rainy day when the Redskins have managed one of their rare pro football victories.

A dive into Bobby Kennedy's pool in Roman toga while reading a first edition of his latest book could not match walking from the crowded stadium at a rainy dusk across a narrow driveway to a carefully attended island of privilege and one's own snug Citroën.

Going to private film showings at the Motion Picture Association of America, a swank residence two blocks from the White House, is a point—and a comfortable one at that. Government officials, members of Congress and correspondents—N.P. or O.P. —are about as attracted to free motion pictures as they are to country places and supper dancing.

To see a major film months before release to the ticket-buying commoners is worth a point when exploited properly. This sometimes is mishandled badly by the new. They volunteer without being asked that they've just seen a private screening of *Lolita*.

The Wonderful Washington Point System

It is much better to wait, for weeks and months if necessary, until a vapid neighbor or a lackluster fellow worker asks, "Seen any good movies lately?"

Persons of this nature may be crushed at once by saying wearily, "I've been so busy translating Proust into Arabic recently that I haven't had the time, but Eloise and I did see the rushes of *Lolita* at MPA the other night with the Rusks and the McNamaras."

The seasoned Washingtonian backs away fast from a sentence dropped in this manner, confining himself to nothing more than an equally weary, "How was it?" To be so gauche as to inquire what in God's name is the MPA is to suffer another crushing blow. In fact, it is a good rule in our town never to ask about a set of initials thrown into a conversation. Nod knowingly and move on.

Letter combinations may apply to humans, as well as agencies. I saw a point-system expert bomb a pushy Pentagon figure unmercifully during a bocci game in Newport.

The Pentagon man had come to Newport purely to deliver papers from McNamara and was trying to build it into a mysterious mission for the President. He was throwing initials all over the bocci box and implied that he heard J.F.K. say something that afternoon about running over to see J.P.K. (the President's father spending the summer in Hyannis).

Our hero let him have it.

"I wonder how that will strike J.B.K.?" he mused.

The poor, poor fool from the Pentagon fell completely asplash into the gruesome well.

"I'm sorry, I thought you knew these people," said our hero. "Jacqueline Bouvier Kennedy, wife of J.F.K. and mother of C.K. and J.F.K.J."

Not drubbed enough, the hapless visitor smiled weakly.

"Oh sure, J.B.K. But J.F.K.J.? You're making these up."

"I don't think John, Jr., would agree," said our man haughtily, in definite possession of three quickly scored points.

There are points to be gleaned in many other little ways, recognized in both O.P. and N.P. circles.

The Good New Days

One system requires experience, good memory and curiosity. This is the ability to identify the True Autocrats of Government, hence known as T.A.G.

These are the quiet people, truly permanent residents of the city who manage to keep the machinery of government going in spite of changing politicians. They are the housekeepers and paperwork experts of the federal system; civil servants who talk constantly of being able to make more money "on the outside," but who seldom leave the security of working for Uncle Sam.

They are not N.P. They wear plastic raincoats and travel in car pools. They live far from Georgetown, Cleveland Park, and Spring Valley in massive complexes of relatively low-cost housing. They make up the bowling teams and blood-bank campaigns. They, far more than the N.P., fill the symphony hall and crowd the Watergate for summer concerts. They picnic on Sundays at the zoo and jam the Monument grounds on the Fourth of July to hear speeches and gasp at the fireworks.

At times they seem to speak a foreign language when discussing their work with each other. This isn't the famed gobbledegook of O.P.A. days, but a bloodless sort of argot made up of numbers and letter combinations which identify the inner workings of government.

They may appear scummy dull to the *avant garde* of the N.P., but these are the squares who protect us. We farm to their formulas and quake at their audits. We pay when they say pay and we rely on them for everything from tide information to insect control.

After they have seen several administrations come and go, they develop tolerance and sympathy frequently not shared by their overlords of the moment. They do, however, contribute more to basic life of the community than many of their more attractive and better-known policy-makers.

It is a point, indeed, for the N.P. who knows and understands the T.A.G.

In every department and agency, including the White House,

there are career administrators, personnel men, and clerks, without whom even the most enlightened new administration could not function. Occasionally there are efforts to displace the T.A.G. and turn over their posts to new political appointees. Not in every case, but certainly in most, such efforts collapse quickly, particularly when it is discovered that the T.A.G. about to be displaced will be snatched up by some other agency of government.

Not that there was any thought of removing him, but there was deep curiosity along the New Frontier shortly after the 1960 election about William Hopkins, executive chief clerk at the White House. Bill Hopkins has been on the job since the early days of F.D.R. as the control point or coordinator of official papers—bills to be signed, executive orders, proclamations and the like. If anyone runs the White House, he does.

Probably no one in Washington knows the intricacies of government better than Hopkins. Probably no one keeps track of more details that would seem piddling to the uninitiated, but which are basic to smooth operation of the Executive branch.

It may be disputable to say that Hopkins is powerful, but there can be no argument about his essentiality. As he was trained for years by such similar experts as Rudolph Forster and Joseph Latta, who dated back to the McKinley administration, Hopkins has a veteran staff in training under him. The new President who tries to divest the White House of these experienced men would be inviting deep confusion.

For all his importance, however, Hopkins would not be recognized on the street or in the White House lobby by any but a handful of N.P. He probably has been to fewer social functions in Washington than many of his rank. Bill also is paid better than many of those widely known to the public.

Thus, to the New Frontiersman who could spot and identify Bill Hopkins on a street corner or waiting patiently for his 1958 sedan at the car wash, a full four points. Assuming, of course, that the Frontiersman patronizes the same place.

CHAPTER EIGHT

Is Culture Decent?

"All my worst moments have been cultural rather than political," said Antrobus, the hard-to-ruffle British diplomat of Lawrence Durrell's hilarious *Esprit de Corps*.

"You see," Antrobus confessed, "we are all supposed to be rather pro than anti in the Old Firm—but as for me, frankly I hate the stuff. It rattles me. It gives me the plain untitivated pip, I don't mind confessing."

Bully for Antrobus, wherever he may be serving today. For his sake, may it not be Washington, for culture has captured the city.

Chamber music flutists without a decent week's work in years are now in demand. The hottest night-club act in town is Charlie Byrd, a fabulous guitarist who plays more Segovia than modern jazz.

Quotations from Shakespeare once again may be heard in places other than classrooms and stages. The Bard sometimes has several units performing his works on the same night. Authors, although this one can think rather rapidly of a few exceptions, are sought socially, even by Mrs. Kennedy. Playwrights and composers are In, for the first time since the late Robert Sherwood moved back to New York after F.D.R.'s death.

It may annoy Frontier people, but they cannot claim full credit for the cultural revival in Washington. Whether N.F. culturists like it or not, the Trumans certainly did more to popularize mass consumption of classical music than the Roosevelts.

Harry Truman's piano tinkling was enough to make a Knabe gnash; the lyric qualities of Margaret's concert soprano did not, in the minds of *some* peevish critics, come up to the endowments of a Pons or Callas.

With no apparent thought of anything but enjoying good music, however, the Trumans were unusually faithful, for a First Family, in attending the symphony. Truman also was the first President to be made a member of the American Federation of Musicians *and* to play a duet with a cornettist named James C. Petrillo.

And at state dinners, the Trumans presented some of the finest musical artists of the opera and the classical concert stage.

For these interests, however, Harry, Bess, and Margaret receive virtually no points from the N.P., many of whom have difficulty for reasons of age in recalling the Truman era. Culture, for many younger N.P., lay in chains for years while Ike and Mamie played cards, thumbed westerns, and stared at TV. This is less than a complete picture.

The Eisenhowers were not cultural in the sense that they surrounded themselves with artists, writers, composers, and professors. Some, but not in mobs. The N.P. tremble at the mere thought of an Ike painting. Also, they fail to consider that, for all of Eisenhower's amateur brush work, more Americans began painting while he was President than at any other time in history. Admittedly, this finding is based on sale of art materials, particularly the carefully engineered kits with which one copied an old master or chintzy illustration by applying color to numbered sections of canvas.

The Eisenhowers also presented fine classicists in the East Room after dinners, but by today's standards, they cast culture aside when they invited Fred Waring and Lawrence Welk to sing and play. By N.P. measurements, only Spade Cooley could have been worse.

References to Truman and Eisenhower are not cited in their defense, but largely to start an argument. Ike painted poor pictures, but thousands of Americans were encouraged to believe they might do nearly as well. Truman played choppy piano, but he also encouraged the careers of a number of young piano artists.

Again, these references are no effort to defend or equate. Only a Right Pole Republican would think of challenging the assertion that certainly not in modern history has a First Family done more than the Kennedys to encourage the arts.

The Kennedys—and in truth, this means largely Mrs. Kennedy —have pushed musicians, singers, actors, authors and painters up front in the political community. Whether this produces any sort of political benefit for the N.F. is debatable, if not doubtful. Despite the persuasive leadership of Jacqueline Kennedy, a great many of her countrymen stubbornly prefer Tennessee Ernie Ford to Pablo Casals.

The show-business section of *Time* magazine once examined the ancient ABC network show, "Breakfast Club" and its corn-dripping star, Don McNeill.

"The show," *Time* said, "is perhaps of limited appeal to the average Vassar graduate who worked at *The New Yorker* for three years before marrying an advertising account-executive and settling in Greenwich, Conn. But there are other kinds of people in the U.S. and they have made Don McNeill the most enduringly successful broadcaster in the country."

It would be amazing happenstance if the more cultural N.F. pewholders had ever heard of Don McNeill. Whether this amounts to a cultural blind side is debatable, and a square-proof existence might be ideal for certain levels of government personnel. Whether high cultural taste is good politics is an entirely different matter.

This is not to argue that government officials of cultural levels equal to or above those of recognized Society should rush to the nearest newsstand for an armload of comics or tune their transistors to Don McNeill. There merely is a possibly presumptuous reminder that, as *Time* said, "there are other kinds of people in the U.S."—those who in the final analysis elect their leaders. Their levels of cultural taste undoubtedly could do with considerable improvement, but it is impolitic, ill-mannered, and stupidly arrogant for some of the N.P. to deride the blueberry slice of American society with its decidedly little s.

The cultural lift in Washington may be linked in part to development of what *Time* identified as New Society as differentiated from the so-called Old Guard. *Time* says of New Society:

> A different and more stimulating social stream of people with more education (than the Old Guard) and more to talk about, who want their friends to be intelligent, active, and amusing (one of their favorite words).
>
> It is a Society to which the Kennedys have given considerable impetus, although it was in the making well before Jack went to the White House. Rockbound in their huge old houses behind iron gates, the Old Guard seldom went anywhere, never saw anybody but one another, and hardly ever worked except as trust officers for the family estate. In the New Society, the term self-made man is not a slur but an accolade, and the New Society is willing to accept anyone with the requisite qualifications.

Time offered some of the qualifications: for men—money, manners, and taste. In women—beauty "and not too cool," intelligence, and "a sure sense of fashion."

Is Culture Decent?

The New Society of which *Time* spoke is centered largely in the East, primarily New York City and environs. But there is a Washington overlap in which qualifications other than those catalogued by *Time* come to bear. These would include influence and/or power born of background, talent, or political acumen. Good examples might be the C. Douglas Dillons and the Robert McNamaras.

Unfortunately, appraisals of current Washington too often confuse society with culture. They may overlap without equating. The editors of *Diplomat* or *Town and Country* may disagree. To them, Society *is* Culture.

Richard Rovere is cultured and social, but not Society. Yet, Mrs. Nicholas Longworth would have to be judged as both cultured and Society. She's well-bred, possessed of 22-karat seniority, has money, and is avidly interested in the world around her. She does not write or paint, but she knows those who do.

We've attempted to point out the N.P. and O.P. levels of Washington Society. There are others. The military, for example, and the diplomats. Each corps is a class distinct with tight structural lines of protocol, rank, and performance. These lines are never crossed except to the detriment of the trespasser.

The cultural divisions of Washington are much less pronounced. A government clerk, listless for having missed dinner, may have the concert seat next to a well-sherried dowager. One of the town's most sought-after economists may be unable to identify a single Cave Dweller (as some second- and third-generation Washingtonians refer to themselves).

Being cultural on the New Frontier is more than having status, knowledge and taste. It is being convincingly and sincerely active. It is being a patron without patronizing.

Culture is more than a spectator sport with the N.P. For one thing, it is ability—and enjoyment therefrom—of being able to speak and read one or more foreign languages. It means an intimate working knowledge of other countries, their people, customs, and problems. Many N.P. came to town thus equipped, giving them time to tackle even other languages.

The linguistic ability noticeable in Washington these days was reflected visibly not long ago by the wife of a starchily conservative O.P. The woman, in her late forties, apologized for being unable to accept invitations on certain nights.

"Those are my Russian classes," she said.

Quietly, for more than a year, she had been studying Russian three hours a week in class, and several times that at home poring over Russian magazines and newspapers.

"I began to wonder about meeting Russians who spoke excellent English," she explained.

Inability to speak understandable French and Spanish is now a source of embarrassment in much of our town. The wife of the President who succeeds Kennedy will appear *déclassée* if her French and Spanish vocabularies are limited to *merci* and *gracias*. Jacqueline has spoiled it for all future First Ladies.

The previously mentioned O.P. woman with rapidly increasing ability to speak Russian is planning to undertake lessons in Japanese in another year. The fact that she manages a residence of more than twenty rooms, entertains frequently and dabbles in numerous community activities would seem to make it difficult for other less-involved Washington wives to offer shortage of time or advanced age as excuses for not attempting to learn another language.

The current D.C. culture also means reading more than newspapers and periodicals. New novels are not nearly as important to N.F. men and women as new book-length nonfiction. The N.P. find it almost incomprehensible when they hear other Washingtonians confess to not having read the latest work on labor-management relations, Southeast Asia, or space.

If some N.P. do not care particularly for art, they at least try to know about it. Better yet, a great many of them budget for a painting as many of their countrymen would buy a new clothes washer.

They're buttoned down and natural-shouldered, to be sure. But don't try arguing art, music, geography, or literature with these babies unless your cultural qualifications go beyond magazine subscriptions and book-club memberships.

Mrs. Kennedy has been responsible for much of the cultural revival, both in personal participation and by creating an atmosphere in which cultural interests are regarded as acceptable.

Use of the word "acceptable" may seem strange, even washed-out and inordinately mild to scholars and artists far removed from the capital. The usage, however, is valid.

There was a time, and not very long ago, when political leaders felt it necessary to conform or identify with the lower denominators of their constituency. It was politically popular and sometimes necessary to appear as homespun and unaffected as possible. Some well-educated politicians actually affected ungrammatical speech to enhance their image of being one of the boys.

With the remotest rural areas now opened up to many new cultural influences, political figures of recent years have found it possible to put aside their bumpkin roles and enjoy some of the finer things of life. Out in the open, too.

Mrs. Kennedy brought to the White House such cultural contributions as a French chef, after-dinner Shakespearean readings and modern ballet performances, and a few Cézannes hanging among the dreadfully stiff portraits of Presidents and famous battles.

It remains to be seen, probably in 1964, whether Jacqueline's Francophile tendencies are thrown back at the White House by political enemies.

You can hear it now: "And if I get to the White House, I'll promise you folks one thing—good old American cooking."

Mrs. Kennedy, however, has history on her side, plus the Common Market, which may lead us to exchanging many items with the French, including recipes. Even such a hard-bitten growler as

The Good New Days

Nietzsche once said, "I believe only in French culture, and regard everything else in Europe which calls itself 'culture' as a misunderstanding."

Cultural advances under the N.P. are regarded questioningly in some quarters, bitterly in others. Outwardly not intending any political allusion, Eisenhower spoke of over-all American moral standards in 1962. Ike, it turns out, had a lot more time in which to worry after he left office and thus was able to extend his active concern into fields which seldom attracted his attention while bossing the Crusade. He said, to an audience in Abilene, Kansas:

"Now I wonder if some of those people [old pioneers of the West] could come back today and see us doing the Twist instead of the minuet—whether they would be particularly struck by the beauty of that dance?"

(Hold it a minute, General Ike. What do you think the same bunch of horny-handed old sodbusters and Indian fighters would say if they could see you chasing a little white ball in an electric cart?)

"When we see movies and the stage, and books and periodicals using vulgarity, sensuality, indeed, downright filth, to sell their wares, you think that our spirit—do you say America has advanced as we have materially when we see our very art forms so changed that the works of Michelangelo and Leonardo da Vinci are scarcely spoken of in terms of a piece of canvas that looks like a broken-down tin lizzie loaded with paint [that] has been broken over it? What has happened to our concept of beauty and decency and morality?"

Before tackling your question, General Ike, let's rest here in the shade of the clubhouse for a moment. Now there: Your remarks quite obviously were not aimed at anyone in particular, but surely you must have read about McNamara and other Cabinet members doing the Twist in the East Room at a private party given by the Kennedys?

You're right. The Twist did represent "some kind of change in

112

our standards." Culturally, but not morally. They still tell a story out in Denver about your performance, General Ike, at parties. You were a young lieutenant then, just married to Mamie. You had a great party trick. You'd clasp your arms to your sides, freeze into a rigid stance, then like a falling tree, topple a-smash to the floor. The trick was to break the fall with your hands at the last split second. The Denver folks say there were a few times when your hands weren't quite quick enough and boy, howdy, the whole house quivered when you hit.

Just imagine, General Ike, the sort of talk there'd be today if Teddy Kennedy tried your same floor-fall in the East Room.

Vulgarity, sensuality, and downright filth are not necessarily the same. One may lead to the other, but the vulgarity of one generation is the propriety of the next. Sport shirts and casual jackets which you wear in public view today would have been regarded as utterly vulgar by my grandfather, who felt a gentleman should wear stiff collar and tie at all times except when bathing or sleeping.

As for comparing the art masters of several hundred years ago with today's moderns, isn't this more a matter of preference? Who is to say what beauty of the future should be? Think back to the outraged cries which first greeted our early ultramodern architecture. How would Michelangelo feel about the superbly modern design of your library at Abilene, General Ike?

You ask what has happened to our concept of beauty and decency and morality. Nothing, really. Our standards seem to be more functional and realistic with time. We know now it is not necessary to put gargoyles at the corners of our buildings to frighten away evil spirits. As for filth in literature, it has been with us always. Today, the distribution system is better. Sadly, but better.

And before we part, General Ike. One thing about your Abilene statement worries me intensely. Do you mean to say that beauty must be accompanied by decency and morality? Here's where we *do* part. I'll go along with you on modern art, simply because I've fallen behind. But beauty is another matter. If a truly beautiful girl strolled through Lafayette Square buck naked, she could be the most indecent and immoral creature on earth—but she'd still be beautiful.

Meanwhile, back at the Frontier, the culture boom shows promise of putting across a long-needed project, construction of a national cultural center. The capital is well-endowed with art galleries, but for years there has been a shameful lack of facilities for proper mounting of fine drama and music. The only concert hall worthy of such designation has been the uncomfortable auditorium owned by the Daughters of the American Revolution.

Along with enthusiasm generated by N.P. for the cultural center have been excited suggestions of forming so-called state ballet and opera companies, a magnificently subsidized symphony, and scholarship grants for aspiring writers, artists, composers, and performers.

Inspiring? Exciting? Badly needed encouragement and recognition of the performing arts? Yes, yes, yes.

But.

Again, to borrow a phrase from Edward R. Murrow, see it now. See it clearly, patrons of the arts, and try to remember what Washington was like *before* the battle.

Conjure, if you will, a vision of a state ballet company director testifying before the House appropriations subcommittee on culture. He is being questioned by Rep. John Rooney, Democrat of New York, a noted anti-frill man.

ROONEY: You say your name is Sergei Deftoe?

DEFTOE:Yes, Mr. Rooney. I am director of the State Ballet Company.

R: American citizen?

D: Of course, sir.

R: That name Sergei threw me.

Is Culture Decent?

D: My name originally was Charles Mump, which I found unsuitable for a career in the dahnce.

R: In the *what?*

D: In the dahnce. (*Swaying sinuously at the witness table.*)

R: Never mind, Charlie.

D: I was just showing—

R: I'd like to ask you about this item—$17,000 for ballet slippers. Seems like a lot of slippers to me.

D: A prima ballerina might wear out as many as two or three pairs of dancing slippers in a single performance.

R: What do these slippers cost us, Uncle Sam (*his voice rising*), the American taxpayer? (*shouting by this time and a little red-faced*). WHAT DO THESE SLIPPERS COST THE AMERICAN GOVERNMENT EVERY TIME A BALLERINA SCUFFS THEM?

D: I can hear quite well, Mr. Rooney. By buying them in bulk, we get the slippers at a reduced rate—twenty-eight dollars a pair, which is dirt cheap.

R (*shakes his head in what seems to be sorrow*): Mr. Chairman, last week it was make-up kits for the state drama company. The week before, fifty thousand dollars' worth of new violins for the state orchestra. And today, satin slippers for toe-dancers. Surely Mr. Chairman, with people on relief, school children in overcrowded classrooms and a shortage of the latest rifles for some of our Army and Marine units overseas, I'll need a lot more convincing before voting seventeen thousand dollars for ballet slippers.

Since the foregoing is entirely imaginary, the figures might be off. But not the reaction of a seasoned money-watcher. In fact, if confronted by a genuine request for ballet funds, Rooney's reaction as approximated here would turn out to be quite an understatement.

And imagine what a West Virginia Senator would do with an appropriation for violins. One does not have to think of the entire speech; just his closing words: ". . . Not while thousands of my people line up each week for unemployment compensation and those miserable bags of surplus government foods."

A West Virginia Senator is not necessarily anti-culture, but in addition to responsibility he may have for betterment of American taste and knowledge, he also has to do something about bread and potatoes for unemployed victims of automation in his own state.

The prospect of a Solomon-like decision on bread or ballet does not have to reach such a definitive point. Washington truly needs a national cultural center; if for no other reason, to help correct the impression in other world areas that we are a people entirely interested in chrome-plated superficialities.

And were it not for possible impairment of the cultural center, the N.P. excitement over helping art forms with tangible federal encouragement would be commendable and do little harm on Capitol Hill. This is a case where practicality must leaven vision. The step-at-a-time approach is by far the better. A rural Congressman might be able to live with legislation to give creative artists, performers, and athletes the right to spread their earnings from peak years over some of the lean periods for tax purposes, or to give composers a better cut of record royalties.

The rural lawmaker, and quite a few city fellers, too, would have some frightful explaining to do back home if they voted bucks for ballet.

The Second Olio

The jargon of Washington is rather interesting at times, and members of Congress are forever putting together little lexicons which they mail to their constituents with "Ha-ha!" added in italics after some of the nifties.

The Congressmen invariably shock their home readers by saying SOB has two meanings, the customary one and the Washington version, Senate Office Building.

They point out that "downtown" means any government department or agency, including the White House, where good Representatives and Senators run frequent errands for their voters.

Washington does have a downtown, but Capitol Hill is not uptown. It is merely "the Hill." People never say Capitol Hill in conversation, only when they're writing about it. If Washington has an uptown, people never refer to it that way although there is an Uptown Theater on Connecticut Avenue. Instead of saying we live uptown, we say northwest. And if you live in southeast, it's just southeast and nothing can be done about it except move.

The Good New Days

In print, members of Congress frequently are referred to as legislators, lawmakers or solons. But these terms are never used conversationally around town except for sarcastic reasons. Members of the House are simply members, Congressmen, or Representatives. A Senator is a Senator.

Bureaucrat is another term that often turns up in print. Senator Stephen M. Young of Ohio, for example, says this means any appointive official who makes more than $10,000 a year. A bureaucrat, however, to the National Association of Manufacturers is anyone eating at the public trough, I believe the phrase is. To the American Medical Association, a bureaucrat is anybody in Washington who does not regularly and loudly denounce socialized medicine.

Without trying to be particularly witty, although some bitterness may creep in now and then, here are other rather conventional words that have peculiar application in Washington.

Hardware: When used by military men, it means guns, tanks, even missiles.

Aide-mémoire: This is a diplomatic term taken from the French, meaning memorandum. Most aides-mémoire are essentially snotty in that they politely accuse the other side of not knowing or forgetting the facts.

Agreement: In Washington it is pronounced "ah-gray-mon," largely because the French seem to have started the entire business of diplomacy. It means what it means to all Americans—agreement. But in the Washington sense, between nations.

Boat: Something the President uses for cruising on the Potomac. His boat by standards of any marina in the world would be classed as a yacht. Ever since Eisenhower called Truman's yacht "a symbol of needless luxury," Presidents have been calling their yachts boats.

News conference: Same as press conference. News conference, for some reason, is a colorless term, but used at the insistence of radio and television people who boggle at the idea of giving the printed word what they regard as free publicity. Thus we have press secretaries announcing that government leaders will hold *news* conferences. But just to keep the record confused, at NBC they insist on calling it "the presidential news conference," but they're mighty proud of a Sunday show called "Meet the Press."

Contribution: Slush fund.

Slush fund: Contribution (the difference being whether you're talking about yours or theirs).

One million dollars: A minor item in your appropriation bill, a mere pittance for those who deserve much more.

One million dollars: In their bill, another raid on the Treasury, a flagrant example of squandering public funds.

Consultation: A sign of trouble for somebody. If an ambassador is called home for consultation, he's either been kicking over the traces or there is new international difficulty. An ambassador is *never* called home for consultation if things are going well with the country where he's stationed.

The Fed: Federal Reserve Board of Governors.

The Feds: U.S. government law enforcement officers. In painful instances, tax collectors. Sometimes known in more colloquial circles by the singular term, The Man.

Farm: Yours.

Country estate: Theirs.

Luxurious country estate: Theirs, in an election year.

Lavish country estate: Gettysburg or Middleburg.

CHAPTER NINE

Dialogue Can Be Dirty Fun

As noted earlier, if there's one thing the N.P. do well and constantly, it's talk.

And it seems only natural that one of their favorite words would be "dialogue." Not something actors say to each other, but an all-covering state of communication.

When J.F.K. and Big Business exchange snarls, he regrets the tone of *their* dialogue. An economist speaks of the unsatisfactory dialogue between labor and management. When a true N.P. takes his boy to the baseball game, a ball-or-strike argument at the plate between umpire and batter may lead to uneasiness in the child's mind.

"The dialogue between those two men," says the youngster, "seems less than friendly."

"They're attempting to reach a viable agreement within their ethical framework," replies the father absently as he studies a draft *aide-mémoire* to Rawalpindi which he tucked into the baseball program.

The Good New Days

Dialogue, in the New Frontier sense, does not always have to be a spoken exchange. It may be merely exposition of stated positions or patterns of conduct. Salvoes in *Pravda* may constitute the latest dialogue from the Kremlin, despite what the dictionary says. Dialogue, in the N.P. reference, is dialectic, but as in many other aspects of new zeal seeming to sweep Washington these days, logic thereby contributed to the fund of public knowledge had damned well better turn out pro-N.P. if it is to be at all acceptable.

Max Lincoln Schuster, the distinguished book publisher, said in 1954 during the McCarthy era, "We are living in a time when you can't collect your thoughts without being accused of unlawful assembly."

The keenly perceptive and often-indignant journalist, Inez Robb, in July, 1962, wrote of an apparently decent and concerned young matron who came to see her with this complaint:

"Peace is a dirty word. Just say you are working for 'peace' and everyone immediately assumes that you are a communist or a member of some crumby communist-front organization . . . it's the semantics that make it so difficult."

Schuster's cogent appraisal of 1954 would not apply to the N.F. sixties, but there is somewhat of a link between the thought-guilt ascribed to many by the late Senator from Wisconsin and the semantic difficulty cited by Miss Robb's visitor in 1962. Any connection between 1954 and 1962 may relate to zest displayed by the N.P. in prosecuting their beliefs and those of their leaders; their totality of dedication.

With engulfing dedication often comes abhorrence and rejection of anything else. To suggest possible moderation of a tenet casts a chill over the faithful.

There is, however, a great difference between the turgid dialogue of 1954 with its dreadful tones of frequently blind hate and the yeasty semantics of the New People. If one can achieve spectator detachment, some current dialogue is downright good fun.

Dialogue Can Be Dirty Fun

There were few smiles in the situation to which Schuster referred, but if one is not too umbilical about it today, there is refreshment, as well as disquisition, to be found among the native hogans of the N.P.

Also, occasional jarring and unsettlement.

For example, it was most disturbing one candle-lit evening to hear a well-oriented charmer, her new *Marienbad* hair arrangement gleaming sleekly in the well-bred light, say to her gentleman, "If you utter one word more about Goldwater, you'll damned well sleep in your tops *and* bottoms tonight."

A Frontiersman of recorded enthusiasm unsurpassed by most save Kennedy blood relatives, swears to the authenticity of another terrifying snippet of N.P. dialogue. His sample shows there are, thankfully, sensible limits which he took with limited grace.

For weeks, this Frontiersman had squired a 36-25-34 member of the N.F. Ladies Auxiliary, Unattached Division, from salon to salon. With mind by Bennington and body by Debby Drake, she aroused in him what he thought was the very best—literate lust.

One night at a highly acceptable In-party, they stood together before a massive Georgetown breakfront gazing at rows of Galbraith, Schlesinger, and Kennedy bindings. The Frontiersman arched his magnificently curried head toward hers and poured out what he thought was the soft sibilance of an attentive swain.

Possibly emboldened by her fourth Castro Curse, a restorative compounded of 151-proof rum, papaya juice, and a dash of Rose's Lime, the young haughty tossed her four pounds of tawny hair angrily.

"For God's sake, Harold," she said, "let's drop the dollar gap."

"Charlie, what's wrong?" he gasped, using the masculine diminutive so popular that season.

"I'm sick of discourse, that's what," she replied. "Doesn't *anyone* ever talk about *intercourse* any more?"

This passing night-sound could be twisted into a grossly unfair generalization, which it is not intended to be. It was relayed to me some days later by the shaken Frontiersman as he sat shuffling cables from Saigon.

"Damn her," he cried, *"and* her intellectual emasculation."

He derived no comfort whatever from my suggestion that she might be a sexually maladjusted traitor to the European Economic Community.

The N.P. on occasion can be less than intellectual about the dialogue of others. As we have mentioned, they seem to have a high degree of sensitivity to criticism. Furthermore, they are as a class exceedingly tender about jokes aimed at their class. Or, for that matter, omnidirectional satire.

This is true to an extent of any political grouping. The barbs are so gay when pointed the other direction. The N.P., however, seem to bleed with unusual ease, which may be due in part to so many of them having come to Washington from other than the ward level of politics.

The Frontier and its leading figures inspired so many night-club and television one-liners, gag bumper stickers, cartoon books, and luncheon-table wisecracks that *Newsweek* in 1962 felt the situation justified a compendium of nasties aimed particularly at the Kennedys.

J.F.K., according to the magazine, was being "subjected to a torrent of adverse comment, quips, scorn and ridicule, much of it witheringly personal. Not since the days of F.D.R. and the New Deal had the level of attack on a President, his family, and his policies seemed quite so heated; and like those days of the thirties, much of the rancor was being generated in Wall Street."

The rancor of this dialogue depends, as all political measurements must, largely on beliefs and dedication of the recipient.

Governor David Lawrence of Pennsylvania, a Democrat and a veteran of such phases of political life, seemed to sum up the situation sensibly. He said, "The jokes are the price a President pays for living in a democracy."

Dialogue Can Be Dirty Fun

Governor Mark Hatfield of Oregon, a Republican, took an unexpectedly dark attitude. "There is real concern about the swimming pool stories, sipping champagne, and all that."

What were the two governors appraising? Such things as Mort Sahl's theory that Caroline Kennedy may have masterminded the Cuban invasion; traveling salesmen who hand out cards saying "I MISS IKE! Hell, I even miss Harry," and the profusion of Big Brother–Little Brother cracks about the President and the Attorney General.

The frequently liberal *Reporter* magazine observed: "There is something quite engaging about these New Frontiersmen; they are overactive and playful; they are dogmatic but their dogmatism is relieved by the absence of dogmas. One must still have confidence that someday they will learn how to move about more sedately, how to stop running around all the time, and how to talk a little less. But when?"

The *Wall Street Journal* worried editorially about a current "propensity to confuse words with action. President Eisenhower could give the country eight years of peace if not tranquillity, and of prosperity if not a millennium, yet seem a failure to men in academic halls and to public commentators because what he did was difficult to articulate," said the *Journal*. "President Kennedy, on the other hand, is suffering from too much articulation by his friends and supporters."

Excessive articulation, if surplus there be, referred to by the *Wall Street Journal,* relates back to what *Newsweek* felt was the most severe ridicule directed at the White House since the New Deal. The more the N.P. talk, the more they let themselves in for shafting.

Political ridicule and comic satire consist chiefly of paraphrase and exaggeration. The native habits of the Frontier people are sufficient to attract much raucous comment quite aside from that of purely political origin. Weren't they the very ones who called Eisenhower "the best President since Truman"? Why, then, should

Frontiersmen bridle surprisedly when their man is tagged as the best since Ike?

Partisan involvement has a way of beclouding history and this may be part of the Frontier problem. Many N.P. may be too young or too preoccupied with the present to have the comforting awareness of history before January 20, 1961.

The previously mentioned totality of dedication makes for poor winners, as well as poor losers. It may be oversimplification, but the pain of a setback in Congress, for example, intensifies with totality of belief or pureness of thought. The reality of roll-call defeat rudely upsets the golden prospectus which shone so brilliantly from the pages of a State of the Union message.

Riding back from Mount Vernon aboard a torpedo boat, on that soft spring night when Jacqueline had entertained on the lawn for President Ayub Khan of Pakistan, a concerned Frontier woman clutched my arm in charming alarm.

"I do hope," she said, "you won't say anything in your story about the strolling violinists during dinner."

Why?

"Because it might seem a little *too much* on the lawn of Mount Vernon."

While I attempted to assimilate this wisdom, my eyes wandered over the procession of yachts and naval craft bearing the handsome and beautiful guests back upriver while small ensembles played dance tunes on each boat.

Personally, I thought Mrs. Kennedy's idea of having a state dinner against the beautiful, historic setting of George Washington's home was outstandingly good. Why one of her more devoted supporters would fear publicity about strolling violinists escaped me. After all, the same musicians had been in well-reported evidence at similar affairs within the White House.

"Outdoors," she reasoned, "it might seem too opulent."

Possibly to my detriment in certain sections of the Frontier, the violins were reported and somehow the Administration remained relatively unshaken.

It was, however, only a few nights later that a comedian on television suggested Jacqueline's next party would be held at the top of the Washington Monument with Lester Lanin circling in a blimp.

On another occasion, I heard a robust Frontiersman denounce what I had thought was a notably fair critique of a J.F.K. speech. The article was written by a columnist usually well disposed to the N.F., but the Frontiersman objected strenuously to the writer's inclusion of "on the other hand" material outlining the position of leading opposition Senators.

"There are times," said the Frontiersman, "when I don't think that man [the columnist] is *really* for us."

I thought back to an earlier experience with practicing politicians.

It was in 1937 and the brilliantly colorful governor of Georgia, the late Gene Talmadge, set out from Atlanta on a speaking tour of the northern counties where the countrymen, known as "wool hat boys" were as totally dedicated as any Frontiersman of today.

At the time, I was a most junior reporter for United Press and went along excitedly to cover the great Gene's woodsy campaigning. I was given a seat in an automobile driven by a state trooper, and seated beside him was the spreading wife of a leading Talmadge official.

Considerately, the lady engaged in polite conversation and asked where I was from. She nodded approvingly when I said I hailed from Savannah, but she was unclear as to the status of my employers. I tried to explain that I worked for a press association which served a great many newspapers. She wanted to know the U.P. editorial policy and I explained that, serving clients of highly varied political convictions, we attempted to stand clear of anything resembling political opinion.

The Good New Days

"Tell me, son," she asked, "are you for us or against us?"

"Neither one," I replied. "Professionally, it is no concern of mine who occupies the state house."

"Then you must be against us," she said sternly. "Trooper, stop the car. We're not hauling any enemy of Gene Talmadge."

Whereupon, with some encouragement, I alighted from the car to a deserted rural highway, but managed a few hours later to thumb my way to the governor's rally.

A few months before this book was completed, the wife of a Cabinet officer said, "This summer, I hope you correspondents won't make *so much* over the President spending his weekends in Hyannis—you make it sound so much like Eisenhower."

Unable to define "so much," I asked for further guidance.

"You know what I mean," she said, "making it appear that he's *never* in Washington."

Here is a classic example of supersensitivity. For five days a week, the newspapers and networks pour out hundreds of thousands of words about J.F.K. activities in the White House. But the Frontier faithful become apprehensive about a few paragraphs over the weekend. To keep this part of the record straight, however, J.F.K. is not nearly as apprehensive about this type of thing as some of his followers.

What struck me as utterly strange about the fear of the Cabinet wife was that her protective emotion was so limited. I mentioned that a recent *Saturday Evening Post* article about New Frontier women had contained dialogue by the good ladies concerning the delightful pleasure of riding to Cape Cod each weekend on the so-called "back-up" Air Force jet which accompanies most presidential movements. This is a plane sent along to haul heavier baggage and overflow personnel, but primarily to provide a duplicate ship in event of mechanical trouble aboard Air Force One.

The article quoted the wife of one White House official about the convenience of reaching her own Cape Cod house, thanks to J.F.K., and the joshing that went on among the girls about whose turn it was to sit in the President's chair (the one he would use if he found occasion to fly aboard the spare plane).

The Cabinet wife saw no analogy or connection.

"The plane is going up there anyway," she said. "Why shouldn't people ride on it?"

"You were speaking, however, of possible adverse publicity."

"The girls, however, are doing nothing to make it appear that the President is away too much," she maintained steadily. "The newspapers do that."

Perhaps the quotations in the *Saturday Evening Post* came more closely to the point of *Reporter*'s recommendation that the Frontier people learn "how to stop running around all the time and how to talk a little less."

To jest about the N.F. dialogue should not be taken as across-the-board disapproval or generalized negation. Washington today is a far more interesting, exciting community because of the dialogue.

The articulation which causes trouble for the N.F. is largely idealistic and thus, easy to shoot at. Brave goals are big targets.

Frontiersmen might be advised to regard some of the satire and sarcasm aimed in their direction as plus marks. Intensity of public reaction to policies and practices of national leaders is more than an indication of political adherence, but of badly needed interest in current events. Lampooning, as well as imitation, is a form of flattery. Hatred can be as much a barometer of political success as adulation.

CHAPTER TEN

How to Use an Ethnic Estoppel

After examining some of the seriocomic aspects of N.P. dialogue, it is only appropriate that several companionate points be made.

The O.P. have their dialogue, too. These days, as one might expect, it is largely defensive. It is possible to guard against inside cultural and political nuances of N.P. conversation, and still emerge socially intact, politically inviolate and, with any acuity, an occasional victor. We'll offer handy hints for survival as we go along.

Mrs. Mesta, I thought, handled the problem exceedingly well in a recent interview with a Philadelphia society columnist. Such people tend to be a bit scratchy at times. Although it was 1962, this Philadelphia person expectedly dredged up the fact that Mrs. Mesta had supported Nixon in 1960, the implication being that Perle perforce now stood Outside in spite of having sold her house to L.B.J.

Mrs. Mesta regarded the snide aside magnificently, as though she'd never heard of 1960.

The Good New Days

"I hope to fly to French Equatorial Africa for Albert Schweitzer's birthday," she said with stunning simplicity.

While the conversation did take place in Philadelphia, it showed Mrs. Mesta was not about to be put down. That, friends, is defense.

Examination of N.P. dialogue also should take into consideration a conversational phenomenon which is truly a product of the Good New Days, beginning under Truman. It is the television panel show. For the networks, this sort of program is gratifyingly economical to produce. It also serves somewhat as an antidote for Newton Minow. More importantly, it gives leading government, political, and diplomatic figures a chance to talk, though labored at times, nervous at others.

Conversational conduct on a Washington TV panel can be of crucial importance for a public figure, and later we will attempt to point out certain pitfalls and how to avoid them.

But first, let us concern ourselves with a program of intellectual muscle building which might be useful in any N.P. forum.

New People have an identifying symptom in their dialogue, particularly when O.P. or outlanders in general are within earshot. You can hear them at dinner, at cocktail parties and at their little dances, complaining about the lack of true meaning in life —the lives of others. Particularly, they deplore the proper or desired depth of meaning in virtually all forms of communication— face-to-face, printed, or broadcast.

In essence, this is a form of intellectual hostility more than snobbery. An N.P. dinner companion will shell hell out of an Out or O.P. with volleys of obscure references to strange authorities, little-known dialects, out-of-the-way places, and writings so current that they've not yet gone to press (the N.P. may be working from page proof).

In such an N.P. ploy, the object of the ployer is to put the ployed in his place, namely, Stupidville. Or, perhaps, Oldtown.

But don't go, O.P. Refuse to be pushed. Ploy right back. The defense at this point may be varied. The ethnic estoppel can be grand fun and destructive, too. Witness:

N.P.: It seems a shame, sir, that a firm as large as yours has not seen fit to liberalize employment policies and get away from a wasteful attitude toward certain nationalities and racial groups.

O.P.: No firm in America employs more Scandinavians than we do. Your attitude, quite frankly, is shocking—what have you got against Swedes?

(The idea is to counterattack when employing the ethnic estoppel. If counterattack is impossible, change directions. This is known to some as the social swivel.)

N.P.: Will we be seeing you at the Clark Cliffords' next week?

O.P.: Oh, drat Clark and Marny. They insist on having their summer tent party at a time when they know perfectly well Evan and I are in Rhodesia with the dogs. They're Ridgebacks, you know, and we try to see that they get back to Rhodesia at least once a summer.

The swivel has many variations, commendable when employed with thought and verve—and always with a crushing topper, or abject underplay. Two examples:

The hard-to-disprove topper:

N.P.: You and Denise going to the Cape this summer?

O.P.: Not on your life—not while Robert Frost is in town.

The N.P. doesn't follow through because he can't possibly tell whether "in town" means Washington or elsewhere. He's not going to be so naïve as to ask, either.

The abject underplay:

N.P.: . . . at least, that's what I told the Secretary the other day. Bob McNamara. You know him, of course?"

O.P.: No, I couldn't say I *really* know him—he's only been at our house a couple of times. . . .

The abject underplay is helped no end by the tactical trail-off which leaves much unsaid, but clearly understood.

We examine next the literary whipping. This is a most common form of N.P. tyranny, used against not only O.P., but N.P. of lesser station, particularly when they display disturbing symptoms of equality. The N.P. technique is to make the subject appear to be hopelessly ignorant of current literature.

A conversation may go like this:

N.P.: Did you read the text of Nehru's speech at Lahore?
O.P.: No, I'm afraid I've been too busy lately—when was it?
N.P.: Two years ago, and I don't see how anyone can discuss Asia intelligently today without having virtually committed the Lahore speech to memory.

Clearly, the O.P. deserved to be crushed in this manner. It was unforgivably fumble-foot on three points: admitting not having read the speech, professing to have been "too busy"; and worst of all, asking when it was delivered.

A thinking O.P. could have handled it several ways—"I'll be a bit more sympathetic to Nehru when he stands up to Krishna Menon," or "I prefer to read Nehru in Hindi, which an uncle in Bombay posts to me every so often."

The N.P. are forever asking if one has read something. Since it is impossible to avoid this trait in Washington without moving almost entirely with Ev and Charlie, it is better to face up to attempted literary whipping—and whip back.

N.P.: Did you read Lippmann this morning?
O.P.: Oh, is Walter back?
N.P.: Where's he been?
O.P.: I shouldn't have mentioned it, I suppose. He may not want it known. I'll give him a call tomorrow. Gladys is so sweet, isn't she?

How to Use an Ethnic Estoppel

No N.P. worth his lifetime subscription to *Lampoon* is going to bite for that. *Gladys* Lippmann? *Gladys* who? The wise N.P. will say something about thinking the world of both of them and pass on to another area of empiricality.

The best anti-N.P. weapon is N.P. dialogue itself, when shifted deftly into reverse.

N.P.: Did you read Lippmann this morning?

O.P.: You know something? I've been a little disturbed by Walter recently. At times, he's seemed so superficial.

If it develops, as it sometimes does, that the N.P. roars back in outrage, one must pick and choose the next defensive move rather carefully.

N.P.: Lippmann superficial? You're certainly in a minority.

Here, one uses all known techniques at once, including the abject underplay, ethnic estoppel, social swivel and crushing topper, if possible. In simpler terms, change directions and leap from your hole while scattering dust and rocks in all directions.

O.P.: Oh, I'm in a *minority,* all right, but I *am* a little surprised to hear a self-styled liberal use the word epithetically. Yes (sadly) I'm in a minority—I think Walter hasn't done his homework on the Billie Sol Estes case and I told him so just before he went away.

The switch in directions should be remembered at all times. Nothing seems to annoy an N.P. more, possibly because he uses the same technique when sorely pressed. This can be regarded for labeling purposes as the power-packed negative. For example:

N.P.: I assume you saw Claiborne Pell's statement on gold?

O.P.: No, but did you read Steinbloch's fascinating letter to the *Post Dispatch** on the same subject?

This is rather cruel since the N.P. must confess ignorance or ignore the entire matter. He has no more clue than the O.P. to

* The St. Louis *Post Dispatch.*

the identity of Steinbloch, but a name of this sort *sounds* as though it should be known. A proper N.P., faced with a possible *contretemps,* will do one of two things: paraphrase the Pell statement sufficiently for the O.P. to grab, as they say in Georgetown, a-hold; or cite another obscure letter to an editor, preferably one of foreign imprimatur.

There are innumerable conversation base-changing sentences which may be employed defensively by O.P. without regard for specific subject of the dialogue in progress. These may be used as grabbers, interrupters, or confusers when the hour and condition of the opposition are favorable. The base-changing sentence should be leaden, falling as a heavy weight on the dialogue underway and leaving little, if any, excuse or opportunity for rejoinder. The following examples are in no way related to each other, having been speared independently from recent nocturnal jousts about the city:

"Poor thing." (This can be mumbled at any time.)

"The one I feel sorry for is *her*." (Also good for disconnected mumbling. Emphasis is so important in a sentence of this nature. Should the N.P. press for details or clarification, the O.P. has but to say softly, "No, no, I'll *not* add to her troubles.")

"Isn't it wonderful about Barry Goldwater's daughter and the Peace Corps? He's *so* happy." (This is a grabber rather than a confuser. The O.P. should beware of being urged to extend his remarks. Keep shifting subjects until the other side hits on one which the O.P. can handle easily.)

> N.P. (Somewhat angrily): I'd like to know what he's got to be happy about. His own children . . . .
>
> O.P.: I hear several Jews have been playing tennis at Chevy Chase. Have *you* seen any there?

The foregoing, of course, is a wildly thrown ethnic estoppel, but in certain N.P. settings it has a fairish chance of hitting home. After all, some of them *do* play tennis and at Chevy Chase. The N.P. we mean.

How to Use an Ethnic Estoppel

Other handy O.P. shafts currently apt might include:

"Tell me, Mr. Secretary, how many Negro ambassadors *do* we have?"

"Why is it the President seems so dead set against having a woman in his Cabinet?"

"I'm surprised so many people at the Labor Department drive foreign automobiles."

Handy hints for O.P. in conversing socially with N.P. may seem a bit churlish, but no more than called for in disquisitive times. The dialogue of Washington today, however, need not be regarded entirely as a matter of jabs and counterthrusts. Eclecticism can be fun.

Or so it would seem on Sunday afternoons when members of the Cabinet, Congress and the diplomatic corps fight to be interviewed on television by panels ranging from seasoned correspondents to squeak-voiced teen-agers whose knowledge of internal politics in the Republic of Chad or highly technical aspects of the Upper Volta Dam can be discouraging.

Some less-than-nimble officials are fools to appear on these shows, particularly at times when their departments or areas of influence have been under attack. They have no way of controlling the questions and as a consequence, sometimes leave the air egg-on-face.

Broadcast interviewees unfortunately at times, and usually in partisan energy, try to control or shape the questioning. Then they're in for real trouble.

Ray Scherer of NBC and I once joined Ned Brooks in a weekly radio network confection called "Report from the White House." The three of us divided fifteen minutes in viewing the local situation, then devoted the last half of the program to a theoretically ad lib interview with a prominent government figure.

The program had jogged along rather well for several weeks until we encountered Ezra Taft Benson, Secretary of Agriculture under Eisenhower.

Benson arrived only a few minutes before air time with wife, daughter, and administrative assistant. As the Secretary seated himself at our broadcast table, the assistant distributed to Scherer, Brooks, and me mimeographed copies of *our questions* plus Benson's answers. Furthermore, the Benson script ran far longer than the ten minutes we had allotted that night.

The producer bordered on collapse as Benson's assistant whispered something to the effect of "No script, no interview." During a commercial before we came to the Secretary, we were able to discuss the situation. Benson was adamant, but willing to accept a few changes in actual language to make the show seem more chatty.

I went to the water cooler with Brooks and we decided to use the first question, then forget the script. Scherer was advised somehow. The first question opened swimmingly with Benson professing surprised gratitude at being offered such a fine inquiry, and proceeded to answer.

Brooks had the next question, and when it failed to follow script there was a gasp from the assistant. The Secretary leafed madly through his script and, not finding the item, proceeded to answer in halting fashion. The rest of the interview bobbled along in this manner and when we left the air, Benson seemed to require all of his powers of charity to depart the premises with civility.

This would not happen today on television—or radio—mainly because Washington air interviews have become more often than not a seller's market. There are, to be sure, some officials hard to sign for broadcast inquisition. The major interview shows such as "Meet the Press" have no trouble, however, in attracting subjects —or interviewers.

Several bits of advice are offered to the N.P. official new to this sort of public exposure.

One, don't drink at Sunday lunch. A few nips of sherry before being thrown to Lawrence Spivak, Jack Bell, May Craig and similarly jolly citizens may be nerve-settling, but in no case should it be overdone. The make-up has yet to be invented to disguise separately focused eyes. The author speaks with a small measure of sad experience.

Two, arm to the teeth with figures. The panel will have figures, too, which its members will have to read. Yours should be committed to memory and need not bear too accurately on the point under discussion. This is base-changing and is regarded as entirely fair on Sunday afternoon, although it may leave the panelists grumbly.

If, for example, Stewart Hensley mentions in a question that A.I.D. figures for Vietnam show only "a million two"—capitalese for $1,200,000—in the last quarter, the harried official should hurl back as "far more to the point" A.I.D. figures for all of Southeast Asia for the preceding fiscal year, referring to "FY 62," which won't impress the panel, but will give the home viewer a feeling of comfortable confusion.

Sunday afternoon TV victims also should practice Old World courtesy (or abject underplay), which will be needed when confronted by some of the ladies—Mrs. Craig, Doris Fleeson, Marianne Means, to name a few. Kindly, attentive, lovely—off-camera. But the subject should remember, these ladies invented the journalistic blowgun.

In the alleys and rest homes of politics and diplomacy lie misshapen hulks of men, quivering from effects of curare darts administered by ladies on Sunday afternoon television. They are the high priestesses of a cult, members of which start the questioning with, "Do you *seriously* expect us to *believe* . . ."

Mrs. Craig is notably adept at slings which begin, "With millions starving, you *still* believe an *expenditure* of this sort . . ."

Their needles are sharp, slender, and expertly administered. So expertly, in fact, that target victims sometimes make it home before slumping flush-faced beside the telephone to hear a colleague inquiring solicitously, "Have you lost your mind, going for a question like that thirty seconds before you left the air?"

Each network has its own version. On ABC, two men do the

questioning; on CBS, one. The *mano a mano* format is better for the interviewed since he has a chance, however slim, to state his case without being interrupted or called to account by four inquisitors. On the other hand, the head-to-head show lacks audience appeal of the larger slaughter. Seated before our silver screens, there's a goodly bit of the old Roman left in many of us.

An interesting aspect of Sunday afternoon dialogue is that it offers O.P. personalities, when invited to appear, a more free-wheeling opportunity than a Frontiersman can afford under the weight of his responsibilities.

An Out may make all sorts of outrageous charges against the Ins and demand that opposite numbers face him in mortal combat before the same cameras. An Out may say to the panel, "I realize *many* of you ladies and gentlemen are pro-Administration, *but . . .*"

If Miss Fleeson then fires harpoon No. One, assume whatever courtliness possible; never reply in kind, and shift immediately into excessive blandishment, such as, "I didn't say *all*, Miss Fleeson, but *many . . .*"

The F.C.C. has yet to lump them with objectionable murder shows, but the Sunday youth question-and-answer periods provide the real blood baths of sociopolitical television. Those innocent little girls in starched cotton and well-scrubbed lads with cowlicks —they're the real monsters. On such outings as "College Press Conference" and "Youth Wants to Know," panelists come by the dozen, each bursting to know such things as why the Senator took his secretary to Africa.

Depending on politics and position of the interview subject, these youth-monsters apparently are recruited from schools for anarchy. They tend to be pro-Frontier when confronted by Republicans, and Nixon relatives when assembled before a Democrat.

The only sound advice here is avoidance. Cabinet-level N.P. cannot escape youth shows entirely, but when shackled and led before their scowling faces, a small vial of chloroform concealed in the handkerchief is recommended.

Meantime, patience. Conceivably there may come a time in Washington, a pleasant Sunday afternoon, when a towering figure of either In or Out connections stares glumly at the television panel and rises slowly from his chair.

"Bums, the whole lot of you," he'll shout. "Ignorant bums."

And walk slowly off-camera ten minutes before the closing commercial.

Of course, he will have ruined himself on that particular show. But he'll be big in the morning papers, a hero at home, and a tragic figure at the office. Also, he will have contributed something new to the dialogue of our city.

CHAPTER ELEVEN

O Little Town of Middleburg

The New People, as they move worshipfully behind their political and/or intellectual leaders (sometimes there is a difference), tend to identify with more than political theories, literary preferences, dress fashions and hair-styling. They have their Meccas—places where the Leader sleeps or slept, bathes or bathed, golfs or golfed.

A Mecca may be so situated that followers camp in the countryside to breathe the same heavenly air. It may have a shoreline sufficiently long to accommodate vast assemblies of baptismees. And at times, a Mecca may be nothing more than a way of life to be emulated, imitated, or at least approximated.

This is the lemming outlook of many political disciples and in truth, not confined to N.P. The O.P. had their Meccas, too.

Hyde Park, New York, was a Mecca. So, of a sort, was Independence, Missouri, and Gettysburg, Pennsylvania. The common denominator was home location of the reigning President.

To have been invited inside one of the three aforementioned shrines while the Leader was in residence was a source of wild

143

happiness to the devoted. To spend a night beneath the same roof, wild, wild happiness. To say nothing of acceptance beyond dispute.

The Roosevelt house at Hyde Park, by Mecca standards, was spacious, graciously but not ornately furnished, and occupied by a family that liked company. The Truman home at Independence was small, the family somewhat more self-contained than the Roosevelts and, as a consequence, few overnight guests outside of blood relatives.

The Eisenhower house at Gettysburg also was no adult hostel for passing Republican Crusaders. Maybe a cookout, but not a sleep-over. Mrs. Eisenhower detested having the place cluttered with the unanointed. She was perfectly agreeable to having all sorts of folks in the yard, but not in the house, which is understandable if one has a highly developed sense of order.

The interior of the Gettysburg house was and presumably still is well-ordered. It's the sort of house in which silver ash trays still gleam in their original shellac. The living room is best described as an intimate museum. An errant bobby pin on the light wall-to-wall rug would cry out for immediate retrieval on, at the very least, a brightly burnished copper dustpan bearing a small medallion proclaiming its origin, "presented by the grateful Young Republicans of Indiana." In fact, there are similar small medallions or silver plates attached to much of the furniture and furnishings. The living room derives its museum quality from these and several large glass-front cabinets in which repose tastefully lighted bric-a-brac and odd-lot treasures (rare china birds from the Queen of England) acquired from social equals and fellow leaders such as Churchill, de Gaulle, and those boys.

Mamie Eisenhower felt strongly against having her spotless home tracked and soiled by political shoes. And her feelings should be understandable, considering the years she spent in Army quarters, borrowed palaces and their limited privacy. She opened the grounds periodically to lavish picnics for the White House staff (at least every staffer including the maids and messengers got at least one visit to the grounds during the Eisenhower Administration, along with a conducted tour of the lower floors of the house where little plastic runners saved the carpets from footmarks in the living and dining rooms). There were several larger affairs for party workers, but these were confined for the most part to a convenient pasture where tents were pitched.

In short, Mrs. Eisenhower wanted the Gettysburg house kept as nongovernmental and nonpolitical as possible. This, of course, applied only to guests. She delighted in federally supplied domestic help when she and her husband were White House occupants, as any housewife would under the same circumstances. There was nothing shrewish about her downhold on guests at Gettysburg. It resembled separation of church and state. When D.D.E. wanted to have official or business guests, there was Camp David, completely owned and operated by the government in the Maryland mountains, easily available by helicopter or car and a constant clutch of Filipino Navy mess stewards and U.S. Marines to keep the place tidy. Camp David also can handle thirty or forty guests at a clip, although they do have to sleep around in little low-roofed bungalows scattered through the heavily guarded woods.

The Mecca aspect of Gettysburg was at first difficult to differentiate from outright tourism. Gettysburg and its hallowed battlefield always attracted visitors. Location of the Eisenhower establishment at the edge of Seminary Ridge brought even larger crowds; but more important from the standpoint of this particular study, it made country living The Thing among those Republicans who could afford it.

As a man of influence with D.D.E., the position of George Allen was towering. Quite aside from George's brilliant job of companionship with other Presidents, he *was,* after all, the man who more or less founded Gettysburg for the Eisenhowers. George had

The Good New Days

his property there first. He sold Mamie on the locale and she in turn assured her husband it was the ideal spot for their long-awaited home.

This left George in an understandably enviable position. Not a soul could accuse him of trailing to Gettysburg behind Ike. It was the other way around, and by every current standard of Washington status this was the highest. Other D.D.E. Crusaders couldn't go dashing around Ike's acreage trying to snap up similar places. This would have been obvious, and perhaps more telling; his arrival shot up land prices terribly.

But there were other sections of nearby Maryland and Virginia open to Republican colonization and as this took place on the Cabinet and agency-head level, quiet cattle raising became about as In as golf. It became incumbent on Mecca travelers to be as knowledgeable about desired straightness of a Black Angus backbone as whether the 16th at Burning Tree was dogleg to the right or left.

It may be roundabout narration to discuss Gettysburg at such length before coming to Middleburg, Virginia, but this sort of sketching may be helpful in appreciating the successor Mecca.

Although they had several other homes between them, the Kennedys selected Middleburg as their personal redoubt for several reasons. One: Middleburg is the epicenter of the horse world, well-bred jumper section. And Mrs. Kennedy from early childhood has been as devoted to riding as Eisenhower was to golf.

The N.P. who thought so poorly of the Eisenhowers for constantly escaping to Gettysburg see nothing wrong when Jackie borrows the helicopter several times a week to ride to the hounds in Middleburg.

For all of their One Worldism, the N.P. relate more comfortably to practices and pursuits of transatlantic origin, particularly British and Irish. This may account for their complete acceptance of the Virginia hunt country as a location for the weekend White House.

O Little Town of Middleburg

A second reason for Middleburg: nearness to Washington.

Then there is the factor of seclusion. This apparently meant much more to J.F.K. than riding, which he doesn't do.

To appreciate the almost total dedication of Middleburg and the surrounding counties of rolling Virginia countryside to horse and horsemanship requires study and time. The people are entirely too polite to make much over the President's not being a rider, just as they speak only under most guarded conditions about his *renting* his estate, Glen Ora, instead of owning property thereabouts. This tolerance, of course, is largely a matter of recognizing presidential license.* The people of Middleburg would be much happier, however, if Mr. Kennedy had acquired his bum back in a riding accident instead of the Solomon Islands.

Mr. Kennedy is accepted in Middleburg not only because of his line of work, but because his wife is a superb rider. She rides in fox hunts with such slashing verve that she falls occasionally at the jumps. Now and then, her spills get into the newspapers. This offends the country hunters as much or more than the First Lady, because her antipathy for counter-image publicity is far surpassed by their morbidity on the same subject.

The hunt country people regard themselves as above the clammy clasp of public prints. They accept primly written horse-show notices, but when it comes to what they regard as popular exploitation, they speak darkly of "doing things" to those responsible. "Doing things" may consist, for example, of refusing to read a certain newspaper and in this they have the heartfelt support of N.P. everywhere; or it may be nothing more than cocktail party castigation of one of their fellows seen in the presence of a scrivener.

The President's custom for several of the more agreeable months of the year is to journey by helicopter to Middleburg Saturday, buzzing back to the south grounds of the White House bright

---

* As this was written, the Kennedys had subleased Glen Ora for a few months during which to scout for another place nearby.

147

and early Monday. During the fall and spring hunting seasons, Mrs. Kennedy may stay down in Middleburg all week unless her presence is required at the White House by a state dinner or the discovery of John Quincy Adams' wig stand.

Mrs. Kennedy rides a great deal and hauls Caroline around to various pony shows in which the younger Kennedy is entered. At this writing, John, Jr., not yet having reached the age of two, still was unsteady in the saddle. At this point in his career, he seemed relatively happy about being led around a small enclosure on a docile pony. He was able to say "horsie," but still was having trouble with "Dean Rusk."

When the Kennedys first established Glen Ora as a primary outpost on the New Frontier, the locals gathered beside their mud-spattered Landrovers parked in front of the Red Fox Tavern and shook their leather-patched elbows in fine F.F.V.* indignation.

With the Kennedys were bound to come "the press" and all manner of tourists, vendors selling Jack and Jackie dinner plates on which the portraits appear to be done by the same men who paint carnival sideshow banners, and miserable little stands of souvenirs—foxtails from Japan, tiny plastic hunting horns, and probably those awful postcards providing spaces in which to check one's sobriety, state of sexual happiness and number of states visited.

Vows that this would not happen proved unnecessary. Save for the first Kennedy weekend, the only press who showed up on following presidential visits were duty-bound servants of the two press associations who disappeared quietly among the early American pine furniture, canopied beds and pewter plates of the Red Fox.

Middleburg wanted so much to remain Middleburg, a sleepy little trade center of about 600 population. The thought of new arrivals was most distasteful at first. Then, when there were no

---

* F.F.V.: First Families of Virginia, or reasonable facsimile thereof.

new arrivals to speak of, the country hunters returned uneasily to their only other subject of conversation—horses.

The dominance of the horse in this section of Virginia is difficult to exaggerate. The village has two drug stores, one primarily for humans. The other features remedies and sundries for horses at a large counter just inside the door. There is an entire shelf of stuff for tired fetlocks, the sight of which can be unnerving to the outlander shopping for a tin of aspirins.

The horsier drug store carries vitamin pills the size of ping-pong balls for ponies. It is said, perhaps with slight distortion so common when these tales are bandied carelessly, that a Secret Service agent assigned to Mrs. Kennedy swallowed one of Caroline's pony pills by mistake and a few hours later was seen jumping fences back of the house. Had he been on a horse it would have attracted little attention.

Life in the area can be droll and uninhibited; it can be stern and competitive. The estates have an air of protective seclusion, and government greats frequent some of the boxwood and pewter establishments for reasons similar to those of the President.

Secretary of State Rusk, for example, visits the farm of one of his associates. Seldom has the Secretary seemed more fun-loving than one Sunday when he was fishing in a small pond. Landing a trout, he raced across a grassy field and threw the wriggling fish into his host's swimming pool then occupied by a group of dog-paddling ladies, who whooped and splashed in mock panic to escape the darting monster of the deep.

Then there was the day Pushinka was lost. Pushinka, a white, furry dog sent to the Kennedys by Khrushchev, is the offspring of the first Russian dog to be launched into space. Pushinka is frisky and wandering; so much so that at the White House it was necessary to string several hundred yards of chicken wire around the base of the cast-iron fence enclosing the south grounds. The wire was necessary to prevent Pushinka from bounding through the iron rods into beckoning arms of tourists or potential dog-stealers.

The Good New Days

The Kennedys have another dog, Charlie, a likable little brown wire-haired tramp who knows a good thing and doesn't wander. Pushinka, being inclined to chase capitalists, is a responsibility. To admit her loss for any reason would be to confirm *Pravda's* worst fears of Yankee hooliganism.

Thus, it was with more than ordinary concern one day that a Secret Service agent called the Virginia State Police and reported gravely that Pushinka had departed the fences of Glen Ora.

Patrol cars were alerted by shortwave radio and before long, upwards of twenty troopers were on the lookout for the small animal. And an effective search it was. Within a few hours, a trooper reported finding Pushinka on an estate several miles away. The dog was rushed back to Glen Ora under police protection because it would have been a frightful tragedy had the Russian pup become involved in a fox hunt. The Master of Hounds would have been mortified to discover a wisp of Russian fur amongst his baying pack.

Some neighbors were huffy and aloof, some even antagonistic, when the Kennedys first moved in shortly after the inauguration— the first inauguration. They felt security devices installed to protect the President were an insult to the community. Who, in God's name, in Middleburg would pillage or plunder except outsiders who could always be detected when they turned at the traffic light in front of the Red Fox?

A few neighbors thought the installation of microwave towers, helicopter landing pads and the like might add an undesirably modern tone to the pastorale. Others said electronic devices were certain, somehow, to frighten the foxes or make stud horses impotent.

Nothing of this sort developed, but some of the more fundamental farmers still regard with less than complete trust the loudhailer installed at the Kennedy gate. This is a remotely controlled public-address system for use when the President is not present and the perimeter of security is withdrawn from the gate to the house itself. The front gate is electronically operated and tucked away is a hidden microphone and loudspeaker.

Push a button and someone several hundred yards away at the house inquires the name and purpose of the caller. Once identity and validity of purpose are established, the gate swings wide and the caller may make his way to the nerve center of the estate.

Farmers, trainers and tradesmen having business at Glen Ora have seen similar arrangements at other country places, but the President's set-up was more impressive in being operated by White House police or Secret Service men.

A farmer-horseman was admitted one day and, as he departed, the loudspeaker at the gate asked him to please hold it open for a procession of limousines just arriving loaded with important personages from Washington. True to security teachings which had been drummed into him, the old fellow slammed the gate shut and roared in the box, "Not on your life—you come out here and take the damned responsibility."

What the President sees in this particular Mecca-in-the-woods remains something of a mystery. Neither riding nor caring much for the unremitting horse-country dialogue, Mr. Kennedy is said to derive most of his Middleburg pleasure from being able to play with the kids without tourists staring through the fence, lolling around the pool in tattered comfort, and the opportunity to read without interruption. He talks on the telephone a great deal from Virginia, frequently placing his own calls rather than asking the White House operator to do it for him.

The Kennedys often have personal friends as weekend guests, but when this was written in the late summer of 1962, they had maintained the separation of office and home even more rigidly than did Ike and Mamie. There hadn't been the first picnic for messengers and maids, nor had there been a political rally, even under a tent far removed from the house. Of course, the summer of 1964 could make a difference.

On occasion, the Kennedys have had house guests who were

The Good New Days

N.P., as well as personal friends, but nonriders and not particularly privy to state secrets. When Jackie was out chasing a fox and the President busy on the telephone to Ruanda or Middle Impala, there was little in the way of guest action or entertainment. This has led some of these guests to drive several miles into town.

Even this pastime has its limits. Outside of three filling stations, two drug stores, a news and candy establishment, the area for browsing is pretty much limited to the Red Fox, a rather uninspired restaurant called the Coach Stop, one supermarket and a half dozen or so antique shops, proprietors of which regard Mrs. Kennedy highly for what she did to renew interest in their trade.

With any orientation at all, the visitor gravitates to the Red Fox, a delightful eighteenth-century hostel boasting seven rooms for rent, a delightful grotto, and basement dining room where the food is prepared by a talented French chef, Gabriel, whose *cordon* is amazingly *bleu*.

The Red Fox catches most of the Mecca travelers. It has become about as In as an inn can be to swoop down from Washington for the evening and sigh over Gabriel's duck and black cherries topped off by crusty-creamy chocolate soufflé.

The Red Fox has no bar as such because of a rather insensitive Virginia law which holds against purchase of strong spirits by the dram. Since conventional bars are illegal, the Red Fox is limited to serving beer and wine, although the pilgrim may go to an upstairs lounge called the J. E. B. Stewart room and get swacked out of his own bottle.

Travelers familiar with Virginia expect to find at any self-respecting colonial inn a menu heavy with spoon bread, tearfully salty Virginia ham which the native-born choke down as a matter of regional pride or utter disregard for cholesterol. Thus it comes as a shock to grope for one's seat beneath gleaming old coach horns in the Red Fox basement and under guttering candlelight, behold a long, handwritten menu listing haute cuisine, Provençal and Upper Pavillon delicacies.

O Little Town of Middleburg

More eye-popping than the menu is the manageress of the Red Fox who could well be lost to some greater area of influence by the time this volume reaches Middleburg. This refers to Mrs. Nettie Michaelis, who looks as N.P. as any lady of Georgetown, as high-fashion as her menu is haut, as well-groomed as Jacqueline at Versailles. Well, almost.

Mrs. Michaelis, in addition to looking recently removed from a *Vogue* cover, can speak Common Market, drop little *bon mots* from *Saturday Review,* ride well enough to speak fluent horse and keep her hi-fi loaded with Bach. N.P.s have been known to lose interest even in road directions to Glen Ora after a one-two punch of Gabriel's cooking and Mrs. Michaelis' glamour.

There seldom seems much mingling between visiting N.P. and the strictly horse people in Mrs. Michaelis' softly candled basement. The horse people, in fact, seem more comfortable when just their crowd is sitting around over champagne or beer and talking the good talk of withers, saddles and stupid bitches who wear rat catcher (a tweedy type of riding costume) to the wrong party.

The N.P. pilgrims, grateful for simple proximity, care little for the indigenous dialogue and adjourn to the upstairs living room to make daiquiris eight-to-one ("to 'one' what, Charlotte? Light to dark?") and bellyflop on the rug before the fireplace on a scrumptious autumn afternoon when leaves fill the bucket seats and Metcalfe's scarf stretched out a yard behind him when he went down that hill on Route 50 between Lenah and Aldie, the settlement immediately east of Middleburg.

The President has not availed himself of the Red Fox at this point, but it could be only a matter of time. There may come a point at which he wonders where his guests go when he's on the telephone. Mrs. Kennedy has dropped in on occasion, but never while he was in town, because his presence at Glen Ora would mean that up somewhere in the Red Fox attic lurked two press association reporters from the White House press room, ready to pounce on any news that moved. The First Lady has dropped in at the Red Fox in midweek for tea or a snack. In fact, she lives rather freely when her husband is not on hand with his necessary entourage.

In casual trousers and shirt and hairdo arranged by the wind, she visits the few stores and trade establishments with no apparent inhibition—in midweek. Oleg Cassini and Mr. Kennedy might object, but there are those who maintain that Jacqueline Kennedy is an entirely different and much more charming person when she's ambling about the Middleburg countryside informally and without being *on*. Even her voice is different when her hair is touseled—none of the semibreathless, pinafore girlishness that sometimes marks her public manner of speech, but the direct, clear conversational tones of a well-educated young woman.

The hunt country seldom sees the President or Mrs. Kennedy in public except on Sundays when they go to the Community Center, a philanthropy of the Paul Mellons, for mass celebrated before an improvised altar by Father Peira. The priest is a Roman Catholic version of a circuit rider whose parish includes at least three different towns on Sunday. During the early summer as many as fifty or a hundred tourists gather outside the yellow-walled hall to watch the Kennedys come and go. No N.P. of standing would be caught in such an assembly beside a church door. It would be entirely too plebeian to watch *anything* from a crowd, save J.F.K.'s inaugurations, and even this would depend largely on the location of one's seats.

The Kennedys leased Glen Ora by the year, at least through 1962. At the time of first renewal, there was talk that they planned to give up the place and purchase one of their own. Then the passage of painter and carpenter trucks along the muddy road to the front gate during the late winter produced word of extensive refurbishing and the lease was renewed. Mrs. Kennedy has been looking at some nearby places which could become available for sale. (There is an interesting divorce rate among some hunt-country circles which naturally produces a certain real estate turnover, to say nothing of fascinating reunions at hunt breakfasts.)

O Little Town of Middleburg

An observer of the Middleburg scene, and incidentally a passionately enamored resident of the area still in possession of his first wife, once told a friend from the outside, "Some of these wonderful people spend so much time breeding horses that they tend to confuse themselves with their animals and this is not always conducive to marital stability as many of us know it." (It is hoped that attribution of this wisdom to one durably married does not result in his quick identification, or attempts thereat. There's more than one, folks. A lot more.)

Evening at the Red Fox is matched by morning at the Coach Stop. The N.P. pilgrims to the hunt country seldom are on hand for this side of Middleburg, having made it back to Georgetown before dawn, or at least in time to unhinge the first coffee break at the C.I.A. or the State Department with a carefully dropped reference to "last night in Middleburg."

The Coach Stop is known affectionately to some of the locals as "the Greek's," obviously because the owner is of Greek origin as are many Southern restaurateurs. The cuisine is a mixture of Old South and Good Greyhound, with emphasis on the latter. This doesn't mean the food lacks quality and charm. It's simply without steak *vivre* or anything *flambé*. But it is a grand place to talk in the morning.

Along with landed gentry, sleepy parents come to visit their daughters at Foxcroft which is outside the village, and mind-your-own-business strangers in dark suits (Signal Corps men come to fix the electric eye at Glen Ora), one may encounter happy trade folk and servitors whose lorries and Thunderbirds service the countryside.

These are the in-area travelers who innocently and interestingly exchange news of the community; not gossip in the destructive sense, but casual items of minor interest were it not for the fact that the subject sometimes is a Mellon or a Kennedy.

In one way or another, news *does* get out of Middleburg. But strangely, much of it does not concern the Kennedys. Most items relayed beyond the county line have to do with horses and their

155

owners. If Mrs. Kennedy is selling or buying a steed, that gets around in a hurry. A leg broken in a hunt, a separated shoulder or torn muscle; all injuries of a Band-aid magnitude to a true horseman—these might be items of exchange at the Coach Stop.

But little of substance, for the chief reason that genuine presidential business would not filter beyond the room in which it was conducted at Glen Ora, much less beyond the fence. Glen Ora, it should be pointed out for the prospective pilgrim, is rather unsatisfactory as a tourist target.

For one thing, it is not marked. Taking the road to the left at the main intersection in Middleburg when going west on Route 50, one travels to the second recognizable road to the right. The entrance to Glen Ora is down that road, but cruising state police cars see to it that no one stops along the rutty clay strip for very long. Even if you were permitted to stop for hours, the sights would be uninspiring unless you had a passion for high grass and bushes which make a view of the main house impossible.

And for the fortunate who have viewed the place up close, they saw only a rambling old, pale yellow stucco dwelling of spacious and handsome lines, but little to warrant visions of a villa, an estate house or a presidential dwelling. Comfortable, but hardly grand.

When the Kennedys first occupied Glen Ora, it was winter and a blanket of snow and ice covered the grounds and added equipment, including a swimming pool. With spring and the drippy thaw which turned dirt roads into sucking auto traps, the tenants beheld a black wagon submerged in the winter run-off that filled the pool. The cast-off vehicle was removed, the pool cleaned, and the family now enjoys an occasional dip; but the word at the Coach Stop is that the thing leaks and it would cost a fortune to fix the cracks.

Foolish little gleanings these may be, but if they're not recorded now, some future historian might present Glen Ora as another Mount Vernon or Monticello, thus leading to erroneous 10th-grade themes for generations to come.

156

O Little Town of Middleburg

On the other hand, it is not superficial to explore Middleburg and its suburb of Glen Ora as a pilot or demonstration unit for the N.P. Were it not for late summer visits to Cape Cod and the Christmas and Easter holidays in Palm Beach, the Kennedys could well hurt the seashore resort business, at least among the wine, cheese and Stravinsky set.

The Kennedys spread their recreational tastes broadly except for one aspect—they're not much for mountains. In fact, it could be that mountains are Out for a few years. There has been a nervous feeling to this effect among the soft ice cream and Happy Hour Lodge people in the Poconos ever since the fall of 1960. Republicans and O.P., of course, still go to the mountains, but they've also been spending on pools at home and motorboats. This sometimes necessitates recreational belt-cinching—even for Republicans.

As a quiet little Mecca, Middleburg is unchallenged. Large enough to be visited, but too small and limited in facilities for vacations, it will grow as a tourist attraction. This will cause dreadful moments for the gentry trying to wheel their horse vans through town, but it will delight the druggists, the Greek's, and the candy store. It probably will delight the management of the Red Fox, too, but Mrs. Michaelis would be far too chic to admit it.

Palm Beach as a Mecca is another matter. There is an outward show of exclusivity, but the merchants love every flower-shirted tourist who shows up—with money. Palm Beach blessedly has withstood the wall-to-wall commercialization of her neighbor spas to the south, but its hotel and motel room count is sufficient to stand considerable paid-up pressure.

Some Meccas can use more publicity than others. Palm Beach had not been exposed so heavily to the golden light of international awareness since the Florida land boom as in late 1960 and during the President's post-election visits. A truly large entourage now swarms into town with the President and sets up shop at the Palm Beach Towers, a slightly confused Taj Mahal which started out to be a cooperative apartment, but changed into a hotel due to pressing economic circumstances such as insufficient long-term lease or purchase argements.

With each presidential visit to Palm Beach, there are more Miami- and Fort Lauderdale-bound visitors who turn off the Sunshine Parkway for a look at the place where J.F.K. dwells. This is hard on the tourist because he dwells at various places, including the fine old Mizener-designed beachfront home of his father and during larger family assemblies, borrowed estates of friends.

Thus, Palm Beach becomes more of a tourist magnet than a real Mecca. Its status as a Mecca derives only from the fact that more and more N.P. seem to have discovered the desirability of that section as a healthful, workingman's resort—a fine place to take the wife and kids at Christmas or Easter.

(See references elsewhere in this volume to the Flexible Sin and Newport, Rhode Island.)

Naturally, when the Republicans win the White House again, the N.P. will shift base and Palm Beach again will become the capital of idle wealth. Unless, of course, enough N.P. buy cooperative apartments in the meantime. Advertisements for co-ops in Palm Beach and its larger sister, West Palm Beach, are fascinating economic indicators. One ad not long ago listed one-bedroom units starting at something over $30,000, with this single added inducement, "Unlimited hot water." For more than $30,000, this would seem only hospitable.

The real people of Palm Beach are much like the real people of Middleburg—they're rich but go to some effort to appear otherwise. Spanking new clothes grate. Except on women at better parties. And the better the party, the less flashy the clothes. This probably is true wherever those of security gather, and in Palm Beach it is underscored by the President as he drives about town in a faded blue cotton pullover, khaki pants, and sunglasses borrowed from the nearest Secret Service man.

Before his unfortunate illness, Joseph P. Kennedy, the President's father, was no faded-khaki wearer. He delighted in scarlet slacks and sky blue shirts with yellow ascots. But the important point with J.P.—his ascot was *old*. And no thready evidence of recent price tags on his crimson trousers.

In Palm Beach, as in Middleburg, there are prigs and would-be prigs (for God's sake, printer, watch it) who regard or pretend to regard the Kennedys as outlanders or, in charitable moments, as temporary. This attitude, however, is particularly susceptible to invitations aboard the Honey Fitz where priggishness quickly shifts to Jack-ism, which is annoying to the recipient of new-found joviality.

As a consequence, the President imports many of his leisure hour companions to Palm Beach. The same goes for Middleburg, although in Virginia Mrs. Kennedy has a number of close horse-set friends who drop by the house on occasion to exchange neighborhood notes.

The Kennedy effect on Palm Beach after his first several presidential visits was interesting. N.P. down to office secretarial level began to show up. Others with no government connections at all checked into motels south of the city and kiddies made sand piles "very near" the excavations of Caroline and John, Jr.

The diamond-encrusted reputation of Palm Beach began to change slightly and Henry Flagler's old social fortress entered what possibly could develop into a second phase of popularity as a combination N.P. Mecca and good workingman's beach.

For the foreseeable future, however, bring money.

CHAPTER TWELVE

The Curious Case
of the Ladies'
Auxiliary

Outside the halls of Congress, bustling departmental offices and other operating units of Washington there exists a frequently sad shadow world of women hopelessly addicted to politics. They are not entirely endemic to the New People, but their number seems to increase as each change of political fortune leaves a few more castaways in the capital.

If reasons for wanting the Presidency are hard to understand and the life of a Congressman or Senator seems harsh and complicated, consider the women who are lured from outwardly normal settings and security into political swamps and hobo jungles; lured by the wild, unchained melody of a politician's mimeograph machine.

Women play an increasingly important part in government and it is only a matter of years before Cabinet status is the rule rather than exception. Their numbers also are increasing in Congress where such Senators as Margaret Chase Smith of Maine and

The Good New Days

Maurine Neuberger of Oregon more than pull their weight in a heavily masculine world.

We are not concerned at the moment, however, with women of such clear-cut accomplishment. Our immediate study is directed at what might be called the Ladies' Auxiliary which gathers loosely around any major political organization.

This unusual category may include wives, daughters and girl friends of political participants and participant-contributors, plus assorted sutlers, camp followers, buffs and broads. There are magnetic elements in national politics that on regrettable occasion draw ordinarily level-headed women from homes, husbands and children to the dizzy excitement of licking envelopes in a candidate's office or dutifully carting his campaign literature around the country.

There seems to be a gravely powerful narcotic blended in mucilage on campaign envelopes, because, after each national election, a carbon-smeared residue of willing women workers is left over in Washington, never to return to their own precincts except for funerals or to get their winter clothes.

This is not to discourage women from participating in national politics. But they don't have to be nutty about it. Reference here is to the apparently intelligent, well-read and educated woman who begins to feel she is Not Doing Enough. Her husband, of course, is busily grubbing for more and more money so that she doesn't have to Do Enough, but the more he provides, the added time she has to brood about her inaction. She becomes too activist for her local League of Women Voters and wants to move into guttier areas.

Whereupon she taps Chester for operating capital and heads for state headquarters, while he hires two more maids and explains to the children that Mother has gone to war. Not in all cases, but with frequency sufficient to make it noticeable, this may be the last time Mother is home for many months and, sometimes, years.

The Curious Case of the Ladies' Auxiliary

Not all of the Ladies' Auxiliary departs husband and kids. Some of them are single, grassly widowed, or generally on the prowl for action.

But however softly spoken, well-groomed and ladylike they may have been back at the country club, they change. They begin to feel at home in rumpled hotel rooms; they learn to exist on awful coffee and pickles which are the last items to disappear at any political buffet; the cultivated tones of Vassar and Wellesley begin to take on harsh qualities of a carnival dressing tent.

Their general migratory pattern is from home to state headquarters to the national nerve center, usually New York or Washington during a presidential campaign. Some of them are politically effective and go into sensible careers with national party organizations. Some, emboldened by the campaigns, return home to run for office. Smarter husbands in such cases contribute to the opponent, heavily.

But many of these ladies never reach a recognizable goal. They brought with them more desire for excitement and escape than deep commitment to improving the political breed. It might be entertaining to think of their hopping in and out of bed periodically to help lift party morale, but in truth, it doesn't work that way. While this is the sort of thing that not even Dr. Gallup would touch, lady zealots seem to derive more sensual pleasure from campaign music and the sound of strident voices through a loudspeaker than the opportunity for casual romping.

What these ladies seem not to sense in advance is that in victory lies deep disappointment for many. A political organization invariably trims the staff harshly after a campaign, even a win; and countless members of the Ladies' Auxiliary find their services no longer needed, even on a volunteer basis. If they're lucky, they may wangle tickets to the inauguration, but they find that after an election, the business of politics becomes almost the private province of the professionals.

It is not unlike cut-time at a major league baseball training camp when the hopefuls are cast adrift without so much as a bus ticket back to Waycross. Ever so nice and mildly talented, but not worth the dismissal of some unspectacular old-timer who can remember the names of county chairmen east of the Mississippi, the detached ladies, clutching their lithographed picture of the new President, must quickly decamp, set up residence with their own money or find work in the bowels of government.

The smart ones go home, politically sated until the off-year congressional elections begin to shape up. But the sad cases try to stick it out. They can become dreadful pests to the organization, popping up at cocktail parties, Senate offices and even in some of the departments, doing their best to lie about being busy on not altogether clearly defined projects. If they have money, they can and do continue in this political shadow world until two or four years hence when they're needed again to lick envelopes. Without money but with the political itch, they hang around Washington, sometimes sinking into minor civil service jobs from which they never emerge again, or picking up scraps of income by working for obscure causist groups dedicated to such things as abolishing the House Rules Committee or attempting to get King Zog's third cousin out of jail in Mississippi.

I don't wish to arouse unduly the defensive spirit of such talented, honorable and attractive professionals as India Edwards or Clare Williams, yet the problems of women in peripheral politics do exist and the results will continue to be distasteful in some instances as long as certain female types intrude themselves unrealistically.

Some Auxiliary members become addicted because of party allegiance or what they take to be political beliefs. They can become distressingly bellicose in their partisanship. In the 1956 campaign, there was an actual exchange of flying fists in the lobby of an Oregon hotel between two ladies, not Democrat and Republican, but two Democrats notably divergent at the moment on how best to elect Stevenson.

The Curious Case of the Ladies' Auxiliary

Then there are the girls and women who are, to be crude about it, queer for politics. Otherwise well-adjusted men get their kicks chasing fire engines. In this subdivision of the Auxiliary, however, the ladies do not seem to care as much for party principle or label as they do for the circus aspects of political activity in general. As the veteran marksman says of beginners, they can't shoot worth a damn but they like to hear the guns go off.

During Eisenhower's second campaign, members of the staff began to notice at rally after rally, from coast to coast, the friendly face of the same woman, bustling about with Ike buttons and pamphlets. She was not attached to the organization, but she was willing and bursting with energy.

After the election, as Eisenhower made occasional speaking trips outside Washington, the woman was spotted frequently in crowds. She turned up when there was unusual activity at Gettysburg and began hauling her children around the country to watch not only the President, but his staff and accompanying press party in action.

Most of the time she was a silent spectator, but in occasional conversations with the travel party, it was determined that she had a loving husband in her home town who sympathized with and was willing to finance her hobby of watching a certain kind of history unfold.

Showing her political flexibility, the same woman, to the amazement of many of us, showed up smiling, active and energetic during the 1960 campaign in both the Nixon and Kennedy entourages; getting coffee for those who needed it, directing visitors to proper offices, and being generally helpful. She had the children with her at times. It was interesting to see how well they grew from tothood to teens and seemed well-nourished on their diet of campaign buttons.

This woman was more fortunate than most of her breed, with an indulgent and apparently well-employed husband. As far as I ever heard, she never asked for a job or for help with her expenses.

The Good New Days

She frankly liked the smoke and fury, and her kids could turn out to be irritatingly knowledgeable civics students for some high school teacher.

Her story is wildly happy compared with case histories of other women who became involved in politics and stormed into Washington with the victors only to find all the jobs taken by Inauguration Day. I know of two amazingly similar and tragic cases.

In her home setting, each girl was the pride of a well-fixed family. Each was popular in and after college where they had respectable, if not spectacular, scholastic records. One of the girls was a stunning beauty and young men swarmed her theoretically happy home in respectable swainship of dances at the country club, dinner and theater dates. The other girl was sufficiently striking to attract second looks on the streets of her metropolitan home city where she moved in an orbit more sophisticated than that of her counterpart.

Neither girl had exhibited any deep interest in politics, or, for that matter, in anything but enjoying life and scanning the field for an attractive husband, until the 1952 campaigns. From widely separated sections of the country, they went first to regional, then national headquarters of the parties as volunteer helpers. They worked eighteen and twenty hours a day, doing the grubbiest sort of work because neither was trained for secretarial duties.

After the election, they both headed for Washington. They were great at cocktail parties, but short on talent; they were smart enough to realize that sleeping out had a dubious future, not smart enough to warrant jobs once the campaign carnival vanished before the reality of operating a government. The prettier one got intermittent employment outside government but in politically connected jobs which required little if any experience. Eventually she ran out of friends with stop-gap jobs and she went home to await the next campaign. The other girl found no berth, whatever. The party no longer needed volunteers and she left Washington with dejected reluctance.

166

The Curious Case of the Ladies' Auxiliary

They were back in the next campaign and, unbelievably, again in the next; still unmarried, without a start on genuine careers; still working the gin and anchovy circuits; not quite as youthfully radiant, but a bit more handy with four-letter words; each still based in her home town, but living apart from family. Each, in short, up a dead end, no longer ingénue, but smarter and harder. What have they done between seasons for ten years? Learned to handle their whisky, even to drink less, except on mournful evenings when looking inwardly. They've worked around local campaigns. Each tried charity drives but found them tasteless. Even a stinking congressional campaign was better than the best United Givers drive with those church people and social workers.

Their future? They're hooked. Various family deaths or continuing family indulgence provide funds for necessities and barely enough luxuries to prevent their being forced into nonpolitical and salaried work. They'll be around in 1964, working in New York or Washington. Which party? They'll take anything. They know the language of both sides and, more, they know that the language of one side is essentially that of the other. The labels are different, but the charges and countercharges sound pretty much alike.

Their identity is clouded for reasons of mercy if not legality, but their parallel experiences are cited as examples of the sad shadow people. There are many like them, plus some weird political wanderers who are truly tragic: mousy little women who confused love with a certain degree of irresponsible fervor that accompanies any sort of war; sad, drab worshipers who trailed their knights and idols to Washington where they learned that knights and idols frequently do not require assistance unless they are attempting to arise; misdirected zealots with sufficient ability to operate office machines while they save money for dancing lessons and contributions to their dead or impossible causes.

To say the more pitiable members of the Auxiliary are representative of Washington or the Establishment would be distortion, but this does not diminish their interesting qualities as tatters on the political canopy. There are, in fact, many more productive females on the job in Washington, but most of these entered government as a professional career or a marital market rather than being drawn to it by shimmering political mesmerism.

There also are a number of women on the Washington scene who are highly successful outside the formal structure of government, but prominent along its periphery. One might expect a discussion at this point of Mrs. Mesta and Mrs. Cafritz, but those dear ladies have been so profiled, extolled and magnified in print and picture that there's scarcely little more to be said about them except, as we hinted earlier, they no longer occupy their once gleaming pinnacles of Command Performance society. The N.P. have their own goddesses.

One recognized goddess doesn't live in Washington, but she packs more punch and commands more attention than the O.P. hostesses where the TIP are concerned. After devoting possibly too much time in morbid curiosity to sad political travelers, it is refreshing to contemplate the elegant blonde beauty, result-producing political elan, intelligent charm and distinctively high pile of money of Mrs. Marietta P. Tree.

When Mrs. Tree, who runs a notable New York salon for visiting nobility of the Democratic party and Great Britain, was named by President Kennedy to membership on the Human Rights Commission of the United Nations, it naturally was an event to be hailed from the Pump Room to El Morocco.

The *Diplomat,* a journal intensely aware of such developments in world affairs, responded almost immediately with a lengthy profile on Marietta. The message was that the attractively leggy N.P. figure was more than qualified for her diplomatic post. An excerpt said:

Mrs. Tree's household at 123 East 79th Street in New York centers around an English butler whom she described as

168

The Curious Case of the Ladies' Auxiliary

"just about perfect." He receives Democratic ward politicians and visitors of varying races and colors without batting an eyelash.

[Which is damned big of the butler and yet, not too unusual, considering that Mr. Tree was a Tory member of the British Parliament for some years before marrying Marietta and becoming an investment banker in New York. The article carefully says nothing about how Mr. Tree receives Democratic ward politicians and visitors of varying races and colors. In fact, the implication might be that Mr. Tree bats his eyelashes, but the butler doesn't.]

Although her home is reputed to be one of the best-run in New York, she herself protests that her English husband's liking for "a certain amount of shabbiness" gives her a little leeway. "Where charm leaves off and Tobacco Road begins—that's hard to judge," she adds.

An ability to remember names, faces and even telephone numbers is another of Marietta Tree's qualifications for her new job in diplomacy. One thing she enjoyed about political canvassing for the Democrats was the opportunity it gave her to see inside so many New York apartments and to observe how they were decorated.

Having never intruded on Mrs. Tree's salon and given the butler a chance to stand there staring winklessly, one does have a certain amount of freedom to envision.

Mr. Tree comes home, possibly weary after a hard day of money-shuffling. He takes one look at the perfect drawing-room *décor* and bawls at the butler, "I thought I asked for a certain amount of shabbiness in this house."

Marietta enters with a seedy fellow in a spotty double-breasted cocoa-brown suit with silver pin-stripe. He's a ward heeler, one of the shabbiest Marietta could find on the way home from the U.N. The butler surveys the trampy-looking politician and remarks rather coolly to Mr. Tree, "Do you still feel the need of shabbiness, Guv'nor?"

As *Diplomat* points out, with Marietta's very own words in support, she may not know where charm leaves off and Tobacco Road begins (surely she could call Erskine Caldwell and ask), but she knows her telephone numbers. *Diplomat* regards this as one of the more important qualifications for diplomacy.

It could have happened during an executive session of the Senate Foreign Relations Committee while they were passing on Marietta's nomination. Maybe one of the Republican members has been giving the appointment hell because she's married to a man who persisted in remaining a British subject. Then Chairman J. William Fulbright takes over in soothingly authoritative tones from Arkansas:

"Come now, Senator," Chairman Fulbright says, "married to a Britisher can't be all that bad. Let me tell you one thing about Marietta—she has a terrific head for telephone numbers. She remembers numbers from year to year, all kinds of numbers—delicatessens, race tracks, hair dressers, Democratic ward clubs, the White House. Telling Marietta a telephone number is like feeding it into one of those computing machines. Punch the button and out comes the number."

The protesting Senator calms down appreciably.

"Gosh, Mr. Chairman, I had no idea she was so well qualified to represent us at the U.N. Please vote me aye."

Diplomat pointed up another interesting aspect of Mrs. Tree's career by telling how much she enjoyed political canvassing for the Democrats because it gave her the chance to see how New York apartments were decorated.

This could have led to interesting developments back at Democratic headquarters during the 1960 campaign.

Suppose a group of campaign workers were reporting after a busy day of doorbell ringing. The precinct captain turns to Mrs. Tree.

The Curious Case of the Ladies' Auxiliary

"And now Marietta?"

"I saw four moderns, two semi-oriental, one French provincial and a simply lovely slum—so American."

"But how are the people going to vote, Marietta?"

"Oh, I was afraid you'd ask that. The truth is that I became so interested in seeing how the apartments were decorated that I forgot to ask. I'll try to do better tomorrow, but let me tell you about one place I saw. In the foyer, there was the most divine . . ."

(Should, by some literary accident, Mr. or Mrs. Tree encounter this fanciful passage, before saying anything to me, I'd think they might want a word with *Diplomat*.)

The Third Olio

Dorothy Parker, whose great writing ability recently has graced *Esquire* for which she reviews books, was disturbed some time back about the cultism surrounding *Derfilthenmeister* Henry Miller. Miss Parker said she had no disrespect for the artistry of the man who wrote *Tropic of Cancer,* but she was "badly put off by the airs put on by its worshipers." She added, however, "in possible extenuation, that it has never been given me to comprehend why people should take so much credit for admiring something."

She was talking about literary buffs; wan, no-talent bums whose only widely circulated writing has been on the backs of checks from home. Without intending it, however, Miss Parker stabbed a nerve that runs throughout Washington; a nerve which seems to lie near the skins of many N.P.

Political fidelity is one thing, but nuttily claiming some sort of glorious self-achievement for having backed a winner is quite different.

The Good New Days

It is as though burning extra candles of admiration lifts the idolater upward.

The New People, Republicans and Democrats as well, can be utterly gaseous in self-claimed credit for creation of a new leader. This leads to an incredible amount of outright lying after an election.

"I predicted it in October," is the sort of thing you hear the day after election from those who strangely would not profit one way or another from the election results. Normally honest men drag sealed envelopes from their desks and vow they wrote the actual electoral-vote count back in September.

Dorothy Parker's puzzlement over people who want and take so much credit for admiring something finds other Washington application.

It is not so much the degree of admiration, but when it began. Heated arguments break out when someone says, "I was for Barry before—" or "I said in 1919 that Jack was sure to be—." Of course, J.F.K. was just two years old at the time, but in the admiration derby, bets must be placed early.

During the 1948 campaign, I never heard one soul outside of Harry Truman and a precious few of his staff members say with any conviction that H.S.T. would beat Governor Dewey. Yet when the November smoke cleared and Truman was re-elected (incidentally, by much more of a margin than Kennedy managed in 1960, Washington was alive with canny gentlemen who had called the outcome in September. There were some cases of men who lied so extravagantly about winning huge sums on Truman that Internal Revenue looked into their bank accounts and found nothing unusual. I.R.S. was decent about it, however, and said nothing.

Feverish political admiration is understandable when the admirer is trying to blandish his way into a job, or when he has taken a truly active part in creation of his leader. But in the words of Miss Parker, it has never been given me to comprehend why some of us feel that by shouting loud enough and wearing enough buttons, we take on some of the greatness of the man whose name we honor.

CHAPTER THIRTEEN

Back to G.O.D.?

A problem peculiar to the Good New Days has been an increase in the number of people who would like to go back to the Good Old Days (G.O.D.), an indistinct era before income taxes, Henry Wallace, and that chemical radicals have been putting in the drinking water to reduce dental cavities.

We have come, temporarily at least, to a system of polar politics—the south pole, naturally, for the right wing and the north pole for everyone else, including the New People. The N.P. frequently live south of the north pole, but failing to move all the way, the right wing rejects them.

Perhaps it might be better to term the new centers of political thought and activity as Right Pole and Left Pole.

The right wing, sometimes referred to as the radical or extremist right, seems to prosper on adversity. These Right thinkers invariably are greater in number when a Democrat is in the White House. This is because the target is better. Prominent Republicans frequently are disliked by the Right, but almost *any* Republican holds more promise for the Right than *most* Democrats. The foregoing italics are necessary because of figures such as Harry F. Byrd of Virginia, a highly respected, highly conservative Democrat who frequently is far to the right of many Republicans.

The left wing, to pursue this theory of inverse political adherence, seems infinitely better off when the Republicans have the White House. We seemed to hear, for example, much more of Walter Reuther and Americans for Democratic Action (A.D.A.) when the Eisenhowers were in town. A genuine liberal swinger such as Philleo Nash of Wisconsin was twanging his guitar all over the upper Midwest and razoring the Republicans nightly during the D.D.E. era. But when Kennedy was elected with considerable encouragement from Philleo in Wisconsin, Nash moved back to Washington. He was made head of the Bureau of Indian Affairs and seldom is heard from except when he goes before a congressional committee in behalf of his appropriation.

The so-called Far Right has been with us for years, but only in the last few has it stepped from the obscurity into which many of its leaders faded during World War II and the subsequent era of Joe McCarthy.

Today, the Far Right is a rather elastic label for a new and/or revived group of social revolutionaries who fear, among other things, engulfment of their native land by a wave of alien treachery. Everything from fluoridation to Earl Warren traces back, in their frame of reference, to Marx and Lenin, neither of whom many of these unsmiling activists have read.

These are unusually comfortable revolutionaries as attempted political upheavals go. They seldom picket in the cold rain before the White House, but meet in moderately comfortable halls and listen to well-dressed speakers. They do not seem to be overly choosy about the origin of their speakers as long as the oratory is a few steps ahead of the listeners' antagonisms. Consequently, the oratory is fearful and denunciatory. Their pamphlets are printed clearly and neatly, not the smudged stuff of the lower class revolutionary who doesn't know where his next soapbox is coming from.

Their coloration is intensely red, white and blue as they equate their brand of fierce patriotism with policies and power needed to solve virtually all problems, national and international.

Their fervor is evangelical. They're the holy rollers of politics. They're also hell at the collection plate, rolling up large treasuries for their faith healers to be used in spreading the gospel.

To question their sincerity is pointless, as far as the rank and file are concerned. Sincerely worried, but not necessarily well informed, about the Soviet challenge to world position and well-being of the United States, the Right Pole people attract uneasy conservatives who feel somehow a way could be found to move us all back in time to a point when Russia was not so menacing.

For a time, these people were regarded by politicians and businessmen of both parties with an air of pained patience normally reserved for vegetarians, single taxers and prohibitionists. As the Far Right folks began to bunch up in regions, however, some politicians began to have second thoughts. And some business executives, particularly on the West Coast where the bunching-up became particularly noticeable, realized these people had money. Whereupon these executives undertook to spend a buck and make a buck from the trend by sponsoring right-wing volcanoes on radio and television and helping out with lecture appearances. For some, it was good business.

At times, the New People have been about as sloppy in their target selection as the Far Righters. The N.P. have been known to attack ridiculous targets and thus move the target into a new position of reality, if not respect. This came close to happening in connection with the American Nazi party operating out of Washington, usually toward the South.

To look at these woebegone weak-chins with their rumpled swastikas, any reasonably detached person would have been moved to some degree of pity. But by kicking them around in several towns and denouncing them far beyond any realistic point

179

of importance, these poor slobs became news-picture personalities and inevitably drew to their forlorn banners a few more nuts.

Scurvy little outcroppings as the American Nazi confuses the picture of the Far Right which, indeed, is a proliferous and splintery faction with divisions and segments intensely competitive in the business of saving the nation. They are allied only against a common foe—the enemy within. Only one basic operating rule seems common to all divisions—if you disagree with them, you're Communist. Witting or unwitting, you're still a Red if you disagree.

Aside from the issue of Communism, the Right Pole has attracted a number of bitter old people who have been relatively dormant since Roosevelt's death. For them, Truman was a political accident to be suffered and endured. Eisenhower, at least, did not increase their taxes and he *was* a Republican, although he persisted foolishly in foreign aid—milk for every Hottentot, that's what it was. The fact that Hottentots had been out of business for some years did nothing to depreciate the allegory.

Then came that damned Kennedy and a lot of crazy schemes for having the provident and thrifty pay medical bills for the slovenly and slothful. Dick Nixon and Barry Goldwater were better than nothing, but barely. Thus, the bitter old people began searching and rumbling and rasping, almost as if brought back to life from the mid-thirties by Peter Arno.

They found voices and causes from the John Birch Society, Robert Welch, William Buckley, Fred Schwartz, and Harry Ward. The good and the nutty were joined together. There was a brief flash of hope from Major General Edwin Walker, a clearly visible and audible Far Righter who had trouble with the Army over the manner in which he sought to indoctrinate his troops against Communism.

Walker tried to run for governor of Texas. Before he was ignominiously defeated, he offered this simple philosophy: "Every

Back to G.O.D.?

American should draw a line—and I mean actually draw a line. You're either on the right side of that line, what is right, or you're on the wrong side."

In his Second Inaugural Address, Abraham Lincoln also discussed the right, but in a somewhat different vein. Lincoln said, "With firmness in the right, as God gives us to see the right, let us strive to finish the work we are in." Old Abe also said something in the same passage about malice, but this is not included here so that we might view the political horizon without the smog of emotional involvement.

Goldwater, the Arizona Republican described in *Look* Magazine as an "apostle of jet-age conservatism," would be regarded by the A.D.A. as Far Right, and if possible, beyond that. On the other hand, the Walker-Welch Right regarded Goldwater as much too close to center for comfort. In fact, there is no center for the Walker-Welch crowd. Only the poles.

Goldwater was highly opposed to Kennedy Administration policies, particularly in the area of social welfare and economics. The Senator also felt much the same about many Eisenhower policies. Goldwater's complaints are based largely on government interference with individual rights. In a proposed statement of Republican principles, he said:

"No nation in all history has achieved the degree of economic security for the overwhelming majority of its citizens which has been reached by the United States in the 20th Century. Unfortunately, during this development, little thought has been given, and less action has been taken, to help the individual to secure, in his individual capacity, the greatest possible scope for effective personal activity."

Despite an occasional unsettlingly kind remark about the Peace Corps which appeals to younger members of his family, Goldwater is regarded by the N.P. as The Enemy, but they have much more respect for him than for some of the lesser Republicans. In fact, it was right out of the J.F.K. book the way Goldwater moved around the college campuses preaching his brand of outwardly simple, but inwardly complicated conservatism.

The steadiness of Goldwater's philosophy attracts wide conservative support. He has had extensive impact on certain types of young people who because of their background—and quite possibly, the lack of it—identify with bondholders, stock owners, and other participants in the world of investment.

The Arizona Senator, however, is pallid when put up against Far Right demands for abandonment of the U.N. and NATO; impeachment of Warren and the fuzzy idea that the mantle of Communist duplicity in this country stretches from Eisenhower to Rockefeller. Furthermore, the entire federal establishment, when viewed from the Right Pole, is a sorry mess of spongy subversion, with spies and infiltrators virtually running, or at least controlling, the show from behind false fronts of intellectuality.

This undoubtedly shocks Nikita S. Khrushchev, who must wonder, if the U.S. spy cries are on the level, why he has to continue spending so many rubles on espionage. This may have been why he was willing to trade U-2 pilot Gary Powers for the Russian professional spy, Colonel Rudolph Abel.

Khrushchev may have wanted to know why, with such reputed Communist influence inside the U.S. government, Abel had to spend such large sums before he was caught. Also, if Ike was a Communist tool, who let him send those U-2 flights over Russia for four years? And if Kennedy is so soft on Communism, what happened to the Red influence when he ordered resumption of atmospheric testing?

Except for the hopelessly emotional and largely idle followers who delight in large meetings and baths of anger, the Far Righters must realize that many of their accusations are, at best, allegorical. This does not reduce the degree of their conviction, nor should it militate against their privilege to feel as they do.

And here we come to the sticky part of the Right vs. Left situation. Should these oddballs be allowed to trumpet as wildly as they do? The oddballs around the Left Pole think not.

Some of the more hoary survivors of Washington politics realize there is a useful, valid place in the national political spectrum for the blazing lights of political extremism. Rants and chants of Far Left and Far Right serve as warnings of thin ice for the larger body of Republicans and Democrats.

The by-God-and-the-Flag omnipotence of the Far Right points up similar ideological blindness on the Far Left. Perhaps nowhere in our national life is there more virulent bigotry and downright intolerance than among extreme liberals in their disdain for the split-level, supermarket, station-wagon squares who make up the great center of America. To disagree with this crowd is to affiliate with the Birch Society or certainly head in that direction.

Professor Irving Howe of the English Department at Stanford examined the detrimental aspects of the Far Right at some length in *Contact,* the San Francisco literary and art monthly. Howe advanced the interesting thought that among conservative extremists, "the very thought of moderation becomes a source of treason."

Amen, Professor. But a comparable situation prevails in the Far Left. There, too, moderation is a dirty word. It means inaction, middle-of-the-road; it means Ike and Mamie and Lawrence Welk. All members of the N.A.M. are bastards per se. Same for the U.S. Chamber of Commerce, American Legion, and the A.M.A. Every single one of them—no good.

This is the same black-and-white world of the Right Pole. The very vigor with which the Far Left may inveigh against a particular social or economic evil too often has the side effect of creating an added area of distortion or bias.

Witness, or recall if possible, the trumpeting manner in political experts of labor announced during the first Eisenhower term that they intended to keep books on the President's absences from town, his weekends away from his work. The same labor leaders, however, have been strangely silent about J.F.K.'s almost solid record of *every* weekend away. (See earlier reference to the Flexible Sin.)

Although liberals are exceedingly jealous of their radical label, it can in all justice be applied also to the Right. Both extremes want vast, quick changes. The Far Right refuses to see the world as it is. The Far Left refuses to see the future as it probably will have to be. Both sides are impatient. The long view becomes moderation and that, of course, becomes terrible.

They may seem uncomfortable about it, but for all their liberalism or pretense thereto, a great many of the N.P. are caught in the middle. They identify with possessions, as well as ideas. If there is anything a Far Lefter hates, it is a man who possesses proudly. Creature comfort is disgustingly soft or an example of decadence. Ideas are the only thing. This disturbs the N.P. and they must turn to a higher power for guidance, notably the nearest *sensible* intellectual.

And perhaps the loneliest, most perturbed N.P. of all is Kennedy himself.

H. L. Mencken wrote in 1933, in the early foaming days of F.D.R. and Harry Hopkins (and Jesse Jones), of "that right to be wrong which Liberals demand for all men." When Lincoln spoke of "the right, as God gives us to see the right," he spoke obviously of justice and good, and not, as the dictionary says, political opinion approaching the reactionary position.

Kennedy in the foreseeable future faces having to ignore the right referred to by Mencken, as well as that of General Walker and Bill Buckley. In the 1960's and for some years thereafter, a President must be right in a thermonuclear world where the ordinary privilege of being wrong, if exercised, might dispose of our problems quite permanently. The President's right must be that of Lincoln and the Lord. His left can be little more than a border.

CHAPTER FOURTEEN

A City of Toadies

A sampling of contemporary accounts of Washington life in the past century reveals an amazing similarity of concern by professional observers over the number of slippery citizens attracted to the capital.

This possibly could be true of any world capital, but Washington is such that some of these men and women rise to stations of eminent notice and with few, if any, legitimate qualifications for the eminence they enjoy.

Frank Carpenter* in the late nineteenth century was most disturbed by the situation and wrote apparently without guile, "Washington is a paradise for curious characters." Carpenter also felt that, more often than not, persons involved in or having business with the government tended to be rather apple-polishing about it. Hence his "city of toadies" label.

The situation doesn't seem to change appreciably. If not toadies, many of us are imitators, name-droppers and victims of a cling-to-

* *Carp's Washington,* edited by Frances Carpenter (McGraw-Hill).

glory syndrome. We have a singularly high ratio of ex-heroes—war, sports, politics, science, education. Ralph Waldo Emerson once said, "Every hero becomes a bore at last." What Emerson did not realize was that most of them seem to gravitate toward where they trade heavily thereafter on what may have been only a fleeting moment of achievement or outright luck.

The unceasing effort to grab a free ride on greatness, or what passes for the moment as greatness, inevitably leads to frequent incidence of poseurs. Those fellows we mentioned earlier—the fifty-year-olds wearing their college blazers to restaurants. They're pitiful, but rarely cause trouble except for their classmates. Some of the fakes or semi-fakes, however, can be so persistent that they worm themselves into the federal structure with expected weakening effects if allowed to gnaw at supporting timbers for any length of time.

The late Elmer Davis, long before his close exposure to government as a participant, wrote in 1924 (*Harper's*), "Anybody who cares enough about politics to give it the greater part of his attention can achieve a considerable participation in the business of government, even if he attains only a nuisance value."

Clinton W. Gilbert wrote in 1933 (*Collier's*), ". . . . do not imagine that our democratic court in Washington is any freer of jealousies than were the royal courts of Europe a century or two ago."

Carlisle Bargeron, the veteran political mechanic, public relations expert and lobbyist, observed in 1947 (*Nation's Business*):

"There is one hobby that will make the person who adopts it a man of distinction, sought after, fawned upon, qualified to hold flattering attention on any subject, or to remain knowingly silent with no risk of being regarded as uninformed. One has only to join that rather indefinite group known as 'men close to the President.' "

The hobby described by Bargeron goes far beyond the White House, but, of course, any contact with a President always offers

A City of Toadies

a fine starting point for a career of trying to belong without being.

Here's the way it works at times. Bargeron tells of a case shortly after the New Deal swept into power. James A. Farley, then the Democratic national chairman, asked some of his friends in the corps of correspondents to advance the possibility of F.D.R.'s naming a well-known publisher to one of the major ambassadorial posts.

Bargeron points out that the man in question did not want the post, did not get it and, as far as anybody knew, was never considered seriously for the job. Furthermore, Farley never said anything to this effect, either. The publisher, however, had supported Roosevelt and, with depressing candor, wanted his name bandied about as one of the inner circle who could have an appointive plum if he so desired, in recognition of his sterling character.

Change the dates and names. The same sort of vainglorious twaddle was spread about the land when the current crop of New People came in. Small political debts were paid off in economical vanity as frequently faceless "men close to . . ." slipped into the pot of public speculation over new government leaders the names of contributors, party hacks and even some completely unconnected oddballs given to delicious quivers at the mere sight of their names in print.

This sort of thing does no lasting harm, but it does contribute to a climate in which counterfeit prominence can flourish. Let us not, however, attempt to destroy the blossoms without first a look at them.

William S. White, the distinguished columnist and Washington observer for *Harper's,* obligingly put together a catalogue in 1958 of what he called *Washington Phonies.* White felt that in the fifties began the Washington era of "the phony rampant."

White had three basic classifications which he described in detail. Briefly, they were:

The Phony Intellectual: ". . . who becomes an intellectual by more or less constantly saying he is one . . ." with unblacked shoes to show that he's interested in more important things . . . asks for sherry but will drink vodka . . . speaks pragmatically until someone else does, then shifts disdainfully to far-out futurism . . . darkly drops the names of opposition leaders in countries formed only yesterday.

The Social Phony: Takes off his unblacked shoes for "bowed evening pumps" . . . regards as completely unlivable "all of Washington except Georgetown" . . . is utterly shaken when he discovers that one of his idols is Presbyterian and not Episcopalian.

The Phony Liberal: ". . . always and automatically right, upon every issue and every conceivable convolution of that issue" and ". . . . distinguished by the most profound illiberalism toward all dissent or opposition . . . nearly always a member of the Democratic party, he is the best possible human argument for the continuation of Republicanism."

Bill White is an old and good friend. I know he won't mind my stealing his catalogue and updating it; but first, in the era of New People, I'd like to say: What's new, Bill?

White is relatively liberal in some leanings, but being liberal is something like being an old-timer in Washington. There's always someone more liberal, phony or otherwise. This is particularly true in the N.P. era. But it is not to say, however, that the N.P. have attracted any more phonies to Washington than any other political pack. Our point is only that political faith has little to do with the ratio of sharpies to the Washington population. In fact, the sharpie birth rate may be a bit higher because no one has paid much attention to developing a specific contraceptive to control their multiplication.

Before attempting to codify the shamsters who grow so well beside the Potomac, there may be sincere beginners who need help in starting their careers as Washington phonies. For these we might offer a home course in name-dropping. This can be awfully important. A name hurled is suspect. The ring of true authority comes from the softly plopped name, and, vastly better, the underhand nickname. The latter takes time and practice.

The underhand nickname never should be wasted on inferiors, but used only in the presence of equals or slightly above. This technique is underhand because the nickname chosen for ploy- ment should be absolutely unknown to anyone, even members of the family.

Say you're waiting in line at a cafeteria and a fellow who has the next desk to yours at Justice says something lobal about con- stitutional law. Slip it to him.

"What you say may be interesting, but I think I'll stick with Curt's judgment on that."

"Curt? Curt who?"

"Oh, I'm sorry—Senator Curtis of Nebraska. We bowl to- gether."

That exchange between two government workers was cited only to show how the game should be played. Consider now the genuine phony, the angle-shooter who lives in the rear of a board- inghouse which he refers to as "my place just off Mass." Through the happy circumstance of a wide-open trade association party the night before, he's conned two out-of-town canners into having him for lunch at the Mayflower where he may suffer himself to be retained as their Washington man for a Big Deal. The conversa- tion all takes place between the time they're shown from the dining room entrance to a rear table. And incidentally, all the conversation is that of our genuine phony:

"Hiya, Gordie, how about my favorite table? (The head waiter, Robert, vaguely wonders if this might be the cheeky chap who ankled a stiff tab something like eight years before.)

"By golly, there's Shep." (Great wave to a puzzled tourist from Iowa). . . . "Mr. Ambassador, how's Dorothy?" (The Surinam envoy wonders about his English.) . . . "Hey, Senator, great party, wasn't it?" (The Senator makes a mental note: find out who that pest is.). . . . "Hiya, Eric, old boy. Hold it, fellows, I want you to meet a great pal of mine, you see him on TV back home all the time; fellows, shake hands with Eric Sevareid." (And after shaking hands with three total strangers, Edward P. Morgan resumes his conversation with a visiting finance minister.). . . . "Ah, here's my table. Gentlemen, as Jack says to the Cabinet, be seated."

Think this may be exaggerated? Ask any Washington public figure about the dimly recalled faces that bob up before him, calling him by his first name, introducing him to smiling strangers. These are the foxies going about their daily trade. What is more amazing, they do indeed have a trade.

I know one of these chaps who shall be unidentified, not from fear of libel, but not wanting to advance his sufficiently sleazy career. His *nom de con* shall be Charles Helper.

Charlie has been around town for roughly thirty years. In that time, he has not held a regular job. He was fired from his first job with a bank in Newark, hooked up with a small advertising outfit and somehow got to Washington as a promotion man for a quick charity drive. He liked the fertile fields which he beheld and decided to stay. His office since has been his hip pocket, various men's rooms, club lobbies and departmental press rooms.

He derives an uncertain existence in several ways. One, he nabs quick, cheap clients in the manner of our friend at the Mayflower dining room. He also digs up business by mail and telephone (collect) in a manner which can be viewed only as an insult to certain American businessmen.

What does Charlie offer? Chiefly, the mildly larcenous hope of an inside chance or special treatment. Charlie has little intellect but unlimited cunning and surprising shrewdness. He reads, far more carefully than most of his so-called clients. He reads, probably in the *Congressional Record* which is his Gideon, that a Congressman is trying to get business for a small metal-fabricating plant in his district. Through research in departmental libraries and public information facilities which are open to Charlie as they are to the public, he gets the name of the plant and its officials. He may dig up similar information on other businesses in the same area.

Borrowing a typewriter and frequently a government letterhead if available, Charlie fires off a brief cryptic letter to one or more prospects, saying he's in a position to give them valuable guidance on landing a government contract. He gives as a return mail address of Helper & Associates the street number of his roominghouse, but suggests that matters might be expedited if the prospect telephones him at the Commerce Department where he'll be in conference. He gives a specific time to be called and the specific extension which is any one of a number of telephones available in or near one of the more or less public areas—a press room, library or information office.

It should be pointed out that Charlie misses far more than he hits, but he does score on occasion. For a retainer plus expenses, he then furnishes the gullible businessman with information he could get from his own local newspaper, but Charlie makes it more romantic and easily understood by whispering over the telephone and making veiled references to his good friend, the Secretary.

Of necessity, Charlie must keep a number of irons in the fire. He must be utterly untouched by insult and shame. He accepts periodic exposure as part of the game and merely shifts his base of operations.

Charlie is not a lobbyist because he influences no one in Washington. This sketch of him is no cartoon. Charlie might have made a reasonably good actor. Sometimes, to get information, he'll call an official of the Interior Department (not a terribly high official, mind you, because he might tangle with a protective secretary) from a pay booth in the Treasury building and announce himself as "Charlie Helper, over at Treasury; when are you going to let the contracts for that dock project in Shreveport?" And on occasion, he gets the answer. This would seem to violate some law, but after all, Charlie only said "over at Treasury."

This particular Charlie managed to stay out of jail for thirty years, but he made a serious mistake that had nothing to do with government. He had several big scores a few years back, bought some new clothes and looked fairly presentable. Thus armed and heeled, he spotted a girl who appealed to him. Figuring her for a few fast sleeps, Charlie snowed her with names and she snowed him right back with an estate somewhere down South.

This was too good to sleep away and, against every rule in his greasy book, Charlie married her. Then followed a horrible year in an airless efficiency apartment with roll-out bed. She got tired of living off of fingerling sandwiches and bad whisky of the lesser mezzanines and dumped Charlie good—with alimony. Charlie dug his own grave, however. He was so accustomed to bloating everything that he boosted his income to the divorce court judge for fear that an accurate statement might lower his standing in the community.

Charlie shortly thereafter was hit from two directions—nonpayment of alimony and income tax evasion. He'll be in prison for quite a while yet, but if I know Charlie, he's promised to get the warden a promotion. Furthermore, the warden knows perfectly well that Charlie is a liar and a crook, but still he *must* have known at least *some* of those people he's forever talking about.

There'll always be Charlies in Washington, so our friend does not relate particularly to the New People. In fact, the phonies to which Bill White referred are that way more for fun and status than cash profit.

In his 1958 catalogue, White could not have been expected to foresee the development of a counterpart for his Phony Liberal. Today we have the Phony Conservative. The N.P. era supposedly brought to town a multitude of liberals, and a great many of them genuine. This was rather hard on the Phony Liberals who had the field of dissent pretty much to themselves during the Ike years. In such circumstances, there's only one thing for the Thinking Phony to do—switch sides.

We are confronted with a situation in which the man ostenta-

A City of Toadies

tiously carrying Barry Goldwater's book through the Metropolitan Club lobby might have *I. F. Stone's Weekly* hidden away in his jacket.

This man in cruder company might be called A.C.-D.C., or political transvestite. His economic status is not affected, but it helps him socially and maybe professionally, if he has any particular calling, to take the other side. The N.P. may argue impressively that this cad never was theirs. But with their rising tide did come a growth in conservatism. Why they should think conservatism is not going to expand is beyond me, since liberalism certainly gained popularity the last time the conservatives were in power. In short, this is the American way. If you like something, I'd better say I don't—until I can find out more about it.

The same sort of criss-cross has led to development of the Phony Anti-Social as opposed to White's Social Phony. It long has been tricky business to separate ersatz socialites from the intellectual pretenders. Funny thing, Bill White's Social Phony seemed to come from "somewhere in New England." Today's Phony Anti-Social is willing to claim almost any geography of origin except the South. (No one comes from there any more except some cute girls, providing they don't lay it on too thickly.)

The Phony Anti-Social, oddly enough, sometimes has a fairly substantial background, but he has never quite hit it off in Washington. Rather than admit he's not invited to the better places, he spends a great deal of time during the day vilifying Washington's social activities of the previous twenty-four hours as reported in the *Post,* which he reads only because of Herblock. At night he goes to art movies or gallery lectures, smokes where he's not supposed to, and talks at length about Washington culture being in the hands of idiot hostesses and government dolts.

The reason this fellow is Phony is that he's not really antisocial. He's just plain lonely. Possibly he would feel better if he fell in with some of the Phony Intellectuals who are with us still but not as happy as they might be.

The Good New Days

The intellectual pretenders today in Washington are frustrated and concerned, due largely to the presence of genuine intellectuals too numerous for comfort. The poseurs had a grand time under Eisenhower. They could attack the military, Big Business and the ridiculous way Mamie spent money on clothes. When they tired of these games, they could tone up their intellectual muscles by pummeling one of their favorite punching bags—Catholicism.

It takes no deep study to appreciate how these stripped-gear brains must be suffering today. Given a choice between Nixon and Kennedy, they could move only in one direction or risk loss of their Intellectual permits. Today, they must stand mute while Oleg Cassini whips up a new wardrobe for Jacqueline. With General Maxwell Taylor at the President's side, they no longer may blast the entire military establishment, merely parts of it. And to say that all Big Business is bad certainly isn't the way Jack would say it. Under the circumstances, the best guide for criticizing is to concentrate only on corporations currently under antitrust prosecution.

As for Catholicism, the Phony Liberal has made a rather easy adjustment. He now is against the narrow-minded Protestants. He never did like them. Now he can be open about it without seeming to be bigoted. God knows, it can't be a crime to be frank about the Baptists, not in his rubbery world, at any rate. And did you see that Billy Graham on the Jack Paar show? You'd never see a Catholic priest—oh, Bishop Sheen was a *long* time ago. Television is bad enough, but can you imagine anyone watching the Paar show? You say Jack and Bobby both appeared and Joe Kennedy is an old friend of Paar?

At this point, our Phony Intellectual may be forgiven and excused from our study group. As we've maintained from the start, Washington once was a town you could count on. But no more.

CHAPTER FIFTEEN

How to Be Dual and Rich

One key to successful living in Washington is duality.

This has been true for years, and it continues no less in the Good New Days.

This may seem senselessly cynical, but there are those who will understand, particularly men and women engaged professionally and avocationally in creating and preserving an image for others.

In government departments, one may hear special assistants explaining over the telephone, "We've looked it over and we're afraid this isn't the sort of thing the boss would do—it's not *like* him."

A Senator tells a colleague, "There may be merit in the bill, but I have to think of how it will *look*."

A Congressman may urge his wife to attend a threateningly dull women's meeting, saying, "I know you hate some of them, dear, but this sort of thing is good for *us*."

The masters of Washington duality, however, are the lobbyists, the men paid by industry, unions, trade and professional associations, and foreign governments to see to it, as far as possible, that the U.S. government operates in their favor. And conversely, the lobbyist also must endeavor to prevent government from working to the detriment of his client. To tackle both chores at the same time often requires tactics which border, to be polite, on the amoral.

Washington morals, and we're speaking here on the conduct of government and not in a personal sense, are flexible at best. As Frederich A. J. Bernhardi wrote many years ago, "Political morality differs from individual morality because there is no power above the State."

And what at times may seem to be a lack of consistent principle may be nothing more than partisan zeal. Socrates said, "The partisan, when he is engaged in a dispute, cares nothing about the rights of the question, but is anxious only to convince his hearers of his own assertions."

Sir Compton Mackenzie, in his *Certain Aspects of Moral Courage* (Doubleday), offered a rather tight definition of moral courage: "When a man acts or speaks without regard to the consequences for his career, his position, or his good name."

Sir Compton, meet Socrates and Bernhardi. You three fellows would have an absolutely grand time together in Washington these days, particularly if you could visit with some of the lobbyists during business hours. Or for that matter, with some of those on the receiving end of lobby pressures.

Morals aside for the moment, it may be helpful to examine the manner in which a lobbyist performs before condemning him, unduly. Lobbyists are accustomed to condemnation; but too often the criticism is as one-sided as the interests of those who employ lobbyists.

As in any form of human endeavor, there are good and bad lobbyists. Determination of category has more to do with effectiveness than morals. The American Medical Association (A.M.A.) maintains a lobby in Washington. Its job in 1962, and apparently for some years to come, was to kill the administration plan for medical care of the elderly financed through Social Security. The bill died in the Senate, and the role of the A.M.A. in its burial was substantial but not total.

There are millions of Americans who agreed with A.M.A. opposition to the Medicare bill. They were ably represented by the lobby which is supported by doctors of the nations.

There were millions of other Americans who thought the bill should pass. The pro-Medicare people wrote letters, some visited Capitol Hill, and others fumed locally. Their feelings, however, were not as well organized as those of the opposition and as a people's lobby, they ended up being ineffectual.

Thus we see a generalized picture of results of lobbying. The professionals were able to get across their story in much more telling fashion than the amateurs. To say that the A.M.A. controlled the fate of Medicare in 1962 is giving the doctors' lobby too much credit. But it is not too much to say that the A.M.A. position was better and more constantly stated within the Congress than even that of the President himself.

Public concept of a lobbyist seems, from recent articles and references in books, to be somewhat outmoded. One of the better and more recent studies of the Washington lobbyist was written by A. L. Todd for *Holiday,* which devoted an entire issue to the nation's capital.

Todd pointed out that the lobbyist not only operates in the halls of Congress, but he represents his clients in dealings with government departments and agencies, serves as the client's Washington-based public relations man and keeps the employer posted on Washington moves which might require even more lobbying.

Then Todd ran over a lobbyist's typical working day, which included the lunchtime hours at the National Press Club to plant stories and see to the distribution of press releases for his client.

This may be typical of some lobbyists, but not the major ones. Charles Patrick Clark, who receives a vast annual retainer from

the Spanish government of Generalissimo Francisco Franco, is
one of the town's better known lobbyists and his visits to the Press
Club are few and far between.

The public for years has been told of lobbyists swarming over
Capitol Hill, buttonholing members of House and Senate, dangling persuasion in many forms and, in general, behaving like so
many friendly wet dogs.

This is a satirical distortion rather than a true picture. Lobbyists, indeed, do visit Congress. Some even testify before committees. But in addition to exercising or attempting influence, a
good lobbyist earns his pay as much by reporting—by keeping his
client informed on what will happen next.

Not to quarrel particularly with Mr. Todd, but my typical
lobbyist operates a bit differently from his man. Maybe mine is
better paid or lazier.

In any case, my man is a master of timing. He does not wear
himself or his client's expense account by racing from Congress
to club to cocktail party.

He arises when he feels like it, usually mid-morning, in a spacious, comfortable but definitely unflashy home in the northwest
residential section of town. Over breakfast, he reads four or five
major morning newspapers. If interested, he skims through the
Congressional Record for the day before.

These are the golden hours of his day. He may earn his keep
more from intelligent reading than from any other single activity.
Years of experience have taught him to read between lines and
to search for indicative but seemingly small details. His client is
a major oil company and his politics are decidedly Republican,
but he also has enough close Democratic friends to keep him
posted.

Once "read" for the day, he may make it to town for luncheon
with one or two key men in government at the Carlton or the
Mayflower. Mostly, they talk about golf or fishing. Possibly in
parting, he may ask casually, "You fellows heard anything new

on depreciation allowances?" Their replies may be as cryptic, but the lobbyist knows from experience that this is no time to press for details. All he needs is a hint, and should he pick up a mere straw pointing to new action on the oil industry's prize tax allowance, there will be enough time to run it down later.

Our man will then drop by his office briefly, look at the mail, sift through messages, and then motor leisurely to Burning Tree for an afternoon round of golf.

He may tarry in the clubhouse for a rubber of bridge, then arrive home for dinner by seven o'clock and retire well before midnight.

He may follow this same sort of half-time schedule day after day, reading carefully, making an occasional offhand inquiry and, above all, listening. He has not been in the office of a Senator or Representative in years. Aside from a rare appearance at a White House social affair, he's not been in a government building. Furthermore, he's not registered, as the law requires, as a lobbyist, because he prosecutes no claims before agencies; he does not seek, outwardly, to influence legislation. He is a retired executive intensely interested in affairs of government.

This man is more effective for his employer than a dozen more energetic fellows patrolling the halls of Senate and House office buildings or attempting to be a lunchtime confidant at the Press Club.

By being highly selective in his friendships, he manages to keep in touch with virtually any government move that might help or hinder his company. He also keeps his executives closely in touch with inside political developments, frequently long before they flame into public domain. His fine grasp of economics also is enhanced by a fishing acquaintance with career specialists at Treasury or a golfing friendship with one of the Federal Reserve board of governors.

Our man's effectiveness would be destroyed if he had to play the lobbyist's conventional role in attempting to push or halt specific bills before Congress. He would never try overtly to get a government contract for his company.

He would, however, supply highly valuable, authentic information which his company could translate into open action by proceeding through a number of channels including trade associations or a company attorney based in Washington.

It would be a mistake to call our man typical in the numerical sense. There are others like him in town, but their number is relatively small when compared with large staffs maintained by such associations as the A.M.A., the National Association of Manufacturers, and the larger labor organizations. The organizational lobbyist is concerned largely with Congress; the men employed by specific corporations often concentrate more on government departments with their regulatory powers, as well as lucrative contracts to be let.

For years, Washingtonians have heard one lobbyist or another justify his existence. God knows, they seem to earn their money. Take the sugar lobbyist, for example. Most of them are retained by foreign countries which are permitted by congressionally approved quotas to sell specific amounts of sugar to this country at above the world market price.

Many sugar lobbyists are paid annual retainers plus a bonus of so much per ton for the quota finally approved by the House and Senate. Sugar nations employ former Cabinet members and one-time departmental officials who usually operate out of well-respected Washington law firms. Their connections are open and above board, a matter of public record. A man who brings in $75,000 a year pushing for his particular sugar interest is doing nothing illegal or, by Washington standards, unethical.

To lean on a tired phrase, some of my best friends in the political world are lobbyists. Of worldly goods and standing in the community, they have far more than I. Furthermore, they need nothing of defense, pity, or charity from me.

Without doubt, the lobbyist performs a specialized service above and beyond the capability of his client. We are not speaking of the miserably ne'er-do-well angle-shooters of a previous chapter. We refer here to the established lobbyist, well-known to political society and in some areas thereof well-respected.

Major lobbies can put before Congress or agencies of government concentrated information which otherwise might be lost or difficult to present in easily assimilated or understood form. Also, any special interest, be it doctor, sugar-producing country, oil company, or labor union, has an ethical right to present its own case.

But for some Washingtonians, including this one, there is a greasy aspect to the *modus operandi,* if not the *modus vivendi* of the big-time lobbyist.

We may forget for sake of this discussion the little eavesdropper and two-bit sutler, their assorted courtesans and courtiers. They work the fringes of all humanity, be it carnival lot or Capitol Hill.

The big Washington lobbyist, however, packs punch. He has a lot to do with laws by which we are governed. Theoretically, the public packs a more potent punch, but only in theory. Former President Truman liked to say in his running battle with the major representatives of what he denounced repeatedly as special interests that one highly important faction lacked a lobby in Washington—the people. He therefore spoke with some frequency of his duty to serve as their protagonist.

Kennedy feels much the same way, although to date, he has not expressed his thoughts quite as bluntly as his Democratic predecessor, once removed.

Lobbying is sometimes lumped with influence peddling which is another favorite Washington phrase of denigration. Influence peddling, however, has more to do with swinging government contracts where they would not be swung ordinarily than it has to do with legislation.

The Truman Administration was plagued by such peddling. There was some of it under Eisenhower and it broke out again in

virulent form under Kennedy, as demonstrated in the Billie Sol
Estes case. The Estes case was influence at its crudest—buying off
minor functionaries of the Agriculture Department to facilitate
transfer of cotton acreage allotments.

The Bernard Goldfine case during Eisenhower's time was an
example, not of peddling, but a variation on the use of influence.
Goldfine, a Boston textile man, was amazingly naïve in his attitude toward those in authority, particularly officials having to do
with taxes and regulatory powers.

Goldfine came to this country from Latvia as a child. At the
knees of his elders, he learned to hate—and bribe—the tax col-
lector. The law in the old country was something to be gotten
around. And before he was twenty years old, Goldfine was involved in rigged bankruptcy cases. He adapted to America
handily.

As business acumen enabled him to start building a fortune,
old man Goldfine became obsessed with the idea of holding on
to his holdings and increasing them.

He learned the valor of cultivating those in high places. He
started out on the state and local level, and the time came when
some of his friends were graduated to Washington. One of them
was Sherman Adams, who went from governor of New Hampshire
to the tremendous power of *The* assistant to the President.

With no intention of rehashing the Adams-Goldfine affair in
detail, I mention it here merely to show another aspect of influence and use thereof in Washington. Adams took a jaundiced view
of the author, particularly after my coverage of the Goldfine
matter.

It may come as a shock to the former governor, however, that
this one moderately detached observer of the Washington scene
never thought he did anything crooked or particularly unethical.
My feeling was that Adams made a severe mistake in judgment by
evidencing White House interest in Goldfine's various involve-

ments with such regulatory bodies as the Federal Trade Commission and the Securities and Exchange Commission.

Hindsight has wonderfully clarifying powers, but it also seemed to me Adams, with all his insistence on efficiency and drum-tight operations in others, might have checked routinely into Goldfine's status with the Internal Revenue Commission at the same time he was asking the Trade Commission the status of various mislabeling claims against Goldfine's textile manufacturing firms. It might have saved Adams a great deal of trouble later.

What truly doused Adams in congressional hot water and turned him into a blazing political potato was penny-ante stuff—a rug, a clock, vicuña cloth, free food and lodging in elegant hostelries of New York and Boston.

Remember the deep-freezes and mink coat of the influence investigations under Truman? And more recently, alligator shoes and $200 suits bought for Agriculture Department flunkies by Billie Sol?

These are cheapness symbols more than sinister payoffs. A member of Congress may let a lobbyist bankroll his daughter's debut and nothing defamatory will come of it; provided, of course, the lobbyist doesn't write off the party with crude frankness as a deductible business expense. A smart lobbyist pays the tax on much of his spent income rather than deduct for business reasons when there is any possible chance of later flareback.

In the broader sense, what Adams did for Goldfine—telephone calls to regulatory agencies—goes on every day in Washington. Officials of the Executive establishment—or, for that matter, powerful members of Congress—inquire for a friend or constituent the status of a particular case. This is not asking the agency to pass on the case one way or the other. It is a simple request for information.

Regulatory officials are, among other things, human. They note with more than passing interest a call from the White House or from the chairman of a congressional committee which may hold enormous power over life of the agency. And the official to whom the inquiry is directed would be only human if, without disturbing his principles or basic equity of the case, he decided in favor of a friend. Or friend of a friend.

As benign and human as this may seem, it *is* influence, Washington style. And punishable as such, not in jail sentences but in the flashy underclothes one seems to be caught in when hauled before a congressional committee and asked either to explain or atone.

Had Sherman Adams confined himself to friendly telephone calls in quest of information for Goldfine, though this may have amounted to exercise or application of influence, it would have been most difficult to raise tempers in Congress without the provable existence of some unfortunately timed gratuities from Goldfine. Without the vicuña, the borrowed rug, or room-service charges at the Waldorf, there would have been no political juice in the Adams-Goldfine friendship and the old woolmaker from Boston would have gone on to his inevitable clash with Internal Revenue with, in all probability, no mention of Adams.

Where the operations of influence and lobbying break down on the sand bars of congressional investigation and subsequent public opinion involves a simple test: without friends in or near the government, would the interests of John Doe be regarded on a par with those of Jake Day who *does* have friendly access to the government? The answer, in many cases—not all, but many— would have to be No. Assuming other things are relatively equal, Jake gets the break.

The break, in turn, attracts little attention in Washington until a congressional investigating committee is moved to inquire into agency or departmental operations, usually because of complaints in volume or information slipped quietly to investigators by dissidents within government.

Even then, congressional inquiry may rock along for months

with no spectacular exposures until someone turns up a questionable *quid pro quo*—a free case of booze on the expense account of a pressure artist, a free weekend at Ocean City for a career man in government who leaps at any surcease from his battle to squeeze three kids through school on $12,000 a year.

Thus, in our brief glance at influence, there would seem to be several simple but possibly cynical moral lessons.

1. Influence and pressure seem more safely exercised in the great open spaces of Washington instead of free hotel rooms.

2. It is far better to give than receive. A federal official who accepts provable minor gratuities is a fool. If he is interested in larger stakes, he should resign from government and become a lobbyist; or, remaining in federal service, hold out for sufficient pelf to tide him over lean days that might result from banishment or a tiresome spell in prison. More takers go to jail than givers.

It would be apple-cheeked and cheery to be able to report any diminution of the forces of influence and lobbying in the N.P. era. The pressures remain, although the techniques may differ from those of the more recent past.

The day of the coarse, powerhouse vote-buyer circling hawk-like over the Capitol dome seems gone. The crude operator who stocks a hotel suite with hooch and broads for pleasurable semi-blackmailing seems rather passé, too.

Although a new breed of lobbyist is evident, the results are much the same. The new lobbyist is for or against specific legislation and he works his side of the street energetically. But operating among the New People, he is careful of his coloration, habits, and habitat.

When the Kennedy Administration took office, there were jokes about more active lobbyists practicing touch football in secret. These were the same jokes, updated, told about the lobbyists in 1953 and their sudden desire for golf lessons.

There seems, under the N.P., to have been an increase in the number and voracity of amateur lobbyists—the idealist pleaders who are regarded in most professional circles as nuisances. A political figure may be forced on occasion to listen to or reckon with the amateurs, but he does not have to fear acting counter to their wishes, because their emotionalism often prevents the degree of organization required for maximum impact.

These, in some instances, are lobbyists of the people, some of the people, but their causes frequently are so divergent that smooth, well-ordered presentation of a professional pressure expert may seem almost welcome to a lawmaker or government executive.

Probably the worst-organized lobbyists in creation are the groups for peace. As if peace of any sort were not almost impossible to achieve, peace pickets, marchers, and pamphleteers quarrel bitterly over the best way to bring about cessation of hostility. Their intramural hostility sometimes matches the emotionalism of South American revolt. They fight to see which group is more against war.

The countless thousands, if not millions, in this country who are opposed to atomic testing are split into a number of factions, most of which express their feelings to Washington with little unity or coordination. They violate the first ethic of a good lobby by, unwittingly or otherwise, embarrassing the men whose help they seek.

The peace and bomb people, as they are generally classified by those who man the main gates of the White House, seem far more interested in public demonstration than truly effective in-fighting. Twenty-five registered constituents of a New York Congressman might scare hell out of him with separate letters promising to work unstintingly for his defeat unless he changed his stand on atomic testing, but fifteen hundred pickets chanting "We want peace" would not cause him to break stride on the way to the Carroll Arms bar.

The men and women who run Washington become interested in pressure in ratio to the distance between cause and effect. They understand a lobbyist with a good record of campaign contributions and his professional ability to help them with pet projects in return for a degree of, at least, friendly consideration. But they are not too impressed by public protestations unless organized to the point of controlling or influencing a section of the electorate.

Does this meandering discussion mean that the single private citizen is without voice in Washington? Singly, yes, unless he happens to be a well-identified contributor. Or a towering, respected authority in his field, capable of swinging public opinion. The individual citizen has power, but it must be organized and applied selectively to be effective.

And the best place for this, at least for a starter, is the bottom layer of government, the local level. For too many of us government has become largely a spectator sport. We leave even the proceedings of city council and county commissioners to others. The state legislature is almost as distant as Congress.

If the base of participation in selection of all levels of government were broadened considerably, the voice of the citizen would be heard increasingly. After all, the lobbyist and the influence-peddler make it their business to participate. Why not more of us who are at the receiving end of their operations?

CHAPTER SIXTEEN

Instant History

It was once observed by a recognizable friend* of the Kennedy Administration that the President and people around him drank printer's ink for breakfast instead of coffee and thus began each day by consuming a frequently bitter brew.

This to a great extent applies to most of the N.P. They don't skim—they devour every available line printed about Washington; and they do it not by the day, but by the hour or whenever new editions of newspapers and late copies of news magazines are available.

The Washington press corps has long looked down on Broadway and Hollywood columnists for the manner in which they are sought out servilely by guys and dolls of the theatre and entertainment world and for their whip-cracking over those who displease them.

Walter Winchell at his mightiest, however, never possesssed or

* James Reston of the *New York Times*.

twirled a club with the smashing quality of Drew Pearson when he zeroes in on an uncooperative news source. Broadway and Hollywood have no counterparts of a Clark Mollenhoff or William McGaffin who can strike terror in a government department merely by walking in and asking if Joe Blow is on the payroll.

A drama critic may be able to kill a new play with a scathing review, but, at worst, he's cost sixty or seventy people their jobs and caused backers to drop several hundred thousand dollars.

Bill White, Roscoe Drummond, Reston and dozens of others could, however, be essentially responsible for adding or cutting hundreds of millions of dollars in the federal budget with resultant ups or downs in employment for thousands of men and women.

Men go to jail because of the burrowing and probing by Washington reporters into the federal structure, which is so large and well-financed that a few rats always are buried somewhere to be turned up at intervals by tough correspondents.

As long as the Washington reporter operates within accuracy's armor, he is, in truth, untouchable. If he turns up the fact that a Cabinet officer is making outside money because of his federal job, it is practically certain the Cabinet officer will leave the neighborhood long before the reporter.

Yet, strangely, there are citizens who object to the zeal with which the Washington corps operates. They don't want Marquis Childs, Fulton Lewis, Jr., David Lawrence or Howard K. Smith putting the blast on anybody. Those who feel deep analysis of those in high places borders on the unpatriotic are, fortunately for the rest of the country, in a clearly seen minority. But they're vocal and write numerous complaining letters.

We are not concerned at this point with fiercely partisan letter-writers who damn you for anything written or broadcast about their side which is not entirely laudatory. The partisan crowd will not accept objectivity, which they regard as either weakness or secret support for the other side.

Letter-writers who object to criticism of those in high places are a class apart, the status quota of our society. I've long had a hunch that they dislike reporters more than being protective of high officials. In fact, many Americans seem to derive quiet pleasure and smiling satisfaction from the sight of a reporter or photographer being assailed.

Seldom, however, is there any prolonged punching of reporters in Washington. Our photographers, on the other hand, seem on occasion to bring out the fistic in witnesses before congressional committees, particularly witnesses attempting to maintain their dignity and the Fifth Amendment at the same time, which can be understandably irritating for such gentlemen of culture and taste as Johnny Dio or Frank Costello.

Washington correspondents seldom are punched by objects of their disaffection because the offended party realizes that such a procedure would merely add many more thorns to the one already in his side. Washington reporters occasionally punch each other, but this usually has to do with vanity or momentary loss of direction.

This intense interest also extends increasingly to television. TV, however, produces a certain intellectual conflict in the N.P. To hear them tell it, they spend spare hours listening to Prokofiev on the hi-fi and wouldn't have a television set in the house. If true, there's some TV bootlegging going on in Georgetown because the N.P. seem to know every word uttered about them and Washington by any one of the better known reporters and commentators.

Thus there has developed in Washington a new class of gleaners and sweepers; men and women of N.P. journalism; the thinkers; opinionated, deeply concerned, frequently acerb, seldom ascetic; instant historians of the press.

These are the Washington correspondents and there are several thousand of them, all as susceptible to the bite of the "right" bug as the President.*

Our city life becomes additionally interesting during the fre-

---

* Use of the term "right" in this sense has nothing whatever to do with the Birch Society. We're talking here about the amazing quality of being damned right as opposed to being downright wrong.

quent juxtaposition of "right" vs. Right. Nothing illustrates deadlock more graphically than a Washington reporter insisting his story is correct and a top government official maintaining that *his* version is correct—and both accounts miles apart.

Before we sink deeper in this discussion, the author of this perishable prose is a Washington correspondent, or was until this book came out. I maintain that the Washington press corps is about the finest in the world when it comes to accuracy, energy and knowledge. But some of us are disturbingly colorful, temperamental and nasty, particularly when our superb qualities are overlooked.

Probably at no point in relatively modern history, and certainly not since the early New Deal days, have ladies and gentlemen of the press and broadcasting industry been intertwined and involved in proceedings of the government as they are today.

Seldom have there been such passionate crushes, such violent hatreds, not only between public and press, but between government and press. And between press.

While the journalistic giants remain rather gigantic, the N.P. have created some of their own oracles—natty, well-combed younger men with terrifyingly extensive scholastic backgrounds; far better-paid in early career than their older colleagues were; academically expert in many tightly specialized fields—except the matter of human relations with some of the grizzled figures in Congress.

Some well-established Washington journalists mutter about the new breed, but in fact, these younger, better-educated, better-backgrounded journalists are good for our town. If not the direct results of the Good New Days, they are the by-products, the badly needed trainees for a bewildering new era of science and technology, of sophisticated finance and complicated economics.

Distressingly, however, many of our brighter, more promising young journalists are tuned too finely to signals of approval or disapproval from the N.P. These signals, of course, begin from the

White House and their intensity tends to build when passed through repeater stations of Georgetown and Cleveland Park.

A frequent attitude among the N.P. is that a young reporter is as friendly as his last story. Among some N.P., and unfortunately in those often underfoot at the White House, "the press" translates roughly as "those bastards." Particularly, non-Ivy peasants who theoretically report without thinking. And thinking in N.P. terms is difficult at times, since N.P. forever change directions without so much as a hand signal.

While wishing to avoid distorted generalization, I may say here with minimal bias that some administration functionaries appear to be downwind from a garbage scow when they wrinkle their well-bred noses and say, "the press."

There is one man rather close to J.F.K. who cannot understand why "the press" must harry the dear fellow on his trips to Palm Beach and Hyannis. This is a man of high responsibility, well-married and well-educated. Yet, in something like two years at the White House, he has not determined clearly how the Presidency must travel with the President. This sort of independent thinking can make the task of a press secretary doubly difficult. It must make this man wonder, and chafe a bit, when Pierre Salinger establishes working headquarters out of town and holds regular press conferences—even in Hyannis and Palm Beach.

Another gentleman who frequently has the President's ear is said to have commented to friends following a Kennedy journey abroad, "Jack might have had a good trip if it had not been for those press along." It should be pointed out that "those press" is an even more derogatory reference than "the press." You can't get much lower than "those press." For one thing, it means that neither Joseph Alsop nor Walter Lippmann was along.

These oddments are cited almost whimsically because their sentiments, while annoying, are not treated too seriously by the man for whom they are intended—J.F.K. He is an intensely political creature; he knows it would accomplish little to make a goodwill trip anonymously; he knows the press is to be used by a President, as well as tolerated.

There must, however, be a natural rise in resentment of middle-grade administration personnel toward reporters. For one thing, each year sees more news personnel in Washington better paid than many government officials. Also, with the advent of television, correspondents and commentators have risen to positions of new eminence in the national and political community. It may be much easier to lasso a Cabinet member for dinner than some of the top news-bureau chiefs.

The Kennedys, themselves, also have enhanced the local standing of many correspondents by including a few of them in virtually all social functions at the White House. The President happens to believe that journalists represent a segment of our culture, and as such should be included in affairs where he attempts to bring together a cross-section of America to dine with visiting heads of state.

Kennedy also maintains frequent, direct contact with certain reporters, columnists and commentators, seeing them off-record, one at a time, in the later afternoons. There are times when he may see as many as eight or ten reporters a week in this fashion, sometimes on his move, but often at their request. These informal meetings beside his office fireplace are largely for background purposes and seldom for attribution; almost never for direct quotation. It serves Kennedy's purpose admirably, and it gives the reporter insight and information undiluted by passage through several echelons of bureaucracy.

The off-record tête-à-tête has one curious drawback. It makes it risky for a lesser official of government to shoot off his opinions of what The Boss is thinking on a specific subject. The mileage that little people of government can get out of supposedly knowing the President's private thinking can be substantial and it terrifies them to be confronted by direct knowledge.

The background contact with the President has other drawbacks. It can have a tendency to place the recipient in a favored position which then begets inhibition. Hearing the President's side of a problem is one thing; becoming so entranced by his personality and savoring the delights of throne-room access to the point of then viewing the problem in a lopsided manner is an entirely different matter.

New Frontier sensitivity to all media of information has, in a larger sense, been beneficial to those media. The Kennedy press conferences on so-called live television irritated many newspaper editors at first. But there is good reason to believe that the public has turned to newspapers in greater number because of the stimulation of televised news conferences. While the number remains relatively small, it still is true that more newspapers today print the transcripts of presidential news conferences than ever before.

There is no example of the Good New Days to match the TV press conference for currency. The effect on public and reporters has been amazing.

For one thing, the conference has become a widely popular sustaining daytime show. It attracts larger audiences than anything on afternoon television. And the viewers react pretty much as TV fans, writing denunciatory letters to some reporters, fan letters to others. It has become quite customary to offer questions for the President. These are noted, but seldom asked.

The conferences, held in a theatre-like auditorium of the new State Department building on 23rd Street, about six blocks from the White House, are barren of the dramatic, close-up banter of the meetings around F.D.R.'s desk. The interplay between President and reporter is cooled somewhat by the formality of the setting as well as presence of TV cameras.

Also, the atmosphere has been changed by some of the reporters' turning, or attempting to turn, into television personalities. This can happen easily and without immediate self-perception. For weeks, for example, I was certain May Craig had better lighting than I received. Many of us on the front row became conscious of other things: chewing gum looks bad on camera, crew haircuts make one seem bald. Lip-biting under the tension of scribbling questions and answers when seen on the TV screen becomes an unsightly tic.

One woman correspondent often wears a white knit dress on apparent theory that it helps attract the President's attention when it is being sought by a dozen or more reporters on their feet at the same time. In all kindness, this seems like overplanning. The lady is sufficiently endowed to attract attention at a Sunday double-header in Yankee Stadium were she to arise, fling out her arms and cry, "Mr. President." And, in a gunny sack.

Mrs. Craig, a friendly little grandmother whose questions have the kindness of a javelin, was well known to the public, as we pointed out earlier, via "Meet the Press" long before J.F.K. faced his first presidential conference. As a result, May and her apparently endless collection of quaint hats, to say nothing of her essayistic questions, have become more than a reporter-in-action to many TV households. She is personality; the lady who seems ready to stick the President with her hatpin if he doesn't come clean. Or pave her street.

Reston and Edward P. Morgan of the American Broadcasting Company have become widely familiar as propounders of what might be classified as the broadly intellectual question. Their inquiries send thousands of people running for the encyclopedia or Sunday's paper. They have a godly, reassuring tone which Kennedy seems to enjoy.

By contrast, Robert Pierpoint of the Columbia Broadcasting System would be classed as a hurler. So would Sander Vanocur and Ray Scherer of the National Broadcasting Company. Their questions seem to have undertones of, "Boy, I bet you wish you didn't have to handle this one."

Frank Holeman of the New York *Daily News* is a delightful questioner. Frank, with a soft North Carolina accent, stands about six feet six. It takes him a little time to uncoil and get to his feet. Consequently, his questions usually come toward the end of a conference. His inquiries are marked by Old South politeness, undertaker solicitude with a hand grenade at the end.

Attendance at a J.F.K. news conference has become a fairish status symbol for those ordinarily not entitled to be on hand. A Washington hostess is slipped in occasionally on one of the rear rows; visiting student groups are admitted at times.

One of the more distinctive visitors recently was a bosomy charmer from Hollywood, who presented an authentic request from the editor of a small Midwestern paper that she be admitted as a representative of his daily. She would have attracted only moderate attention from the physical culture students seated near her had it not been for her dog.

Being an affectionate person, she couldn't think of leaving her toy poodle at the hotel, so she brought the tiny animal along in her ample handbag. The President was holding forth sonorously on the gold outflow when a tiny but clearly audible "arf, arf" came from the woman's purse. The President may have fluttered a mite in mid-sentence, but plowed resolutely ahead.

Embarrassed White House police officers began thinking up excuses, Russian correspondents seemed deeply puzzled, and reporters in the vicinity of the dog leaned away in mortification. To be caught on camera with a poodle would not add to their eminence in the journalistic community.

Needless to say, following the conference and delighted interviews by the dog woman, there was a new understanding among the security officers—no dogs.

Aside from new prominence conferred by living-room status of the President's news conferences, the standing of many Washington correspondents has risen with the N.P.

The Truman brand of N.P. made close, lasting friendships with a number of reporters. Under Eisenhower, the bureau chief, par-

ticularly for a Republican newspaper, had a certain social acceptance, but his staff was another matter. Today, the N.P. interest in
writers is sufficiently broad to include many journalists, although
the semi-savant does outrank the functional reporter.

To say J.F.K. has a freer policy on access to information than
his predecessor is to start all kinds of arguments. Here again it is
a matter of standpoint.

No administration is *ever* going to make it easy for the public
to have information which tends to show the administration in a
poor light. Not as long, as we've pointed out in other cases, as the
government is a collection of human beings.

It seems establishable, however:

—There is more direct contact between Kennedy and journalists, albeit mostly for background purposes, than in recent years.
And to avoid becoming enmeshed in new political arguments, no
effort will be made here to compare with the Eisenhower era.
F.D.R. will serve as a fine point of comparison. J.F.K. is in more
direct, across-the-desk discourse with more reporters, broadcasters
and authors than Roosevelt at his friendliest.

—The N.P. who do look down on the press socially and professionally are, for the most part, rather dumb or—charitably—out
of touch.

—It seems to have become easier to see public officials, and,
equally important, to reach them by telephone. Not that they
always give the reporter what he's after, but contact can be established.

—In return for easier access, New Frontiersmen would like to
exact a dividend of friendly treatment and understanding. When
such a dividend is not paid, disappointment and even carping
may result. Human this may be, but often unrealistic.

—Frontiersmen dislike very much doing business with their
enemies. The degree to which this becomes apparent varies with
the dedication of the enemy. Also, it can be poor politics. Truman,

to illustrate a different approach, saw to it on several occasions that some of his more irritating journalistic critics were slipped bell-ringing exclusive stories. This would be most unlikely today. The faithful would be too bowed and might take to hardening sharp sticks in the fires of their discontent.

—These things are difficult to measure, but seldom has an administration or its leaders developed so rapidly what has been described as Potomac sunburn—a stinging allergy to printed and broadcast disapproval. All Presidents eventually come to a point of disliking much of what is printed and broadcast about them, but this painful sensitivity usually does not peak until later years of service. Possibly because he reads so much, sunburn came early to J.F.K.

The only remedies for this sensitivity seem to be swearing off printer's ink for breakfast, or gradually narrowing one's list of selected reading. The latter is the more frequent restorative.

There was an afternoon not too many months after Kennedy took office when he glowered at an article in one of the leading weekly news magazines, hurled the offending publication across the room and said darkly, "Maybe Eisenhower had the right idea."

This, of course, was an emotional reference to the belief popular among N.P. that D.D.E. read little more than his Burning Tree scorecard, the *Herald Tribune,* and the more uncontroversial westerns. Conversely, Pierre Salinger has devoted hours to popularizing the idea that Kennedy reads several hundred newspapers daily, plus *Grit* and the *Economist* on weekends. It seems true that the current President does read more, a great deal more, than his predecessor. But if he continues to throw offending material in the fireplace, he may reach a point of hunting through seldom-used closets of the White House for some of Ike's old westerns.

Many N.P. are people of Eastern culture and affluence, reared in the daily shadow of the *Herald Tribune*. Thus, it was a confused day in many Georgetown breakfast nooks when the dispatch-case crowd discovered via the Washington *Post* that the *Herald Tribune* was Out. J.F.K. canceled twenty-two subscriptions; and the delivery boy, furthermore, was told to keep his mouth shut about the whole business.

Were it possible to retrieve this decision, there is reason to believe J.F.K. might have done so. True, the *Herald Tribune* had been needling him. It was at the outset of the Billie Sol Estes case and mere mention of the Texas fertilizer financier seemed then to be an unkindness to Agriculture Secretary Orville L. Freeman. For some months, the *Herald Tribune* also had treated some of Mrs. Kennedy's divertissements a bit raffishly.

The *Herald Tribune* is owned by a prominent Republican, John Hay Whitney, and there could have been little reason inside the Frontier to believe Jock Whitney's paper would fail to exploit frailties in a Democratic administration.

Those more conditioned to Potomac sunburn felt the President might have handled his displeasure toward the *Herald Tribune* more effectively by letting daily deliveries continue, then donating them to the Salvation Army. As he was bound to be asked sooner or later, when questioned at a press conference about a *Herald Tribune* story, J.F.K. could have commented airily that he hadn't read the paper in weeks because of having to devote available reading time to more complete, informative publications.

But instead, the newspaper was put in an almost favorable light. In Washington, people in and out of government began reading it more closely than ever before, hoping to come across some gem for later conversation—and relay to the nearest Frontiersman.

With time, there will be other *Herald Tribunes* removed or dropped from the New Frontier required-reading list. This is inevitable. By the time J.F.K. leaves office, he will dislike many publications intensely. And if bets this far ahead are worth anything, a worthwhile wager might be that Kennedy and some of his company shortly after departing 1600 Pennsylvania will be writing for some of the same public prints they now find increasingly unpleasant.

Since he has the economic means, it would be somewhat of a poetic first if J.F.K. bought a newspaper and it turned out to be the first to be banned at the White House by the New, New People.

The Fourth Olio

If there's anything truly loathed and despised in Washington, it is the American tourist.

If they read this, members of the Board of Trade will deny it quickly and in soothing tones, tell all America that if there's anything truly loved and desired in Washington, it is the tourist. But, sadly, this is not true.

Of course, hotels, restaurants and stores like tourists as long as they put down their money and depart rather quickly. (If the tourists want to be really liked in Washington, they'll mail the money and stay home.) What benefits the merchant, however, produces revulsion in the heart of Washingtonians in and around government.

Why? Well, for some reason, when people swarm into town from Memphis and Boise, they have some fool idea that this is *their* capital. It is theirs much more if they stay in Memphis and Boise. Then they can be sentimental about it. But if they come to town and clutter the streets, there's bound to be talk.

The Good New Days

Frequently Washingtonians, although they may not have lived here more than a month, say cruelly harsh things about the way tourists dress. Women in shorts and slacks walking through the Capitol; men in rumpled pants and sport shirts worn with the tail out, looking up at the beautiful Lincoln Memorial; kids dripping ice cream from a stick while waiting to go up the Washington Monument; a youth in a T-shirt on the steps of the amphitheater at Arlington National Cemetery.

Furthermore, there are so many of them. Sometimes, more than ten thousand a day marching through the White House, restrained by ropes from touching the furniture, almost as though they had a right to be there.

The Washington *Post* carried on quite a campaign a while back to have the tourists dress properly, saying, "They don't dress properly because no one has told them how . . . no one has put it in black and white, 'THIS IS WHAT SHOULD BE WORN WHILE SIGHTSEEING.' "

Obviously, this is a serious situation that needs, if not immediate correction, certainly some helpful hints on clothes and accessories while visiting Washington.

Portable radar sets: These are helpful to strangers in determining when to cross a street, because the traffic lights will never tell you. Washington probably is the only town in the world with semi-stop lights. The same light may mean stop for one lane; not for the next. Not even lifelong residents can master the traffic light system, because city officials apparently receive some sort of bonus for the frequency with which lights are changed.

Salt pills, oxygen tanks and portable air conditioners: For summer visitors. July, August and September in Washington have the lovely atmosphere of equatorial jungle. Temperature and humidity usually run neck-and-neck. If you have relatives in Washington, they won't be here.

Oh yes, the clothes: It does look odd, if not downright disrespectful, going into a famous national shrine in capri pants.

So, if you ladies are going to wear these pants, be sure to wear a top, too.

And girls, under no conditions, absolutely none, should you go into the Capitol in shorts and halter. Only an exceedingly reckless woman would dress in such a manner while passing the halls of Congress.

For the men, it would look much better when visiting the White House if you dressed completely—coat, trousers, shirt and tie. Of course, you'll be a lot more comfortable in the summer if they're made of Kleenex. And feel free to go barefooted.

And a final word of advice. Things are bad enough in the summer. But even if you're out of work, don't come in the winter. Probably no city of its size and weather zone knows so little about snow. A slightly chilly white vapor slows traffic; a delicate rime stops it; and a real snow—nobody comes to work but J. Edgar Hoover. Tourists who persist in coming to Washington while snow is on the ground will find no place to stay. Hotels will be filled by Washingtonians who were unable to get home before the snow fell.

CHAPTER SEVENTEEN

One Vast Boarding House

The relationship of food to business is an odd nicety. It could have originated shortly after men learned to cook and the gesture of two or more of them eating together symbolized tentative, mutual acceptance for at least as long as the food lasted.

The gesture remains much the same today in the Good New Days which have seen business-eating develop to an almost ridiculous extent, possibly reflecting an interestingly growing need for oral satisfaction. The constant mixture of food and business casts other reflections. For one, a shortage of time. Vanity is another. No one seems to simper quite like a Washington banquet host as he leads his already over-gravied honor guest to the center of a head table while guests rammed together in a stadium-like hall applaud.

Washington business-eating begins shortly after dawn. Congressmen meet constituents at 7:30 A.M. in hotel coffee shops, often shooting the visiting farmer voters a sleepy-eyed line about having been "up for hours."

The Good New Days

The President meets over breakfast with Cabinet officers, congressional leaders, ambassadors, stray potentates and, on rare occasions, his wife and children. The same process is repeated at lunch and dinner, not only at the White House but all over town. The cocktail hour is a mixture of bitters and business, vermouth and visitors.

Harry Truman once uttered an immortal line which we have quoted many times to show the sometimes sad side of Washington eating. He commented after some months in the White House, "It seems like there's always somebody for supper."

Indeed there is, and for all other meals, too.

Each Cabinet officer has a private dining room and if he were to eat alone, his staff would suspect one of two things: either the Old Man had fallen from favor or become unhinged.

Higher-rank government officials as a matter of standing in the community would never be caught lunching alone. Faced with a lunch hour for which there are no invitations, a smart official will eat at his desk, thus appearing too bogged down in vital matters to spare a moment from work.

An assistant secretary who *brings* lunch from home is regarded either as a health faddist, an ulcer patient, or a shifty one to be watched.

Some government officials, particularly Cabinet and sub-Cabinet level, keep dinner jackets, clean shirts, and toilet articles at the office. These reverse supplies enable them to work until the last possible minute, shift uniforms, and dash to an intimate little affair for twenty to two thousand.

The N.P. should be commended, however, for one social pattern. While they're keen for business-eating, they have brought back the relatively small dinner party for eight or ten couples. This may rise from so many N.P. living in Georgetown where narrow old houses cannot accommodate more than fifteen or twenty people on the same floor.

Among more active business-eaters are members of the armed

228

services. True or not, many officers seem to feel their chances for promotion depend on ability of the little lady to dish up something toothsome while the officer of the house pushes grog.

Pentagon neighborhood dinner parties produce ghastly tension, particularly when a colonel's wife has invited several generals and their ladies. A spilled glass of wine on the Paris original of a general's spouse can give a lower-ranking host instant vision of faraway, muddy stations. It is interesting to watch terror spread through a military household when the mildly smashed wife of a field-grade officer begins to play chuckle-chin, sometimes known as "you dear boy," with a junior officer, preferably the colonel-host.

The hapless host can't win. If he spurns the old waffle, she'll turn out to be equipped with an elephantine memory which will haunt him until the blessed day of his retirement. If he plays the game and starts snapping her girdle, the general will either lunge for *his* younger, more attractive wife or retire behind a cloud of cigar smoke to make mental notes on the colonel's future.

The syndromic business-food relationship reaches its peak, or low point, depending on digestive tract durability of the analyst, in the banquet.

From early fall until late spring, with closed seasons only at Christmas and Lent, government officers and large groups of often hedonistic simpletons gather in enormous Washington ballrooms, ice palaces and armories to be seen together; to hear speeches but not converse, because this is impossible over usual banquet clatter; and, during the course of such torture, they eat.

Trade and professional associations meeting in national convention, fraternal orders, journalistic clubs and organizations, pressure groups, and even the Boy Scouts—one at a time and in deadly number, they bankroll large assaults on midriffs and minds of men who are having enough trouble as it is running the government.

Including the worst of all, the $100- or $200-a-plate gatherings given by his political party to raise new campaign funds or pay off old debts, a President is asked to several hundred banquets a year. He usually ends up having to attend twenty or thirty. And if he has a genuinely enjoyable time at one out of thirty, he's far ahead of the game.

Roosevelt reached the point of having his own chow shipped to banquets from the White House to avoid some of the creamy slum offered as food. Truman, once a gusty eater, eventually became a banquet dabbler. H.S.T. loved going out more than most Presidents, but the caloric intake became too much for him and he took to mashing his baked Alaska instead of eating it.

Until his 1955 heart attack, Eisenhower did his best to appear pleased by banquet life, but once armed with a clearly defined and well publicized excuse for avoiding high calories and late hours, he began skipping many usual stops along the banquet circuit. Also, he struck a happy compromise of arriving at the few banquets he did attend after the eating was over.

J.F.K. has had his banquet problems, too. His attendance record continues to be high, but he's turned into an Ike-type "drop-in" banquet guest when he can get away with it without causing political insurrection or calloused insult to the host organization.

Kennedy has another factor in his favor. He has let it be known that short of raising a million dollars for the party by eating in Boston, Chicago or Los Angeles, he wants his Saturday nights off. He has established what future Presidents may be wise to follow as a behavior pattern by almost never being in Washington on Saturday evening. This has a decided damping effect on many banquet promoters, the bulk of whose patrons hate to get overly boozed on weekday nights.

With few exceptions such as the Boy Scouts, although what their adult patrons may do in private is another matter, most big banquets are quite boozy. Many members of host organizations regard this their one big night of the year, failing to realize that their more distinguished guests plow through this same ruck night after night.

A perceptive Cabinet member can take one look at soup and tell what his hosts paid wholesale for an entire dinner. With no aspersion of any hotel intended, but in hard-headed realism, Kennedy frequently eats just before leaving the White House. Stoked in advance, he may devote most of the banquet to talking, writing his ad libs on the back of a menu and shaking hands with faithful who press through waiters and Secret Service men to touch the hem of his tablecloth.

Out-of-town host organization members seem to whoop it up a bit more than in-town counterparts. For one thing, locals who think they derive some advantage from this sort of affair may belong to several organizations and they spend almost as much time picking over celery and olives as, say, a Supreme Court Justice.

Freshmen Congressmen go to these dinners with relish, as do lower-executive echelons, particularly in early days of a national administration. At the outset of a new regime, many officials are afraid to stay home nights, Thursday through Saturday. But as time goes along, they become more selective—except Supreme Court Justices who lead such ordinarily lonely lives that they're grateful for the opportunity to be introduced from almost any head table.

There are in any administration, however, a few square pegs who seem to like Washington's mass eating. Possibly they dislike their wives. Perhaps the old ladies lounge squiffed before TV sets and refuse to cook. A few are bachelors, and some never achieve a degree of job or political security which would permit them to decline an invitation.

Whatever the reason, such men—these more-than-willing banquet guests—could be detrimental to national welfare, particularly if occupying federal posts of judgment and trust. To demonstrate a healthy attitude, one almost never sees J. Edgar Hoover at a banquet unless it is to award him another gold medal or engraved brass plaque for having kept the nation secure from crime and subversion. Hoover is not alone in this sensible attitude, but unfortunately, the number is few.

In fact, the F.B.I. director might take a discreet look into public servants who show up every time a Florida fruit cup is unveiled. Any man who, of free will and preference, would frequent Washington banquets when given the chance to dine instead at the Golden Rule Bible Mission has, to put it charitably, a quirk. Such a man is afraid of the dark, unable to live with himself and possessed of aberrational lust for gravy.

Produce a man who genuinely likes Washington banquets and we'll be gazing upon a nut.

Yet, why do we go? Why do Presidents and those of similarly high station and theoretical devotion to preservation of their faculties suffer such punishment? Aside from aforementioned fears, it shakes down to a matter of professional necessity or what seems to be a business-related need to see and be seen.

Armed with such philosophic acceptance of a bad but necessary situation, it is possible to banquet and survive.

Before we seem to stray afield from the Good New Days and the focal point of this book, it should be pointed out that banqueting has increased under the N.P., not because of their taste for such affairs as much as proliferation of host organizations, and also, aggressive hotel sales staffs.

Our handy guide to Wahington banquet attendance and easy rules for survival are not directed at the one-shot guest. He can sober up, administer any one of various commercial packs of alumna gel the next morning and return to Des Moines nearly intact. Our immediate concern is for the young or middle-aged male who has come to work for the government recently and must show up at a number of these fiestas before feeling sufficiently secure to stay at home occasionally.

First, get a large bulletin board for the home and pin up invitations in chronological order. This helps the family with laundry, pressing, and knowing when the subject is liable to have a cranky morning.

Virtually all invitations are for one of three or four larger hotels. The engraved card will specify two target hours—cocktails and dinner. A wise man gulps a shooter at home while changing clothes. This prepares him for later vicissitudes, the first of which will be finding a parking place if he's fool enough to drive his own car. In most cases, unless one lives in Baltimore or Richmond, it is wiser to leave the car at home and travel by cab. Washington police circle banquet hotels in the manner of Apache scouts attempting to pick off the sick and wounded from "Wagon Train." The combination of a slightly grinning driver *and* evening clothes is almost too much for a normal traffic officer to resist.

Once on the scene, our new official will find fifteen hundred similarly clad males herded into a room suitable for occupancy by about five hundred. This is the cocktail party. Before entering, however, be sure to ask *whose* party. At some of the larger hotels, there may be several simultaneous but carbon-copy affairs under different sponsorship. One would not want to spend an entire evening with the National Rifle Association when you accepted for the Mohawk Iron and Steel dinner. This is very important, because once inside the cocktail party, movement of personnel is likely to be *en bloc*.

Because of this same *en bloc* peculiarity, be selective as the devil in speaking to anyone immediately upon entering a cocktail party. Cut your closest friend utterly cold if necessary. Why? Because of crowded conditions which make the going-home bus at 5:15 seem airy by comparison, you'll be jammed against the first person to whom you speak and thus joined together until off-duty subway guards push you into dinner.

Even a dear friend can become a bore, drag or pest under such circumstances. It is distinctly preferable to fall into acquaintance with a stranger because your growing irritability at being unable to move will be focused on a target of little or no lasting importance. If this first voice contact happens to be an official who outranks you in your own department, forbearance is the word.

As for drink, should you be fortunate enough to be pushed against the bar, never under any circumstances ask for a prepared cocktail. Under most opulent sponsorship, you'd only be able to get a Martini or Manhattan. Banquet cocktails are made up in ten-gallon lots—one part whisky or gin; one part vermouth, and then apparently a lacing of kerosene or refrigerator drippings.

By all means, stick to highballs. Even better, another straight shooter to top off your home fuel. A straight shot avoids spilling, and those jammed against you will be grateful.

Upon reaching your table by following number cards (it'll take time, because these cards never are in any logical sequence; only Sicilian banquet waiters know the order and only God knows how they count in Sicily), grab a program immediately. Check the seating list. The better banquets include a capsule identification behind the name of each guest. Then check the place cards. If you're on the spot first, rearrange the cards as you think best, careful to select your own seat facing the head table and away from a folding stand which will be used later for stacking dirty dishes, if such a selection is geographically possible.

Often it is more fun to sit between two strangers from out of town, because they're easier to impress and, conversely, easier to shut off should they attempt to fascinate you with tales of life at home. If there is a higher ranking guest at the table, naturally you'll want to switch place cards so that he's seated at your side.

At Washington affairs where both men and women are present, place-card switching presents a problem. There might be a lustrous tomato whom you cannot identify as such from the printed list. Don't rely on name alone. Miss Gloria Svelte may look fine in print, but she could be the toastmaster's eighty-two-year-old first-grade teacher. Also, Mrs. Minerva Munch could be the legal name of a ravishing visitor from Poland. These, however, are occupational risks and old banquet hands have been known to race to their table, destroy all place cards, then shift as the table mates arrive.

The start of a banquet is the busy period. In addition to maneuvering for table position, one must keep an eye open for passing dignitaries who should be greeted as fine old friends. Carry a small pencil for noting the numbers of suites where after-dinner cocktail parties are held; start moving the rolls, water pitcher, and dish of celery and olives toward your place.

At most Washington banquets, individual tables are set for ten or twelve guests. In any case, they're really eight-guest tables, so one must first learn to sit and eat with elbows pressed in closely. For ten guests, the hotel usually provides six stalks of celery, five ripe olives and six green ones. Needless to say, get yours first. Same for seafood cocktail sauce. It apparently comes only in containers for six.

Before taking your seat or greeting other guests at the table, check your program again. Are you at the right banquet? Check the sign over the head table. If it matches the program, shake hands and be seated.

Maneuvering for proper guest placement is highly important, because the young official will talk to only two people the entire evening—those to his right and left. A boxing announcer at Madison Square Garden could not project sufficiently to reach two seats away. To converse beyond the more immediate dining companions requires leaning in another's salad and screaming.

This occurs at all two hundred tables at once—leaning and screaming. Only society columnists and Senators seem to last beyond the soup course at this forced communication.

Conversationally, the traps are many. Once your screaming period of getting acquainted is over and you're contemplating the limp salad, you'll be expected to exchange occasional remarks with immediate companions.

Several rules here: For one, don't attempt a story, anecdote, or statement of position with a telling time of more than a minute. Otherwise you'll be interrupted by a new medley from the Marine Corps Band, members of which seem to reach virtuoso peaks of instrumental volume just as you explain why this is no time to reduce taxes. For a bureaucrat to have such a delicate discussion with the member of the Senate Finance Committee interrupted by a brass choir version of "In a Persian Market" can be hazardous.

Trying to pick up the conversation at point of interruption is equally risky.

At the moment you say, "Senator, I'm afraid the band stopped me at a point where I seemed to oppose your bill—" there will come a dreadful gavel-knocking from the head table.

The room will squabble down to an undertone of discontent while the toastmaster introduces sixty-five VIP's and semi-VIP's at the head table from right to left when he should have started from left to right. A thin, worried clerky-looking individual will sneak up behind the toastmaster, hastily rearrange his note cards, and the instructions will be repeated obversely.

Meantime, the Senator sits back glaring at you, the young junior official who may end up being responsible for having your departmental appropriation sharply questioned in committee. The fact that you're in trouble becomes moot should the Senator inquire, after the head table introductions, "What was your name *again,* son?" You may have been a big man in the Bergen County Democratic organization, but you lost several points when he said "son."

Thus, obvious rules of banquet safety would indicate short, snappy and loud sentences. When the larded tenderloin of beef or seafood thermidor is served, should one of your seatmates be your host or member of the host organization, say something about the food *looking* fine.

"My, doesn't that *look* wonderful," is adequate. The emphasis is protective should you later determine that consumption is above and beyond the call of duty, politics, or sensitive gullet.

One Vast Boarding House

Never run down the food to an out-of-town guest or a dentist. They're having fun and will regard you as a jaded spoilsport. What is a dentist doing at the annual banquet for the President given by the White House photographers and reporters? Don't be naïve. A sensible correspondent, when torn between inviting his dentist or Congressman to dine with the President, is far more inclined toward the dentist. And few Congressmen would blame him.

If one is seated in a clump of Democrats, it may be advisable to look expertly at the head table and say, "Everett Dirksen *is* getting older, isn't he?" Should your table be predominantly Republican, "Do you think Kennedy is going downhill?" might be a starter. Don't worry about the replies. You'll not hear them, but those who do respond will feel the better for it. If a guest on the far side of the table grows red-faced as he attempts speaking to you, particularly if he waves his celery, this means either he heard you incorrectly or was quite moved by what you said. Pay him no heed for the moment, but after dinner say something about having enjoyed hearing his opinions.

Club banquets sometimes serve several wine courses, but at most affairs, the so-called commercial or standard banquets, one wine is par. The waiters usually slap two bottles on the table and go about their business. Banquetmanship comes to play here if one is a bibber. Grab one bottle immediately and, with flowery graciousness, serve your immediate tablemates first. Then your glass. A veteran then will shove the bottle forward into the protective covering of the floral centerpiece, removing it only upon need. It is considered civil to offer refills to your closer two tablemates, but not absolutely requisite. Should others at the table ask, "Any wine left?" remain silent. Your side-by-side beneficiaries will not give you away since this would interfere with their source of supply.

Following demitasse, there will be from two to five speeches of varying length. It is inadvisable to complain about a five-speech banquet, because an official never knows when he might be invited to speak on some future occasion. It is important, however, particularly when the speakers are of one's political faith, to stay awake.

Nothing sticks in a Cabinet member's mind more than the vision of a slumbering assistant seated beneath the dais. A drunken assistant would be more forgivable, assuming, of course, he remained ambulatory and that he applauded, not independently in mid-sentence, but along with the others.

This is not meant to be a compleat banqueter, but a set of rudimentary warnings. Time, space and sadness prohibit pointing out many pitfalls. For example, the need to eat sparingly. Fill up on hard rolls. They induce sleepiness much less than meat, gravy, or the inevitable potato puffs which have the specific gravity of raw lead when kept long enough in the great warming compartments of a hotel banquet kitchen.

Nor shall we dwell at any length on after-banquet partying in upstairs suites, except to advise avoidance of any gathering which features a strolling accordionist. While this may be regarded as posh and hospitable by the host, sound of accordion music in a crowded hotel room coming on top of a long evening of high-decibels in the banquet hall has been known to drive otherwise sensible men to over-anesthesia.

Another warning: after-banquet bartenders get off when all the liquor is consumed. Consequently, they become heavy-handed as evening wears into morning. Too many one-drink-after-dinner men have been stacked like cordwood in strange hotel bedrooms due to stiffness imparted by hospitality suite bartenders trying to get home for the Late, Late Show.

Forseeable necessity of survival of the writer on the Washington banquet circuit in other seasons moves him to point out that in some of the local hotels, large banquets are about as good as they can be.

Friends on the staffs of such fine hotels as the Sheraton Park, the Statler and the Mayflower surely will understand that any application of the foregoing to their hospices would be nothing more than witless coincidence.

Furthermore, any hotel this close to as many willing victims would be foolish not to push the banquet business. The larger establishments employ specialized salesmen for this purpose. They seek not only banquets, but conventions and meetings.

For some idea of the big-business aspect of a banquet, we asked Barbara Norton of the Sheraton Park to give us a partial breakdown of the economics of a typical banquet for two thousand. The President was a guest, as were many higher-ranking administration officials, associate justices and military commanders. The hosts are not being identified, however, to avoid their becoming embroiled in intramural punting over prices.

The hosts paid $6.75 a plate for a dinner featuring broiled breast of chicken served on a thin slice of ham. The bill for the dinner was $13,500 plus a mandatory tip of about $1,800, which meant a hundred extra waiters and waitresses hired for the evening received each nearly $16 in tips for serving about twenty guests. The balance of the $1,800 in tips was split between two waiter captains, the banquet manager and the maître d'hôtel, giving each of them close to $50. Several banquets during the season make this a lucrative business not only for the hotel, but for the help, too.

Most of the guests either lived in Washington or stayed at other hotels. The Sheraton Park, however, did rent 125 rooms to out-of-town dinner guests plus thirty-eight hospitality suites. In these thirty-eight suites, the hotel grossed almost as much as it did in the enormous banquet hall—$8,177 in whisky, beer and soft drinks plus $1,327 in food. And $9,504 for hooch and snacks in thirty-eight suites before and after dinner, while it may not be anywhere near a record, shows, at the very least, a willingness to try.

There were other food and bar sales throughout the hotel in connection with the evening. One bar did $365 over its norm for that night of the week. Of the 125 rooms rented because of the dinner, it may be assumed that each represented at least $25 to the hotel.

There was entertainment at dinner and this involved an expenditure of more than $7,000 on music, transportation of performers and other related items. Printing for the affair cost more than $2,000 in tickets and programs. Other outlays for which precise figures are not at hand would include money spent by guests staying at other hotels, transportation to and from Washington, for cabs and meals outside the Sheraton Park, cost of manpower hired by the host organization to handle ticket sales, preparation of programs, hundreds of dollars in long distance calls and telegrams.

Traceable money spent within the Sheraton Park comes to around $37,000 for the one night. For a fuller economic picture, the untraceable expenditures would have to be added. This item would amount to several thousand dollars more. It would seem to make the party at least a $40,000 affair, probably a bit more.

The $40,000-plus represents money that in all probability would not have changed hands or been otherwise pumped into circulation had there been no banquet.

What were the results? What did those who spent about $20 per ticket receive in return? Who gained prestige?

Very little of a tangible nature except for the hotel and those employed in connection with the dinner. For those who paid the bills, fleeting pleasure and prestige, fulfillment of tradition and a sense of having associated agreeably with those of higher station, plus the hard-to-measure advantage of having made or renewed theoretically valuable business contacts. And, too, the payment of social obligations.

What did the guests get out of it? It varied with individuals. A relative or neighbor outside the normal spectrum of government celebrities, the previously noted dentist—they had the write-home

240

thrill of having dinner in the same room with the Chief Executive of, as some are inclined to say, *these* United States.

For the more case-hardened Washingtonians, the entertainment probably was the high spot. The dinner and company? There would be other evenings much like this one, and next week, too. For the lobbyist, an expense account gem, a chance to write the client an eyes-only report on significant conversation with significant officials while appending thereto the bill for one of those hospitality suites.

For the President? A duty plus some surcease provided by the show. Cabinet, court, and others of similar status? About the same return as that for the President, but with decidedly more freedom to move around and talk with the others. In addition to the type of banquet described here, the President and his top men also must spend dozens of evenings each year at so-called official or state dinners for visiting foreign dignitaries. These are held at the White House, the State Department, and in embassies of the visitors.

Put them all together and it would seem that official Washington plus its widening circles of attached or related personnel spend an incredible amount of time in ceremonious eating. Whether the hours so devoted could be more wisely spent might be argued, but never determined.

In time, we may develop a Washington culture in which the banquet does not figure so prominently, but there are those who hope devoutly that day—or night—never comes.

There they stand, beside their gleaming kitchens, rolling bar carts, huge warming ovens, freshly made beds and dusted suites, and naturally, their cash registers. And beside them, with checkbooks cocked, dinner jackets pressed and a new sign to hang over the head table—the ever-ready hosts.

CHAPTER EIGHTEEN

A Great Town for Drunks

After President Rutherford B. Hayes left the White House, he looked back not so much in anger as in justifiable regret over the waspish criticism he and his wife suffered for not serving whisky while they were in office.

"When I became President," Hayes said in 1881, "I was fully convinced that whatever might be the case in other countries and with other people, in our climate and with the excitable, nervous temperament of our people, the habitual use of intoxicating drinks was not safe. I regarded the danger of the habit as especially great in political and official life. It seemed to me that to exclude liquors from the White House would be wise and useful as an example, and would be approved by good people everywhere."

(Hayes, incidentally, took an occasional dram before he became President, but after his election he swore off for good.)

The climate has not changed appreciably since 1881, nor has the excitable, nervous temperament of the people. But their drinking habits . . . Rutherford, you'd be positively amazed.

The Good New Days

It must be said for the New People, they don't seem to sluice the hard stuff as much as some of their predecessors. As we pointed out earlier, beer is more popular. Knowledge of good little wines is more of a status factor than a cellar of bourbon. And as of this writing, I know of no bona fide tosspot in the present Cabinet, although this was not always the case in years past.

There always have been, there are now and there always will be several medium to active shellshock cases in Congress, but without attempting a statistical survey, I offer my impression that even on Capitol Hill there has been a decline in the incidence of bottle fever in recent years.

What has not inclined, however, is the cocktail party. Writers from T. S. Eliot to Ann Landers have taken their turns at bat against the cocktail party, but they have not endured Washington's marathon version. It is not uncommon to hear a government official, at the end of a rigorous day, moan to his secretary, "I have to get out of here—three cocktail parties before dinner."

Earlier, we pointed out Kenneth Crawford's theory that the cocktail glass is one of the more powerful instruments of government. Actually, many Washington cocktail parties represent the opposite of power—rather, a manifestation of insecurity, not knowing really what to do about meeting new people, an almost meaningless gesture.

Because of the never-ending drinking parties and large number of out-of-town visitors who avail themselves of some of the country's lowest per bottle prices, Washington year after year has the largest per capita whisky consumption of any major city in the nation—the recent range was between five and seven gallons a year per person, which, if consumed by local residents, would have even the kiddies going to school on the bleary side.

There's no accurate method of computing the number of cocktail parties given here every day, but it runs into dozens in the main hotels. Added to these must be several drinking jousts at

A Great Town for Drunks

lunch or before dinner at various embassies and many more in private clubs and homes.

Why are they given? To introduce, to do honor, to promote, to publicize—and particularly, to bring together the known and the unknown who wouldn't be caught dead with each other in any other setting.

A Cabinet member, a leading Senator, a Supreme Court Justice would not think of going to the office of a corporation executive to have a drink with him. But they'll go to his cocktail party largely as a matter of tagging the better bases, leaving no possible stone of friendship unturned.

Government officials quickly become accustomed to being entertained far more than they entertain, with the exception of certain State Department officials who must pour almost nightly, it seems, for the steady stream of foreign dignitaries who must be given cocktail parties, frequently called receptions, even if they don't touch the stuff.

Embassies give countless cocktail parties, sometimes two a day, to launch new members of the staff or visiting firemen from the old country; to celebrate various national holidays, or simply because the ambassador feels that some of his colleagues are working into the federal structure more intimately than he can claim.

There are members of Congress mightily opposed to official expenditure on hooch, at home or by our embassies abroad. These men can take this attitude rather freely because they're never very far from free hooch themselves, not as long as they open their invitations and can recall the location of varied mezzanines.

Where the Washington cocktail system reaches its most pointless stage is in the afternoon spreads of industrial, commercial, civic and fraternal groups plus lobbyists, pressure packs and even out-of-town individuals striving for any audience. Major automobile companies give Washington cocktail parties to introduce new models. Motion picture companies pour before advance showings for government elite. These parties usually are given in hotel

245

suites, parlors or, for some of the larger affairs, in ballrooms. Sometimes, when business is slow, even the hotels give parties apparently for the sheer hell of it.

The sad thing about this type of party is its waste of time and effort. It may be an overrated instrument of business, but also a terrific bore—a tax-deductible bore, however. The waste results in important part from the fact that most commercial cocktail parties are frightfully easy to get into, and this tends to lower the caliber of the guest list.

A man with a clean shirt and halfway presentable suit, but known only to God and his landlady, can remain well-fed and moderately drunk six nights a week at the better hotels. If he stays on this circuit and doesn't throw up on a host, he's bound to make friends and thus line up some action for Sunday when Washington bars are closed theoretically (oh, they close all right, but it is possible to give a cocktail party in a hotel on Sunday by ordering and paying for the whisky on Saturday).

There are slumps in late summer when our strange hobbyist would be forced to go dry occasionally, but with any cleverness and the right exposure, he could work onto a few embassy invitation lists and get through the dog days with the Indonesians or Malayans, who serve a lot of fruit juice but usually have a jug around for American guests.

Hard-pressed public relations men, during the busy season, will set up well-stocked bars for mid-morning press conferences where new products are unveiled or corporation executives satisfy strange vanities by reading aloud completely unnewsworthy statements to a handful of trade-paper correspondents.

This has to be a somewhat misguided folkway rather than a hard-headed, cause-and-effect business relationship. The corporate or trade association cocktail party may gratify the hosts by the misty idea that if a Cabinet member makes an appearance, this means the host will be able to get him on the telephone a few days hence. It does not mean that at all. If the host could not get

A Great Town for Drunks

the Cabinet member on the phone *before* the party, chances of his ability appreciating in ratio to cocktails served is dim indeed.

But this does nothing to deter the enthusiasm of the party givers, even though many of their guests may be present entirely due to a mixup in dates, times or places.

Some few years back, Earl Godwin was one of the nation's most noted radio commentators. The late Godwin was a highly sought-after cocktail party guest, as David Brinkley, Howard K. Smith or William Lawrence would be today in some circles. Earl dropped by the White House press room one afternoon and we discovered that both of us were headed for the same party. It was being given at the Statler for some visiting executives of the National Broadcasting Company for which Earl broadcast.

Arriving on the mezzanine floor, Earl and I looked into the first private banquet room we passed and saw a number of familiar faces around the bar, including a number of big names at NBC such as Richard Harkness and Morgan Beatty.

"This must be us," Earl said, and in we barged.

After about an hour, several of us at the bar started to leave—for another party. A smiling man at the door obviously was the host, because he was shaking hands with the departees.

Grasping the man's hand, I gushed, "Thanks for having me—NBC always gives such swell parties."

"They do?" he said rather coolly. "Well, I'm glad you came to our party, too."

Earl, who knew everybody in creation, was bothered that he didn't know the host's name. So he asked.

"I'm Earl Godwin and I work for you people," he said. "I thought I knew everybody in the organization."

"Really, Mr. Godwin?" the man said in obvious confusion. "I didn't know that. I'm Joe Blank of the Cement Manufacturers Association and we're delighted to have you with us today."

Only then did we discover that the NBC party was two doors down the hall.

The Good New Days

The cheapest form of Washington cocktail party—and I suppose this blight afflicts other cities, too—is the one where only Martinis and Manhattans are served. The Martinis at such affairs are prefabricated from what seems to be a mixture of olive juice and kerosene, possibly left over from a banquet. The Manhattans are equally deadly in their economy—two parts prune juice, one part paregoric.

The economy party usually is given in desperation by individuals or organizations on spidery financial shoestrings. They arrange with a hotel to serve drinks at the lowest possible price per head. Knowing full well that there are thirsty people who will drink even this prestirred hemlock, the hotels protect their slender profit by closing the bar in exactly two hours.

This sends the guest away fighting mad. He did not like the drinks to begin with, but after two or three jolts of alcoholic algae offered as cocktails, he dislikes even more being cut off from the source of supply.

What's more, he pays a quarter to go to the bathroom, another quarter to retrieve his hat and coat. On the way out of the hotel, he stops in the regular bar for a few bourbons to kill the taste of the horrible free stuff, arrives home bright-eyed, aromatic and two hours late for dinner, has a swacking good row with his wife, and next day he must buy dinner and theater tickets to emerge from her doghouse. And forever more, he devotes part of each day to blackening the name of the man or organization responsible for that cocktail party.

Older hands at giving Washington parties seem to have mastered the trick of appearing completely generous while actually pinching pennies. This is best accomplished by covering the bar at the start with cocktail glasses filled to the brim with Martinis and Manhattans, but having the bartender secretly armed with Scotch, bourbon and a supply of ice and highball glasses. This smart host never displays his full stock of highball whisky. He permits it to show only a bottle at a time.

248

A Great Town for Drunks

And when he wants to end his party, he weans his guests. The bottled goods gradually disappear, leaving only the array of, by now, lukewarm cocktails. Any guest who quaffed several highballs and topped them off with a Martini or two is going to leave shortly, if not entirely under his own power.

There also is the lavish party, the cost of which can be borne only by ambassadors in quest of increased American aid, the Russian embassy to remember the October Revolution, or by genuine moguls. These fellows watch the gate carefully. Their guests are many, but well-screened. The sharpies don't crash many of these affairs, the portals of which are guarded by experts on the current crop of floaters.

The economy party has nothing but lousy drinks and potato chips. As the drinks improve, so does the food—and the cost. Any party offering hot and cold canapés plus shrimp and stuffed celery is getting close to the top. Even on the rarefied level, however, a constant guest must be blessed with the insides of a concrete mixer. No lion of the Seregenti plains could make it through the evening without a digestive remedy after stuffing on fried shrimp and oysters which have been slowly ossified in a Washington cocktail party chafing dish.

The people who inhabit these affairs are frequently as indigestible as the food.

One must expect to encounter certain types at any Washington gathering. Perhaps they exist in other cities, but not with the intensity and devotion to duty, nutriment and other forms of self-improvement.

Join us at a late afternoon affair given to introduce the new officers of the International Cough Drop Association. If you were here last week, you could have met virtually the same people who're also the new officers of the International Nose Drop Association. And their guests are virtually the same, too.

The room, the drinks, the canapés, the bartenders—all the same.

The Good New Days

The man at the door—this is the Federal Room of the Statler Hilton—is not the ICDA president, but a Lutheran pastor looking for a meeting, on the same mezzanine floor, of a group dedicated to the International Control of Drug Addiction (also ICDA). Because he sees dimly familiar faces streaming before him, he thinks he's in the right place, but he'll catch on in a few minutes when a half-smashed Congressman arrives, claps him on the back and says, "You old son of a bitch, how's the cough-drop business?"

That fellow moving toward you with a broad, hearty smile and arms outstretched, well-dressed, well-groomed but with slightly crossed eyes? The reason for his effusive hospitality is that you're a stranger. Not knowing you, he's taking no chance that you might be important. This gentleman has no known means of existence, but he's always on hand—in the front row of Congressional hearings, at prominent funerals (sometimes the less prominent, if there's nothing much doing in town), in the box seat section of the baseball park although he never sits. He is as typical of Washington as the majority leader of the Senate. His hidden means of livelihood, and a miserable one it is, involve the mixed duties of tout, pimp, gossip and errand boy. (One of our earlier-mentioned Charlies.)

This particular fellow claims to know every cop. He should, for the manner in which he patrols the hotels, checking up on scheduled parties for the evening. He made $100 yesterday for taking a senile Oregon lumberman to the International Plywood Association offices in a $15 limousine ("I'll get you in with no trouble at all").

That glamorous woman by the buffet, stoking away fried oysters and hot cheese balls. She's also typical of Washington. How does she keep that wonderful figure and eat all that stuff? First, that's all she does eat, and man, if you covered territory like that baby, you'd stay slim, too. She's a stenographer down at Agriculture and she heard about this party through her boss in the Sugar

250

division (cough drops use an important amount of sugar). She and the seven girls with whom she shares a two-room apartment operate an efficient intelligence service on the location of free food and hooch.

Sure, she's well-dressed—her cocktail sheath must have cost somebody $300. It did, the original owner. This girl bought it secondhand. These are her working clothes. She can get falling-down stewed but never spill a drop of cocktail sauce on the dress. She has what must be a ten-gallon stomach. She hopes to meet a Credit Card who'll take her to dinner, but against the possibility of a miss-out, she'll put away at least 2,000 calories at the buffet table.

Does she sleep around? Not as much as you might think. Of course, every now and then you run into a Miss Punchboard at one of these cookouts, but the percentage is low. There's a reason. This girl and many like her in Washington are playing for keeps. They do this sort of party-hopping to stay in circulation, to cut the cost of groceries, and, more important, to spot a husband. In the office where she works, most of the men are married and make little more than she does.

After a few exploratory jousts when she first arrived here from Chattanooga, she learned there was little future in backseat love with one of the office Romeos. She's on the party circuit as an alternative to the girls' bowling league or Y.W.C.A. cooking school. If you want to take a try at her, walk on over, introduce yourself, invite her to dinner. Don't worry about where, she'll know a good place. And take money. But this girl is not a gold digger in the classic sense. She doesn't want your cash, but when you look at the tab in the flickering light of the cherries jubilee, take it like a man.

Those four men together at the bar. They're junior officials in the same office where the girl works. True, they look like average guys from your town of Scranton. They are. Each has a wife, a young child and a leaden mortgage on identical $13,500 shacks in Barony Estates. They get to only a couple of these parties a year (they usually make the Beet Sugar Producers reception) and for an hour or two (time makes little difference since they *are* the car pool) they can get a little spiffed and escape the dreadful sameness of their lives.

You'll notice that with fresh drinks (fine bourbon with ginger ale because they've become accustomed to drinking cheap blended rye and ginger on Saturday nights) they move in a group toward the food. Yes, one might think they'd split up and try to meet new people, possibly open a way to advancement or opportunity outside the government. Not these poor guys. They're out of their league, they know it and they'd be struck dumb before a man of importance. Their world is horribly limited. Listen to their conversation.

"When Mr. Giles brought the QM-4 reports in to me today, I thought I'd had it."

"Why, Jer? What's so tough about QM-4's? Y'oughta have some of my ID-8's."

"Yeah, Jer, I've just worked through a stack of AR-50's and, brother, a QM-4 would be a relief."

"Rob, you know as well as I do—the QM-4 may be bulky but it's simple. When Mr. Giles came in, however, I'd just finished my QM-5's and the thought of QM-4's was too much. I was about ready to put in for my T-I-I."

"T-I-I? What's that, Jer?"

"This Is It."

They broke into uproarious laughter, and, almost choking on a stalk of stuffed celery, Rob whooped, "Holy cow, I must remember that."

There are thousands of men and women in Washington who can and do talk like this for hours, days and even years. It is the language of certain levels of government, a dismally sparse argot of serial numbers, initials and bloodless symbols which guide the flood of forms where there is never enough space for your full

A Great Town for Drunks

name and home address; the make-work credentials of bureaucracy; the papers of our existence.

We'll have time to study only one or two more of the guests here if we're going to get to the next party. The Shovel-Makers League, down the hall. This crowd will move there, anyway, so you won't miss much.

That man working his way through the crowd like a fellow giving away money? He's the Congressman who ran into the Lutheran preacher. The biggest cough-drop plant in America is in this Congressman's district. There are 452 workers in the plant, and every two years he goes to the front gate of the plant and shakes hands with employees as they leave for the day, smelling of licorice, horehound, menthol and wild cherry.

Notice the way he shakes hands. A simple handclasp for a stranger. For a casual acquaintance, the handshake with the other hand at the acquaintance's elbow; for any woman under eighty, a handshake with both hands; for a real friend, the shake with one hand and vigorous shoulder-slapping with the other. And for another Congressman who only this afternoon denounced him as a scab on the behind of progress, the double-armed *embrazo* with a cry of delirious joy, "Why, *Clyde*, you old son of a bitch, how's that beautiful wife of yours?"

We'll be visiting other wigwams as this baleful Baedeker continues, but, for the moment, the guide must step outside for a breath of fresh air. Oh, those three lonely men over in the corner? They have not spoken to a soul for the past thirty minutes, not even to each other. This is understandable. They're the honor guests. The new officers of the ICDA.

Because our survey has been largely limited to the more distasteful type of Washington drink-outs, mention should be made as a matter of fairness of a device that marks the upper echelon assemblies. This is the eternal champagne punch fountain.

These gurgling re-circulators are seen in other cities as conversation pieces for wedding receptions, but they are used frequently

253

in Washington to ram home the idea that this is a cut above other cocktail parties. This could be very well true—until a bibber bibs some of the frothy fluid trickling from silver spouts into a catch basin suggestive of the swirling bowl beside a dentist's chair. The liquid apparently at one time contained a few jiggers of champagne mixed with orange juice and corn syrup, but any early life has been flailed thoroughly from the champagne by the time it makes several trips through the pump.

Observing one of these horrors piddling its faint song of conviviality at a party away from the White House, the then President Truman said to a friend, with deep feeling that could have come only from bitter experience, "That, my boy, is pure slop. It'll rust your innards."

CHAPTER NINETEEN

Sights and Sounds Unavailable on the $3 Tour

Before ending this visit with the New People and *their* Washington, it might be wise to accent some of the positive rather than depart in a mood of cynicism and hooting.

It is impossible to poke fun at the N.P., because they *are* fun in many of their moments; but this isn't to say they are to be measured solely by superficialities.

History takes care of the more definitive appraisal of a political era, but sadly, the historians sometimes become so overburdened with monumental matters that they fail to tell us how the people lived or behaved.

Obviously all Washington today does not consist of clever young marrieds leaping into distinguished swimming pools or shouting flawless French from Porsche to Porsche.

Our town contains important human elements and countless scenes which are never heard or seen by millions of tourists who trail through the capital each year from California to Chad. They see handsome buildings and majestic monuments; chambers of

Congress, art galleries and museums; historic residences such as Mount Vernon and the home of Robert E. Lee. During the spring and summer they tour public rooms of the White House at a rate of better than five thousand persons an hour.

This is the proud and handsome face of Washington. Behind it are countless and deeply interesting sights and sounds which could never be available on a $3 tour—or, for that matter, $300 or $3,000.

Being in town for relatively short periods, tourists start their sightseeing early in the morning after jamming hotel coffee shops and cafeterias for breakfast. Those four fellows at the next table in the Statler coffee shop look like businessmen here to confer with the Commerce Department. Also, they may be some of the government's top administrators jamming in a 7 A.M. breakfast conference before getting to their offices a little after eight o'clock.

Probably in no major city in the world are so many gilt-edged celebrities so hard to recognize. Tourists, for example, stare at big limousines in street traffic, not realizing that many of the government's more important officials move in fleets of black Fords or Chevrolets.

Sightseeing buses would never see my next-door neighbor, Senator Carl Curtis of Nebraska, a decidedly conservative Republican, standing patiently in line with his cart of groceries in a suburban supermarket. The public at times forgets or fails to realize that prominent political figures, leaders of government, and diplomats have families and home responsibilities.

Carl Curtis certainly is not cited here as an example of the N.P. We mention him fleetingly to illustrate that Senators have stepped far from their broad-rimmed, string-tied image of a few decades ago and are now found quite commonly in habitats other than the Mayflower and Sheraton Park hotels.

The cartoon image of Washington personalities persists in many minds, the shape depending largely on the source of information—glamorous slick magazines, newspaper society sections, weekly news magazines, TV and radio accounts and commentaries.

The typical wife of a Washington official is, to many non-Washingtonians, a vivacious, ever-active lady, always stunningly gowned, squired by a handsome husband in dinner clothes, and more important to the out-of-town housewife, the typical Washington official couple seem *always* together except during bothersome daytime working hours. Even then, we see the Washington wife at exciting luncheons or standing in receiving lines for visiting dignitaries.

Naturally, the story-tellers—the sightseers—miss Mrs. Smiling Little Cabinet on more representative evenings when she dines with the children after Father's good-night call from the office; driving kids to various schools; endless telephone chants entreating her to help at still another charity bazaar; weekly Spanish class; Chinese cooking school; occasional urgent calls from Henry —jump into a dinner dress and make it from Spring Valley to the Pentagon in twenty minutes with his evening clothes; they've just been asked to sub for a cancellation at the Secretary's dinner.

Neither would it make particularly attractive reading or telling to go into the dreary, low-paid loneliness of wives on a much lower echelon, the slowly neurotic wives of federal men whose jobs are highly classified and require frequent, unheralded and prolonged absences from home.

These are the wives of the law enforcement and intelligence agency men, trouble-shooters for the armed forces, investigators of everything vile and sad from narcotics to airline crashes.

There are literally thousands of such job-widows in Washington. Their comfort and ability to stave off unstabilizing worry must come in great part from each other, and from the sometimes blessed daytime preoccupation with children. Many have jobs. This may help ease pressure on Mike's paycheck, but there comes a time at night when money and children are no substitute for the man.

Starting in World War II but reaching new heights of responsibility and prominence in more recent years is a seldom-seen group which in time might become the new aristocracy of government—the friendly killers. This is perhaps an unkind label for scientists who devote themselves largely to developing better nuclear weapons—the missile designers and space experts.

I have a friend who lives in our suburban section of Chevy Chase, outwardly one of the most peaceable, conventional civic club and youth movement types imaginable. His rambling house is a clutter of dogs and children, where seldom is heard even a phrase that might identify his profession. He and his wife devote long hours to church and neighborhood activities. When he stands bony-kneed in shorts that make him seem thinner than he is, and calls with affectionate gruffness to a pack of Cub Scouts, "Let's get a move on, men," it is hard to realize his professional hours are devoted to designing and testing some of the more murderous rockets and missiles in the arsenal of the West.

Even before Eisenhower left office, this man and his wife were decidedly N.P. in political philosophy, behavior and intellectual taste. Seen on the street by out-of-town visitors, it would be amazing if he attracted even a passing glance, because he looks for all the world like another tourist.

Dr. Glenn T. Seaborg, chairman of the Atomic Energy Commission, or John A. McCone, director of Central Intelligence, two of the more important officials in our teeter-board avoidance of conflict no nation can afford, move freely about the city with little or no recognition, even from long-time residents.

In a hotel lobby, one might take tall, gangling Seaborg for a touring professor. Compact, gray-haired and with noticeably assured, penetrating eyes, McCone has the look of an all-business banker.

Sights and Sounds Unavailable on the $3 Tour

Ted Sorensen, one of the closer and more constant advisers to President Kennedy and certainly one of the more influential figures on the New Frontier, seems like the headmaster of a good boys' school or a competent slide-rule man from the Budget Bureau as he strolls across Lafayette Square to the quiet dining room of the Hay Adams House for lunch.

The Hay Adams dining room, incidentally, probably has more influential figures from the executive branch of government and journalism per square inch during the midday hours than most comparable eating establishments.

The Hay Adams is a quietly venerable hotel just across the square from the White House. The dining room has an atmosphere of hushed conservatism which often is counterimage to some of the torrid issues being discussed at its lamp-lighted luncheon tables. A taproom in the basement where lunch also is served might be a better place to seek out the sports-car wing of the N.P. The mood below stairs at the Hay Adams has zip.

And speaking of new or current modes in Washington food and drink purveyors, note was made earlier of the Red Fox Tavern in Middleburg which would darned well be spoiled if much more note is made. We've also mentioned The Place Where Louie Dwells as a better *boite*.

The Red Fox is about an hour to ninety minutes from the center of Washington, depending on traffic conditions, and thus would be rather difficult to reach for luncheon if one had to return to work. For the visitor, however, it is a somewhat surprising experience in *haute cuisine* at lunch or dinner.

Louie's is another matter. Take money, but prepare to eat well. It is one of the darkest restaurants since the discovery of electricity. This may well be one of the prime attractions for so many top political figures. Vice President Johnson and Dick Nixon could be dining at adjoining tables and never see each other.

The restaurant is a wasp-waisted series of tiny red-walled (I'm

259

told) dining rooms on the ground floor. The owner-operators are Bill and Pat Reisinger, an affable couple who seemed to have gotten in the *boite* business because they were tired of being gouged by others. The Reisingers are now getting even, but feeding their clients extremely well. At midday they feature a special luncheon for New Frontier women—two vodka Martinis, a low-calorie salad and iced coffee. This keeps the young matron slim and sluiced.

Upstairs at Louie's is an even darker area. It is a living-room type of bar, lighted in dark blue. Ghostly streaks of dim white at about knee level are long, narrow cocktail tables of marble obviously obtained from a headstone establishment during a slack season. All drinks—cocktails, highballs, sarsaparilla—are served in enormous brandy inhalers.

Drinking in the dark apparently can be fun, but seasoned patrons manage to leave before 2 A.M. when, I also am told, the lights suddenly flare up to full mazda, women scream into their compact mirrors, and kindly attendants begin shepherding the flock down a flight of narrow stairs matched in pitch only by those of the Washington Monument.

Louie's is at Third and G Streets, NW, and no more unlikely neighborhood for a fine spa could have been selected. On the other hand, one would expect Georgetown to abound in sophisticated dining and drinking spots—and it does. Billy Martin's Carriage House, for one, is a handsome oaken reminder of colonial tavern days. Martin's appears just old enough to be fashionable for the N.P.

One of the newer Georgetown shrines is a spanking modern hotel, which we mentioned before, the Georgetown Inn. The *décor* and service, however, are quite Old World. Some Washingtonians have been struck more by the parking-lot attendants than four restaurants in the Inn.

One alights from his car in a covered driveway to confront a

Sights and Sounds Unavailable on the $3 Tour

platoon of husky young men, all of whom appear to be blood relatives of Jungle Jim. After adjusting to the sight of white T-shirts, khaki shorts and simulated cork helmets, the next step is the doorman, a startling vision of scarlet uniform which seems to have drawn together the finer points of dress from the 'Lasses White Minstrels, *Guarde Republicaine* of Elysées Palace and the Canadian Royal Mounted. There are other scenic treats inside which we won't attempt to spoil for potential visitors, except to say the *décor* is a most welcome relief from too-functional modernity that marks many newer hotels.

Before we veered off into a dilute version of Duncan Hines, there was, at least, the start of an effort to correct possible impressions that because the social customs and behavior patterns of Washington N.P. frequently are so entertaining and attractive that a tendency develops to judge them superficially.

To their credit, the N.P. have injected a long-needed element of firsthand knowledge of international affairs into life of the American political community which for too many years had deferred to diplomats in this field.

Speaking of a new political fashion whereby candidates of the sixties enhance their position at home by far-swinging field trips overseas, the *New York Times* noted not long ago:

"Nobody stays home any more talking about stopped drains or other local problems, but moves out on the world stage and lets the voters see him yonder brooding prominently on the larger fate of mankind."

There are conformists, conservatives and the generally uncomfortable who would prefer to see their political figures less preoccupied with foreign affairs. While this attitude may warrant a certain amount of sympathy, it fails to consider the way in which nations are being pushed closer together by high-speed transportation and such instantaneous communications as Telstar.

261

The Good New Days

Aside from destructive gadgets which have been under constant development since the dawn of the sharpened stick, one of the truly great marks of the Good New Days was Telstar.

After this intercontinental space relay system for television and telephone calls is perfected to put us in instantaneous audio-visual contact with the rest of the world, it might develop into a great deterrent to savagery. Should man's social development continue to lag behind scientific progress, Telstar also might be able to keep us posted pictorially and with up-to-the-second audio on genuine killing as it happens from Southeast Asian jungles to the Berlin Wall.

This, of course, would make it difficult to keep kiddies interested in make-believe bloodletting of some of the current TV favorites. Even box-top premiums could not be expected to compete for youthful viewer interest with the actual sight and sound of an East German refugee being riddled by submachine-gun fire while attempting to swim the canal leading to West Berlin.

It may offend the O.P., but the N.P. have been responsible for a more informal atmosphere in Washington and less rigorous conduct of government, particularly its ceremonial aspects, along inflexible lines of protocol and tradition. Preservation of meaningful tradition is one thing, and desirable, but to continue an uncomfortable custom simply because it has been in effect for years is inconsistent with other areas of progress in the sixties.

Rightly or wrongly, the N.P. have injected into national life a steady stream of new schemes, plans and ideas, some so advanced as to defeat practicality; others startlingly simple.

In any loosely contained flood of new ideas lies danger for a national administration. Political opponents invariably select the wilder, more impractical suggestions as representative of an over-all program. This, of course, distorts the true picture, but it frequently makes for good negative politics.

With zest, zeal and intellectual overtime displayed in abun-

dance by the N.P., they also have their moments of shortsighted-
ness, bias, prejudice and needlessly argumentative verbosity.

As we pointed out earlier, some N.P. are so overflowing in the
intellectual endowment, to say nothing of financial security, that
they regard government as a marvelous game. Some of their
women folk view political recruitment with the gleeful excitement of a Junior League Tag Day.

Some N.P. seem surprisingly impressed by the appurtenances
of high federal station; the social rights and privileges that go
with even middle-rank government jobs. Professors who are back
in good Washington graces again after having spent some years
as underground eggheads seem to be among the larger suckers
for local social bait. This may be understandable, if not forgivable, considering some of their unglittering moments in
campus social life.

Morally, the N.P. seem to be about as good as any politically
motivated faction but they profess to such high dedication that
there is always a danger their purity may interfere with detection
of termites that bore into any political structure. Referring back
to Sherman Adams, it seemed to some relatively dispassionate
students of his plight that, as one of the prime architects of the
Eisenhower Crusade, he inveighed against evil (particularly as
he found it under Truman) for so long that he developed an air
of some immunity.

Although Adams might want to quarrel with this idea, it
seemed to some competent outsiders that his vision became so
directed to sins of the other side that similar faults in those allied
with him became difficult to detect.

This is meant as no Adams analogy but the politicians crying
out against sin in others may bring to mind the classic tragedy of
the preacher who hurls fire and brimstone from the pulpit, then
pads around the choir loft after hours with a toothsome beauty.

The analogy of the miscreant pastor, however, might be applied in a loose way to some of the more vocal N.P. who see total evil and/or granite stupidity in the O.P.; the particularly young N.P. who date history from Jan. 20, 1961. To this history-blind sect, Eisenhower represented eight lost years; Truman a period of crude valor; F.D.R., the Leader, without question, but primarily great for *his* time.

Unrelieved totality of political belief also is a mark of awkward newness. The more experienced activist does not attempt balance in his beliefs but he reaches a stage where he accepts an occasional point for the opposition. He may go so far as to confide to a highly trusted associate, "I wish we had a man like Joe Blow gunning for our side."

We have catalogued the N.P. largely as Democrats but Republicans are working energetically to recruit their own N.P. and, while Frontiersmen dislike the thought, the G.O.P. is making what its leaders regard as heartening progress.

Should Republican efforts in this direction bear fruit in any volume, the intellectual traffic jam in Washington could be terrifying. God knows what would happen to real estate prices in Georgetown with a second wave of eggheads. Establishment of a second Youth Front in Washington would mean still more new styles, new oracles and new thought; probably more of those annoying foreign motorcars; new guest lists; unreliable stag lines.

It would be awful for the O.P. and particularly the Cave Dwellers if the Republicans entice hundreds of bright young people to the city. For one thing, it would be a trying experience just in keeping the two Youth Fronts well and separately identified. The Young Republicans would have money, too, and clutter every club in town.

This would leave Constitution Hall and possibly the Sulgrave Club available for meetings where the O.P. could recall with indignant anger, as well as nostalgia, what they refer to in their softly complaining voices as the Good Old Days.

Sights and Sounds Unavailable on the $3 Tour

Nostalgia may have certain comforts but not among them is the ability to resurrect time. The O.P. know this in their hearts but when they look out on what once was such a graceful city, where one *knew* position and stuck to it, little wonder they recoil from sounds of so many new languages, strange dark men in striped robes, brisk young strangers looking out from the society pages, new talk, or what was that word he used the other day—"dialogue?"

CHAPTER TWENTY

Eventide on the Potomac

In a third-floor rented bedroom of a slightly bowed Georgetown house two girls gabbed excitedly as they stood bare shoulder to shoulder in their slips before a single murky mirror, busily fluffing, combing and anointing for the evening ahead.

"You'll love Ab," Doris said as she carefully lined the upper lid of an eye in luminescent blue. "He's a fifteen."

"Funny, I've never been out with a fifteen before," Milly said to her hairbrush. "Is he old or queer or something?"

Doris shifted to the other eye with jeweler's precision.

"Why do you have to say something like that? Why should Ab be queer?"

"He's not married and he's a fifteen."

"Sure, lots of them in that grade are not married. He had a good job in electronics and got blanketed in when the Democrats were elected."

"A fifteen makes an awfully good salary."

"You're not kidding. If I weren't going with Joe who's just a ten, I sure wouldn't be fixing you up with Ab. He's cute, and a fifteen at that. . . ."

Three blocks away in another Georgetown establishment a remotely similar appraisal was in progress. It was a handsome house on Prospect Place, elegantly furnished. The attention of all who entered was forced to a ceiling-high picture window at the southern end of the living room.

A pouchy man with carefully combed, thinning gray hair stood beside the window gazing idly at early season canoeists on the Potomac and the drab, squat outline of the Arlington business buildings on the other side. While he sipped a Martini with one hand, a handsome woman put a cuff link in the other sleeve of his frilly dinner shirt.

With the remaining cuff link in her mouth, her words were a trifle garbled.

"Vi, I cannot translate your gibberish," he said. One sleeve finished, she spat the cuff link into her hand and addressed him.

"If I had been quoting a price on mollybend steel, you would have understood," she said with laughter flickering in her shrewd brown eyes. Her dress, a short dinner sheath of white raw silk, showed a tanned, firm bosom. Her teeth spoke of physical good fortune or a fortunately good dentist.

The man made a kissing motion toward her.

"Switch hands so I can get the other sleeve," she said. He obeyed with a quiet smile.

"What I said," she continued, "was why is the man Duncan so important to us?"

With the second cuff link placed, the man walked to a rolling bar with its own electric ice chest and freshened his drink from a crystal pitcher.

"He is highly important if you want to travel this summer in the style to which you have become accustomed," he said. "Duncan is quite a bore. In fact, he's something of a shit. We are, however, thirty days from the end of the fiscal year and Mr.

Eventide on the Potomac

Duncan is in charge of one phase of the space program which still has some twenty million dollars in uncommitted funds.

"If this money is not committed very shortly, it will revert to the general treasury and one of the companies I represent will have lost a golden opportunity to place a highly lucrative contract for something the government will have to buy sooner or later. Now, my dear sister, are you convinced that Mr. Duncan is a man of superb charm, exquisite taste and a joy to behold?"

Her smooth helmet of golden hair shone in the fading sunlight reflected from the river.

"Mr. Duncan just became Tab Hunter, my sweet," she said. "But please, Paul, when there's just the two of us like this, don't call me your sister. . . ."

At the White House, a suddenly called meeting of the National Security Council was breaking up. Most of the participants moved across the lawn to government cars waiting in the south driveway while the President paused at his door for a few final words with the Secretary of State.

The meeting had been in the Cabinet room. Trusted Negro messengers walked around the coffin-shaped table, carefully picking up scratch pads in hard leather holders with automatic pencils. The top sheet of each pad, some with doodles and scribbled words, were ripped off and stuffed in a canvas bag for later burning in a special basement furnace.

"Be sure to call me tonight if we hear from Bangkok," the President said.

"By all means," said the Cabinet officer, fastening the catch on his brief case, "but it might be late."

"I'll be up late anyway," the President said resignedly. "We're having a small dinner, some of my wife's friends. I know I'll be up until after midnight. . . ."

In an enormous mansion astride a low wooded hill on Foxhall Road, a fat old woman walked with puffed-ankle effort around her sparkling dinner table. She was trailed by a milky young man in a white dinner jacket. She jabbed a wrinkled finger at a gleaming wineglass.

"That one is chipped," she said in a flat voice. Her brown lace gown caught on the edge of one of the twenty dinner chairs. The household manager bent quickly to free it.

She checked a place card.

"Yes," she said absently. "He wanted his sister seated by Mr. Duncan. . . ."

In the society department of a newspaper downtown, a middle-aged woman ruffled her sheaf of notes and began to type, "Mrs. Edgar Landsdown chose a Space Age motif last night for her season's curtain call. It was the last of her traditional dinners-for-twenty before the famous hostess flies away to Switzerland for a restful summer at her chalet. . . ."

Out in the suburbs, the fast check-out counter for no more than six items at the Giant Food Market buzzed with action. A short, perspiring man in heavy spectacles put down three cans of dog food, a steak, a box of frozen peas and a carton of Cokes.

"Does the carton of Cokes violate your six-item rule?" he asked the checker.

"No sir, they're all in one package," the youth replied. "Say, aren't you a Senator or something?"

The customer smiled weakly. "Yes, thank you, I'm Senator Berkstrom of Iowa."

"I had you spotted, Senator," the checker said. "I seen you on 'Meet the Press' or 'Huntley-Brinkley' or one of them shows. My wife and me watch TV all the time. That will be five twenty-five. . . ."

Late afternoon also was a busy time in other parts of the capital. Not far from Chevy Chase Circle, in the wing of a house that served as the doctor's office, a patient leaned back in a comfortable leather chair and toyed with his cigaret lighter as he talked to a psychiatrist.

"There is nothing wrong," said the doctor in a firm, low voice, "with being a Congressman and still trying to improve one's mental health."

"But if it ever gets out that I've been seeing a psychiatrist—"

"What so terribly awful would happen?"

"I'd get my pants licked in the next election, that's what."

"Do you think you're the only member of Congress receiving psychiatric treatment?"

"I've heard about one Senator, but those fellows only run every six years; and besides, he's just a drunk."

"And you are to be censured for trying to help your wife and children have a better life?"

"You don't know what a backwoods politician can do with a thing like this—'I've never said my opponent was crazy, but I don't know about this sick-ee-attry stuff.' I can just hear 'em."

"What else do you hear?"

"Now, by God, you're getting as bad as my opposition."

Five blocks from the shining Capitol dome, two police officers in summer shirts stood inside a jumbled, fetid living room where a negress lay sobbing on a lumpy couch, one side of her formless cotton dress ripped in an angry tear. One of the officers stepped across the room and cut off the TV set. There was an empty bottle and glass on top of the set.

"The man is alive," the policeman said coldly. "He didn't have any heart attack. He was just drunk."

"You'll get him down there to the jail and kill him," she moaned without raising her head.

"No," the officer said wearily, "but you better go down to the jail tomorrow if you have enough money to get him out. How many times is this for him?"

She sat up and turned angrily on the officers.

"You police always know when it's payday, don't you? . . ."

In the patio of a pleasant low-roofed home in Virginia, just south of Alexandria, a young woman in khaki shirt and denim shorts brushed the hair from her eyes as she retrieved a tennis shoe from the driveway. The last of several station wagons pulled away bearing fudge-smeared Brownies as a small car zipped into the drive.

The woman walked swiftly with a clean, assured stride to throw her arms around the handsome man who stepped from the auto.

"And how is my great bureaucrat this lovely night?" she asked.

"Delighted," he said, "utterly delighted—and a bit shocked, I might say, to find the wife of the Assistant Secretary of Interior looking like a beautiful teen-ager—a teen-ager who's been around."

"Don't kid me, mister, I've had my moments—you've never lived until you have made fudge with a pack of Brownies."

"Where's Karen?"

"Soaking off ten pounds of chocolate."

"Did the office call just before I got here?"

"Unless they called loudly, I don't think I could have heard over the Brownies."

"There's a meeting I may have to look in on tonight."

Her pretty, mobile face deadened.

"Not again."

"At least, I'll be able to eat at home. . . ."

The meeting which the Assistant Secretary might attend, if his boss, the Secretary of Interior, could not, was in early progress at one of the large mid-town hotels. There was the inevitable cocktail party at six to be followed by dinner at eight, all under the auspices of an organization of petroleum producers.

The first guests were arriving in an enormous cocktail room

across a red-carpeted corridor from the banquet hall. Impassive, mess-jacketed bartenders waited behind four imitation bamboo bars, two men at each station.

One of the bartenders, a Cuban understandably nicknamed Fidel, sliced lemon peel slowly as he chatted with his partner, a Filipino known to thousands of Washington cocktail party guests as MacArthur.

"What's this thing tonight, Mac?"

Scooping ice into highball glasses in preparation for the on-coming crush, MacArthur replied languidly, "Something about oil."

"Christ, another load of oil men."

"You don't like oil men?"

"Oh sure, buddy, I like everybody. Is this the same bunch that tore the clothes off some girl after dinner last year?"

"No, that was concrete."

"I musta been off for the oil thing last year."

"They tip good, real good."

"That makes 'em A-okay in my book."

"Lotsa girls. Good-lookin' ones, too."

"Lotsa government brass?"

"Oh sure, the same—Congress, a few Supreme Court. . . ."

As the hour neared seven, the alternating current of Washington life cast lights and shadows of many colors.

In the spacious, quiet office of the Secretary of Interior, a tired man reached for a white telephone.

"Get me Jackson at home, please."

He put down the telephone and picked up a voluminous report bound in stiff black cardboard. A light blinked on the base of the instrument and he picked up the receiver.

"Jack, I'm sorry as hell, but you'll have to make that oil dinner for me. I've already called them. Give them our straight pitch on resource development, but stay out of trouble on import quotas.

I explained, but you'd better explain again—I'm tied up on a matter of national security, but as Assistant Secretary, you're fully authorized to present my views.

"Sure, Jack. And one thing more. Stay away from that fellow McCabe if you can. He may not know it, but he has us by the balls on that land deal in Idaho. Until we figure a way out, let's keep our distance. Okay, good boy, Jack. Give 'em hell. My love to your wife and Karen. . . ."

In a brightly lighted fourth-floor apartment atop one of the new buildings in southeast Washington overlooking the putrid Anacostia River, two couples were drinking beer in the living room.

"By golly, I've waited a full year for some of Mabel's chili," said one of the men.

His wife backed up his point.

"Mabel, Joe isn't kidding. He must have mentioned your chili a dozen times."

Mabel smiled with proper modesty and glanced at her husband, Sinclair. She was shamefully proud of him. Sinnie was four years younger than Joe, but both of them had entered the F.B.I. at the same time; both earned the same salary.

A telephone rang in the apartment's only bedroom and Sinclair went to answer. The wives exchanged brief glances while Joe swirled the beer in his sweaty can. After several minutes, Mabel, the hostess, got up and smoothed her new rayon knit dress.

Sinclair walked back into the room, beer can still in hand. He took a last gulp and looked at Mabel almost imploringly as he spoke to Joe.

"The girls better go ahead and eat, Joe. We've got business."

"Not again," said Mabel with a frown.

"It's always this way," said the other wife.

"Overnight?" Joe asked.

"Several. I'll pack a bag in a couple of minutes and pick you up at your place. I'll drive and we can leave your car here for the girls. . . ."

Across the Anacostia and down Pennsylvania Avenue at the Justice Department, the Attorney General sat behind his table-like desk, face drawn and worried in the greenish glow of a single desk lamp. Across from him with stone-idol impassiveness and tapping a heavy blue file folder on his knee, sat the F.B.I. director.

"These are two of our best men, as you know," the director said, "and if any of our agents can handle this one, these men can. They're quite familiar with the situation."

"Yes, I know, Charlie," the Attorney General said impatiently. "But be sure you back them up with plenty of support."

"Everything of that nature will be in order," the director said drily.

"Don't give me that 'everything in order' crap," the Cabinet officer said loudly. Then he drooped. "I'm sorry, Charlie, but these cases are piling up, aren't they?"

"There's no closed season for sabotage or espionage, General. . . ."

Several blocks down Pennsylvania Avenue, in the grill of one of the hotels, four young people sat around a corner table, away from the full effects of the electric organ played on a dais behind the bar by an intently smiling woman who in two more pounds would be mildly overweight.

Two young men, two younger women. Heads together over bottles of Dutch beer. The men had short haircuts, button-down narrow-striped shirts, small dark ties, subdued and unpadded jackets. The girls were in similar good, but in somewhat un-decorative dark dresses, their hair done rather plainly, and little makeup except mascara.

Their common denominator was intensity in conversation, their utter imperviousness to the cocktail clutter and sounds around them. The men worked at C.I.A., the girls at the State Department.

"I don't care what he says," said one of the men, staring straight into the rapt eyes of his date across the table, "the M.G. without a doubt is a vastly superior buy to any Karman-Gia made."

"But you'll never get the mileage and still the performance that I get out of my Gia," the other man insisted. . . .

Many lights still burned in the new Senate Office Building; and in one of the more select offices, location of which indicated rank of the lawmaker, three Senators sat around a paper-piled desk. There was space cleared for a bourbon bottle, ice dish, a water pitcher and several plain tumblers.

"Gentlemen, the company and the whisky are grand," said one of the men, "but I think we've about exhausted the subject."

"I guess you're right, Frank. There's no point in rushing tear-ass into hearings until we get some solid word from the White House."

"The President is hoping for something tonight from Bangkok."

"I'd feel a lot better if he'd sent someone else to Bangkok. That fellow really disturbs me. I don't care if he's the world's greatest trouble-shooter—he talks funny. He can't say a simple declarative sentence unless he's on television."

"Say, friend," the host Senator exploded, "you might have an idea. Tell the President to keep a TV camera with that guy while he's negotiating. . . ."

At a church not far from the center of Washington, the rector was in his upstairs study with a weeping woman. She was over the hill in looks, but well-dressed. Through the cracked emulsion of her face there was evidence that she'd once been quite attractive as would befit a so-called leader of society.

She tried to smooth away her tears with tissue.

"I'm dreadfully sorry, John."

"Grace, we've known each other many years."

"John, you're the first person I've breathed this to. . . ."

"Where is he now?"

"Here in town, at our—or his apartment."

"Do you *know* she's there with him?"

"Well, there was the letter and then the telephone calls. I've driven by the place."

"If you suspect this, why do you remain in Warrentown?"

"I suppose I just don't want to face the awful truth."

"Maybe there isn't any awful truth, Grace. Maybe it is just as he says—he's tied up so late in town and so tired that he just can't drive that distance every day."

"But these horrible, nasty calls."

"These things happen, Grace. Why don't you do this?—when he's home next weekend, say to him that you want to spend several nights in town and will come to the apartment with him."

"John, I simply cannot, I simply can't."

"Why not, my dear?"

"I hate to say it, but he has only a double bed there."

By now her tears had stopped and she fished in her bag for a mirror.

"It would make no difference, John. I wouldn't get a wink of sleep. I cannot—I'm sorry, but I'm so high-strung—I absolutely cannot sleep in a bed with another person. I haven't for years. . . ."

In the church basement, a room used during morning hours for nursery school, more than two dozen men hunched awkwardly in small, bright red chairs around the low-level tables.

A man at the head of the room tapped a pencil against a soft drink bottle.

"Fellows, it is seven-thirty and we'd better get started because we have some new men here tonight. Before we begin, I think we'd should revert to our old rule of first names only. I haven't had a chance to meet all of our visitors and they may not appreciate the

277

fact that us old drunks gave up long ago on anonymity because we're so damned proud of being sober.

"Like I say, I don't know all you new guys. Some of you probably are in government and you're saying to yourselves, 'I'll get the boot if my boss finds I've turned to A.A. for help with my drinking. . . .'

"It may make you feel better to know that among us tonight is a line admiral on active duty, a man pretty high at State."

In a night duty office at the Pentagon across the Potomac, two Army colonels stood before a top-secret war map covering an entire side of the room.

"There she is, buddy, and you're welcome to her," said the colonel going off duty.

"I'm glad to see the pins haven't moved since last night."

"You may get to move a pin yet."

"Not tonight?"

"Yep, tonight. Maybe. That thing in Southeast Asia is touch-and-go. You'll find a mess of orders. The Secretary is downriver on the Sequoia with the German defense people. Give the Sequoia a hot rocket the minute anything comes in from Bangkok. I don't think the Secretary will want to use the scrambler, but he may want to hightail it home. There's all the poop."

"Say, our wives have a big drill worked up for Sunday. Rita tell you?"

"No, we've been busy as hell all day and I couldn't get out to call her."

"She'll tell you tonight, Ev, and get ready to spend and spend and spend. They want to do the Shoreham Terrace."

"Okay, fellow, I'll go rob my money belt. And peace. . . ."

One of nation's more famous TV news shows was about to go on the air from a large air-cooled studio over in town. The commentator, toupee in place and light tan pancake makeup saving a late shave, mumbled a dry run over his script ". . . the future of world peace may well depend tonight on a meeting scheduled to start within a few hours in the steamy Asian city of Bangkok . . . say, Hoot, or whoever wrote this crud . . . isn't 'steamy Asian city' a little corny? . . . why not just plain Bangkok?"

A voice came over the flat-toned studio intercom.

"Don't forget, Clyde, you're the world's most colorful reporter."

"Color-schmolor. I'm not Lowell Thomas."

An assistant director on the brightly lighted set muttered not too softly to a camerman, "Brother, you can say that again."

"I heard that, you bastard," the commentator said without looking up from his script.

The camera crew cackled appreciatively. The old boy was in a good mood. The show oughta swing tonight.

"One minute to air," the loudspeaker blurped.

"How about that Bangkok line?" the commentator wanted to know.

"Clyde, will you settle for 'ancient Bangkok'? Don't forget you're over film at that point."

"Ancient Bangkok it is."

He reached behind the aspirin sign which proclaimed the show's sponsorship and swigged at a small medicine bottle filled with sherry.

"Fifteen seconds," the hidden voice boomed. . . .

In Lafayette Square facing the White House, a police corporal came to the door of the men's comfort station and motioned to his partner waiting in a squad car at the curb.

"There's two of 'em in here about to claw each other to pieces," the corporal said, "and I ain't tackling two queens alone with my bare hands."

"Why don't you let 'em finish it and we just send for the ambulance?" the other cop said as he climbed from the cruiser.

"We may have to do that anyway. They got beer openers."

The Good New Days

"This a little early at night for 'em, isn't it?"

"Watch it inside. There may be a third one in the toilet."

From the eighth floor of one of the cheaper hotels, visiting high school boys bombed passers-by with paper bags of water. On the lobby level, there were delighted squeals by girls in the party from Elmhurst, Long Island, as they peered daringly through the door. An Indian couple glared up from the sidewalk, dark splotches of water showing on the woman's purple sari. . . .

In the penthouse of a nearby modernistic office building, the president of a powerful labor union was calling it a day. He pushed a buzzer on his desk and a motherly-looking woman came through the paneled door.

"Well, Margaret, what say we close shop?"

"I still have a few letters."

"Leave them till morning. You know there isn't a member of this union who would put in the hours we do, is there?"

"But you never strike."

The union president laughed and reached for a box on his desk.

"By golly, Margaret, that's good. I think I'll have a cigar on that. Will you call my car for me, please? . . ."

"You're not going to change clothes?"

"For that old Landsdown woman? Hell, I won't even wash for her."

"If you dislike her so much, Mr. Edwards, why do you go to her house?"

"This is only the second time in three years. I'll tell you why I'm going tonight. The guest list interests me. There just might be something going on that I ought to know about. . . ."

This was eventide in Washington, capital of the nation and, some say, of the world. The free world, or what we call the free world.

280

Quite obviously much of the foregoing must be allegorical lest an author find himself looking down the business end of a libel suit. But the allegory is neither invalid nor farfetched. Aside from literary liberty with names and places, it IS our town at the close of a fairly normal day. Not all of the town, of course. But the selected components are faithful.

As Frank Carpenter wrote nearly seventy years ago, the town is a living curiosity, almost make-believe in its instability.

Postlude

The Good New Days was written largely as a contemporary sketchbook and not a definitive effort at socio-political analysis.

For the highly sensitive participant, there may be sections of the book which seem too raffish, too given to rock-throwing. Be at peace, dear friends. This is an anti-monument book.

Too often learned history tends to resemble monuments in that one sees the classic outline without being able to capture the flavor or personality of those memorialized.

And as any sensible sightseer would agree, Washington has entirely too many monuments.

Acknowledgments

The author is deeply grateful to those who assisted in preparation of *The Good New Days,* including Mrs. Eleanor Baustien of Stroudsburg, Pennsylvania, and Miss Susie Silverman of Washington.

A special note of appreciation, too, to Timothy and Allison Smith for their help.

Written 1961-62 at:
  Washington
  Swiftwater Lake
  Middleburg
  Hyannis
  Newport
  Palm Beach
  Boothbay Harbor
  And other rugged outposts.